D1105934

Studies in Diplomacy

General Editor: **G. R. Berridge**, Professor of International Politics and Director of Research, Centre for the Study of Diplomacy, University of Leicester.

In association with the ADST–DACOR Diplomats and Diplomacy Series, Publishing Director: Margery B. Thompson.

The series was launched in 1994. Its chief purpose is to encourage original scholarship on the theory and practice of international diplomacy, including its legal regulation. The interests of the series thus embrace such diplomatic functions as signalling, negotiation and consular work, and methods such as summitry and the multilateral conference. Whilst it has a sharp focus on diplomacy at the expense of foreign policy, therefore, the series has no prejudice as to historical period or approach. It also aims to include manuals on protocol and other aspects of diplomatic practice which will be of immediate, day-to-day relevance to professional diplomats. A final ambition is to reprint inaccessible classic works on diplomacy.

Titles include:

Herman J. Cohen
INTERVENING IN AFRICA
Superpower Peacemaking in a Troubled Continent

Andrew F. Cooper (*editor*)
NICHE DIPLOMACY
Middle Powers after the Cold War

David H. Dunn (*editor*)
DIPLOMACY AT THE HIGHEST LEVEL
The Evolution of International Summitry

Brian Hocking (*editor*)
FOREIGN MINISTRIES
Change and Adaptation

Michael Hughes
DIPLOMACY BEFORE THE RUSSIAN REVOLUTION
Britain, Russia and the Old Diplomacy, 1894–1917

Donna Lee
MIDDLE POWERS AND COMMERCIAL DIPLOMACY
British Influence at the Kennedy Trade Round

Jan Melissen (*editor*)
INNOVATION IN DIPLOMATIC PRACTICE

Peter Neville
APPEASING HITLER
The Diplomacy of Sir Nevile Henderson, 1937–39

Gary D. Rawnsley
RADIO DIPLOMACY AND PROPAGANDA
The BBC and VOA in International Politics, 1956–64

TAIWAN'S INFORMAL DIPLOMACY AND PROPAGANDA

Studies in Diplomacy
Series Standing Order ISBN 0–333–71495–4
(*outside North America only*)

You can receive future titles in this series as they are published by placing a standing order. Please contact your bookseller or, in case of difficulty, write to us at the address below with your name and address, the title of the series and the ISBN quoted above.

Customer Services Department, Macmillan Distribution Ltd, Houndmills, Basingstoke, Hampshire RG21 6XS, England

Intervening in Africa

Superpower Peacemaking in a Troubled Continent

Herman J. Cohen

An ADST–DACOR Diplomats and Diplomacy Book

First published in Great Britain 2000 by

MACMILLAN PRESS LTD

Houndmills, Basingstoke, Hampshire RG21 6XS and London
Companies and representatives throughout the world

A catalogue record for this book is available from the British Library.

ISBN 0–333–77929–0

First published in the United States of America 2000 by

ST. MARTIN'S PRESS, LLC,

Scholarly and Reference Division,
175 Fifth Avenue, New York, N.Y. 10010

ISBN 0–312–23221–7

The Department of State has reviewed the manuscript of this book to ensure its contents do not compromise national security. This review should not be construed as concurrence with the text. Opinions and characterizations are those of the author and do not necessarily represent official positions of the United States Government.

Library of Congress Cataloging-in-Publication Data
Cohen, Herman J.
Intervening in Africa : superpower peacemaking in a troubled continent / Herman J. Cohen.
p.   cm. — (Studies in diplomacy)
Includes bibliographical references and index.
ISBN 0–312–23221–7 (cloth)
1. Africa, Sub-Saharan—Foreign relations—United States. 2. United States–
–Foreign relations—Africa, Sub-Saharan. 3. Mediation, International—History–
–20th century. 4. Civil war—Africa, Sub-Saharan—History—20th century. I.
Title. II. Series.

DT353.5.U6 C64   2000
327.67073—dc21

99–087453

This book is printed on paper suitable for recycling and made from fully managed and sustained forest sources.

10   9   8   7   6   5   4   3   2
09   08   07   06   05   04   03   02   01

Printed and bound in Great Britain by Antony Rowe Ltd, Chippenham, Wiltshire

To Suzanne, Marc, and Alain

Contents

The ADST-DACOR Diplomats and Diplomacy Series

For more than 220 years extraordinary men and women have represented the United States abroad under all kinds of circumstances. What they did and how and why they did it remain little known to their compatriots. In 1995 the Association for Diplomatic Studies and Training (ADST) and Diplomatic and Consular Officers, Retired (DACOR) created a book series to increase public knowledge and appreciation of the involvement of American diplomats in world history. The series seeks to demystify diplomacy by telling the story of those who have conducted our foreign relations, as they saw them and lived them.

Herman J. "Hank" Cohen has been a pioneer in promoting democratic transition, good governance, and civilian control of the military in Africa. From 1977 to 1980 he was US ambassador to Senegal and the Gambia, having previously served in Uganda, Zimbabwe, Zambia, Zaire (Congo), and Paris. One of a very few named Career Ambassador in the United States Foreign Service, he was a top specialist in African affairs, serving as Senior Advisor on Africa to President Ronald Reagan (1987–89) and Assistant Secretary of State for African Affairs under President George Bush (1989–93).

Under Hank Cohen's creative diplomacy and skillful leadership, the Bureau of African Affairs initiated an assertive policy of diplomatic intervention in major violent conflicts and attention to their dire human consequences. With characteristic candor and insight, Ambassador Cohen reveals his search for peace in seven civil wars, the many horrific circumstances on the ground, and the frequent frustrations of power struggles and bureaucratic obstacles, in Washington as well as in Africa. The results, ranging from heady triumph to deep disappointment and outright failure, yield complex lessons of continuing value to governments, practitioners, and citizens.

EDWARD M. ROWELL
President, Association for Diplomatic Studies and Training

KENNETH N. ROGERS
President, Diplomatic and Consular Officers, Retired

Preface

Civil wars in seven African countries absorbed the attention of the US State Department's Bureau of African Affairs when I was assistant secretary there during the administration of President George Bush (1989–93). Since then, scholars and policy analysts have completed and published a considerable amount of research on the nature, causes, and evolution of each of these wars. This volume is not just another study and analysis of African conflict. Rather, it is a review and analysis of how the United States government addressed these seven conflicts as it assumed the mantle of the world's only remaining superpower.[1]

In this volume, I look at how the United States exercised leadership or failed to do so. In particular, I describe how the Bureau of African Affairs took charge of the policy process within the national security interagency system and critique how the bureau organized itself in dealing with African crises – its approaches, procedures, strategies, and tactics. In short, this volume is the story of what the practitioners did and how they did it, replete with triumphs, stalemates, disappointments, and outright checkmates.

When the Bush administration took office in January 1989, the problem of African conflict was not at the top of anyone's policy priority list, neither in Washington nor in most foreign capitals, including those in Africa. Policymakers generally saw civil war in Africa as a normal backdrop to African underdevelopment. It remained the domain mainly of the humanitarian agencies such as the International Committee of Red Cross Societies (ICRC), the UN High Commission for Refugees (UNHCR), and the World Food Program (WFP).

Starting in 1989, the Bureau of African Affairs pioneered in implementing a comprehensive policy to address violent conflict as a third party intervenor. When the Bush administration took office, we in the Africa Bureau were more or less alone in this field. By the time I left office in 1993, conflict management, prevention, and resolution had become a growth industry among foundations, humanitarian agencies, nongovernmental organizations, think tanks, and academic institutions.

The idea of my writing this volume grew with the proliferation since 1992 of conferences, seminars, and publications on conflict in Africa. For a number of these efforts, I was invited to present papers and write chapters in collective volumes on such subjects as the American intervention in Somalia, security in Africa, and how the United States could contribute to the effectiveness of Africa's own conflict resolution program.[2] In writing for these contributions to overall knowledge of African conflict, I decided that our record as practitioners in the Bureau of African Affairs constituted a treasure trove of experiences meriting description and analysis.

Though official archives will eventually provide most of the basic data surrounding US actions as a third party intervenor in African conflict, they lack the personal reflections that tell the story of why we approached problems the way we did and what lessons we learned from our experiences. That is what I try to do in this volume: to provide such personal recollections and describe the lessons learned, thereby rounding out those official despatches and memoranda and putting them in perspective.

This volume is not a practitioner's guide, but a practitioner's memoir. Nonetheless, if it helps to guide and instruct present and future practitioners, especially in what not to do, it will have served a useful purpose. To the extent other analysts draw lessons not found in this book's specific case studies or overall conclusions, so much the better. Stimulating thought and analysis on the role of a superpower as a third party intervenor is important. This is true because, unfortunately, Third World civil conflict in Africa and elsewhere, with all of its accoutrements of terrorism, refugee flows, and arms proliferation, now appears to be a permanent factor on the world scene.

HERMAN J. COHEN

Acknowledgments

With gratitude I acknowledge the financial assistance of the United States Institute of Peace in Washington, D.C., whose generous grant enabled me to curtail my employment as a consultant in order to do research and to write during the period October 1995 to November 1996. The Association for Diplomatic Studies and Training reviewed and accepted my manuscript for its ADST-DACOR Diplomats and Diplomacy Series, and ADST Publishing Director Margery Thompson gave me valued editorial support and guidance throughout the publication process.

For their assistance in reading and criticizing specific case studies, I want to express appreciation to:

- Ambassador John Davison, one of the Foreign Service's great conceptualizers, who served as my director for East African Affairs (Ethiopia and Sudan);
- Aileen Marshall, my brilliant colleague at the Global Coalition for Africa, who lived in Mozambique during much of the fighting there (Mozambique);
- Stephen Morrison of the State Department Policy Planning Staff, who witnessed the Angola crisis firsthand as a congressional staffer and a USAID humanitarian-response official (Angola);
- James L. Woods, my wise opposite number in the Defense Department, who was such a valuable member of the US government's Africa team for over fifteen years (Somalia, Liberia);
- Donald Lieber, the "super memory" in the Office of Southern African Affairs, who provided valuable research assistance for the Angola case study;
- Ambassador Antonio Deinde Fernandez, who was always available to undertake confidential unofficial missions at the highest levels in Zaire, Angola, and Mozambique and who contributed substantially to conflict resolution without fanfare, self-promotion, or publicity;
- And especially my dear wife Suzanne, who proofread the original manuscript, finding and correcting errors and inconsistencies.

To all I say thank you, with the caveat that only I am responsible for the contents and conclusions.

HERMAN J. COHEN

Map of Africa

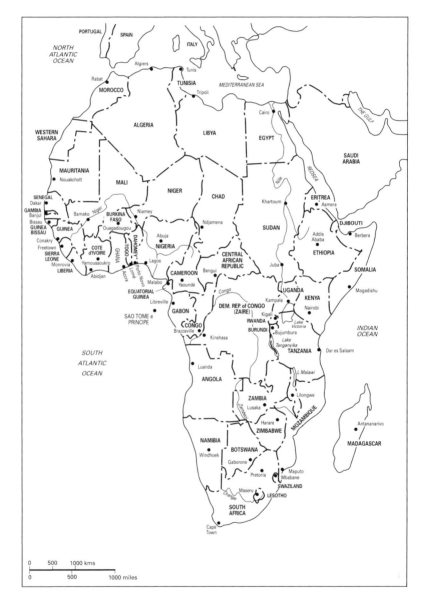

1
Forging a New US Policy for Africa

It was a career diplomat's dream come true. When I took charge of the State Department's Bureau of African Affairs in March 1989, the Cold War was winding down. The shackles of the East–West struggle no longer bound our hands in Africa. The team of Foreign Service officers I had assembled to help manage the bureau were all veterans of the days when we helped sleazy African dictators principally because they were deemed "pro-West." Now, at long last, we had a great opportunity to formulate new policies unencumbered by the "communist menace."

To help matters along, President George Bush, Secretary of State James A. Baker III, and their top advisors were encouraging us to be creative. They were telling us to make the administration look good and work with the Soviets to find solutions to regional problems. Who could ask for better policy guidance than that? Needless to say, we began enthusiastically to lay the groundwork for a new and productive relationship between the United States and Africa.

We all remembered the ideals of the 1960s, when the newly independent African states assigned high priority to economic development. For thirty years, both Democratic and Republican administrations had consistently tried to make development the keystone of their Africa policies. Unfortunately, policy imperatives external to Africa, especially the Cold War and the endless Middle East crisis, impeded US concentration on economics. Within Africa, the issue of *apartheid* in South Africa also complicated the development agenda, especially in the southern third of the continent.

Nevertheless, at the beginning of the Bush administration, the prospects for a return to our "development roots" looked fairly bright. The Soviets were asking us for advice about their situation in Africa, and in South Africa we sensed the first stirrings of political change as a

1

new generation of more enlightened Afrikaner leaders was coming to power. Although the Middle East problem was still out there, we saw far less pressure for involvement of the African countries of the eastern Horn in our defense posture than had been the case ten years earlier. It might just be possible, we reasoned, to restore the policy balance in favor of economic development.

Few African countries could be considered development success stories in 1989. Three decades of misguided policies that emphasized state ownership of the major enterprises, highly centralized economic command structures, and mistreatment of the main wealth-producing farming sector had caused most African economies to regress from their preindependence levels. In addition, the African "one-party state," which African elites had greeted with enthusiasm in the 1960s, had become repressive and corrupt in many countries, causing deep political conflict and, in some cases, civil wars. Against this backdrop, the question we posed to ourselves as the Bush administration got underway was what role US foreign policy could play at that point to help African countries return to the path of economic growth.

Considerable work on economic policy reform in Africa was already being done by the International Monetary Fund, the World Bank, and the United States Agency for International Development (USAID). "Structural adjustment" had become the term of choice for economic reform. State Department diplomacy could add little in this area except to provide the usual high-level support. As secretary of the treasury in the preceding Reagan administration, James Baker had been one of the architects of the economic reform policies the international financial institutions were promoting. As Bush's secretary of state, he missed no opportunity to promote those same policies during meetings with African counterparts.

Where we in the Africa Bureau might be able to support these economic efforts, we believed, was in the area of conflict resolution and political reform. At the beginning of 1989, four major civil wars were raging in Africa – in Ethiopia, Angola, Mozambique, and Sudan. All of these wars had caused massive economic regression as well as humanitarian disasters, not only in the countries themselves but in the surrounding subregions, which also suffered from massive refugee flows, arms proliferation, and lost trading opportunities. Civil war was clearly the great impediment to economic development.

Political reform, too, was vital to development, because repressive, corrupt states lacking effective governance and the rule of law could not possibly hope to attract the private investments that are the engines of economic growth. We decided, therefore, to make conflict resolution and democratization the centerpieces of our African policy.

We had no problems achieving consensus on this policy within the State Department Bureau of African Affairs. The question remained, however, as to how we could sell this to the department's senior political levels, as well as to the other agencies in the national security community. In our favor was the major diplomatic success achieved by my predecessor, Dr Chester A. Crocker, who mediated the negotiations involving South Africa, Angola, and Cuba that led to the New York agreements of December 1988. Those agreements brought about the independence of Namibia and the withdrawal of South African and Cuban military forces from Angola. That the United States played the key external role in bringing the New York agreements to fruition was a most important precedent in US policy toward Africa.

Crocker's success during the Reagan administration gave solid momentum at the start of the Bush administration to the idea of the United States as a third party intervenor in African conflict.[1] Nevertheless, because we were talking about intervening diplomatically in conflict situations in which the United States had no "vital" interests, we knew we had to proceed with caution.

The art of "piggybacking" on other people's priorities

In my first policy conversation with Secretary Baker in April 1989, he emphasized two "global" priorities for the Bush administration: to demonstrate active cooperation with the Soviet Union in solving "regional problems" and to improve relations with the Congress on foreign policy issues. He said President Bush felt strongly that Soviet President Mikhail Gorbachev merited US support. Consequently, Bush wanted every assistant secretary to maintain close contact with his or her Soviet counterpart to determine how the two superpowers could collaborate. As to Congress, the Reagan administration had left some bad feelings on the Hill, especially on the Contra affair in Nicaragua and the question of *apartheid* in South Africa. Baker wanted me to do whatever I could to diminish congressional ill will on the South Africa question.

In response, I told Baker about my plan to concentrate on conflict resolution and democratization. On democratization, Baker did not hesitate. The promotion of democracy worldwide was something he said Bush was thinking about to replace anticommunism, and he had no hesitation in approving that aspect of my proposal. On conflict resolution, however, he hesitated but did not reject it. He suggested I look for ways to dovetail conflict resolution with the president's priorities and in any event to keep in close touch with Under Secretary for Political Affairs Robert Kimmitt on a case-by-case basis. Kimmitt would be the Africa Bureau's direct line to Baker.

Baker's reaction to my conflict resolution idea led me to conclude that I should not seek to introduce the subject as a national security policy issue by initiating the lengthy formal process needed to develop a policy document for the president's signature. In the Bush administration, such formal policymaking procedure began with the Policy Coordinating Committee for Africa, which I chaired. All government departments with an interest in Africa took part in the meetings, depending on the subject. State, Defense, USAID, the United States Information Agency, the Central Intelligence Agency, the National Security Council (NSC) staff, and Treasury were present for all meetings. Recommendations from this body were sent to the next-higher level in the NSC system, the Deputies Committee, composed of the second-highest-ranking person in these agencies and chaired by the deputy national security advisor. The highest policymaking level, the NSC itself, chaired by the president, produced a final presidential national security decision, then called a Presidential Decision Directive, or PDD.

Instead of going through the laborious process of seeking a PDD on African conflict resolution, we decided we should proceed cautiously, one country at a time, keeping in touch with higher authority as we advanced.

Baker's emphasis on collaboration with the Soviets to solve regional problems led me to seek an early meeting with my Soviet counterpart, Anatoly Adamishin, vice minister of foreign affairs for Africa and human rights. I had gotten to know Adamishin during 1987–88 when he and Chester Crocker were consulting on the Namibian independence negotiations. (I was senior director for Africa on the National Security Council staff at the time.) The Soviets had been helpful in nudging both the Angolans and the Cubans toward flexibility. I found that he was quite anxious to meet with me, and a meeting was arranged to take place in Rome at the end of May 1989.

In Rome, Adamishin was quite frank about the Soviet view of "collaboration to solve regional problems." When Gorbachev came to power and reviewed Soviet foreign policy around the globe, he was horrified to see the costly Soviet commitments in Angola and Ethiopia. Both governments were Marxist, and both were Soviet client states.

Ethiopia had been fighting an unwinnable civil war for thirty years on two fronts – against Eritrean secessionists and Tigrean "freedom fighters." Angola's regime had been fighting a war against the National Union for the Total Independence of Angola (UNITA) since 1975, when chaos ensued after Portugal gave Angola its independence without any preparation. That same year, Cuban troops had come to install the communist Popular Movement for the Liberation of Angola (MPLA) in power. In response, the neighboring South African regime began arming UNITA, which embarked on a guerrilla war that was still raging fourteen years later.

In both countries, the Soviets were spending the equivalent of $1 billion per year for arms deliveries and in-country military technical assistance. Adamishin said the Soviets could no longer afford these costly burdens in Africa and did not believe either conflict could be resolved through military means. They wanted to bow out but did not want to withdraw in a way that would cause their clients to be defeated or humiliated. They were hoping that US–Soviet collaboration could focus on promoting negotiated settlements.

I told Adamishin that our collaboration on Angola should be feasible because we were both involved. The Soviets and the Cubans were arming and advising their clients in the Angolan government. We had been engaged since 1986 in a "covert action" program in support of the UNITA rebels, who were popular with US conservatives. Our assistance to UNITA was part of the "Reagan Doctrine," designed to counter the spread of Soviet military power throughout the world. The presence of Cuban troops in Angola also made our aid to UNITA popular within the Cuban exile community in the United States. While UNITA's main support came from the *apartheid* regime in South Africa, UNITA leader Jonas Savimbi considered US support essential, both materially and politically. US assistance, worth about $25 million per year, consisted of defensive equipment, including Stinger shoulder-fired antiaircraft missiles and TOW antitank missiles.

I proposed to Adamishin that we work together to push our respective Angolan clients to the negotiating table. He agreed, although he could not resist chiding me. The Soviets, he said, were supporting the legitimate regime in power in Angola, while the United States was assisting the "illegitimate" rebel group UNITA. The answer to the Angolan conflict, he suggested, was for us to stop helping UNITA. Nevertheless, he acknowledged that the war was unwinnable on the battlefield and that negotiations were necessary.

On Ethiopia, I told Adamishin I was less sanguine about our ability to be helpful. US relations with the harsh Stalinist regime in Ethiopia under dictator Mengistu Haile Mariam were at rock bottom. We had not had an ambassador there since 1981, and during the Reagan administration Ethiopia had remained on the list of pariah Marxist states publicly condemned by the president and other senior officials. No high-level US officials had visited Ethiopia since the regime took over in a coup against Emperor Haile Selassie in 1974. Prior to the coup, we had supplied arms to Ethiopia and maintained an important military communications station in Asmara, the capital of the province of Eritrea. After the coup, when it looked certain that the regime was coming under the control of Marxists, the United States cut off all military assistance. This decision by Secretary of State Henry Kissinger inevitably led the regime to turn to the Soviets for arms and thereby hardened their Marxist tendencies. When I explained all this to Adamishin, he smiled and said, "Mengistu wants to make friends with you. Will you accept an invitation to make an official visit to Ethiopia?"

I could not immediately agree to go to Ethiopia, however, because of political sensitivities in Washington. The Ethiopia relationship was comparable to the one with Cuba. Officials at the assistant secretary of state level did not routinely go to Cuba. The same was true for Ethiopia. Adamishin predicted that an invitation would be forthcoming. I told him that I would need to consult with the "political levels" before I could accept.

Back in Washington, I raised the issue with Under Secretary Kimmitt, who said I should accept an invitation to go to Ethiopia. He would tell Baker that the visit fell under the US-Soviet worldwide collaboration policy and that I should be protected from the "hard-line" folks in some parts of the White House and the Heritage Foundation. In effect, Kimmitt agreed that we could begin to engage in conflict resolution work in Ethiopia.

To begin work on resolving the conflict in Angola required no such persuasive efforts. Bringing the warring parties to the negotiating table was the main objective of both ourselves and our client, UNITA. Our assistance to UNITA was not designed to help UNITA win the war but to prevent the Angolan government from winning. Not surprisingly, the Angolan government, like their Soviet mentors, saw the solution coming from an end to US "covert action," but we continued to insist that this would happen only after "national reconciliation" was achieved in Angola through negotiations.

Even before I could get together with my Soviet counterpart to discuss collaborating on Ethiopia and Angola, I received a call from Deputy Secretary of State Lawrence Eagleburger, who spent a large percentage of his time stroking key members of the Congress involved with national security and foreign policy. In April 1989, Eagleburger told me he was being besieged by the "Hunger Caucus" about starvation and malnutrition in the Sudan. The chairman of the congressional Select Committee on Hunger, Democratic Representative Tony Hall of Ohio, and other committee members, especially Republican Representative Frank Wolf of Virginia, were highly energized by the nongovernmental organizations working to alleviate hunger and malnutrition in southern Sudan, caused by the never-ending civil war.

Beyond the absolute horrors of the guerrilla war and repression in southern Sudan was the added factor that the victims were mainly Nilotic African Christians and Animists, while those in the Sudanese government repressing them were mainly Arabic-speaking Muslims. Particularly egregious was the existence of significant evidence that the regime, although democratically elected, was using hunger as a weapon against the south. For these reasons, the Hunger Caucus was highly effective in getting Eagleburger's attention.

Because of this pressure on the hunger issue, Eagleburger instructed me to "go to Sudan right away to demonstrate that we are on top of the problem." Thus, on my first overseas trip after becoming assistant secretary, I spent most of my time persuading those in power in Khartoum to cooperate with the United Nations by allowing humanitarian relief convoys to transit government-controlled areas into the war zones in the south.[2] While my colleagues in the Africa Bureau and I knew that the government could probably be persuaded to do the right thing that year with respect to food shipments, we also knew that we had to attack the fundamental problem, which was the war itself. Otherwise, we would be faced year after year with the same problem of negotiating food shipments with the government while people were dying of starvation. While in Khartoum, therefore, we decided to add conflict resolution in the Sudan to our checklist of diplomatic priorities. In this case, I knew that I could count on being fully protected by Deputy Secretary Eagleburger.

By the middle of 1989, the door had been opened for us to become third party intervenors in three of the four major African conflicts then in progress. For Ethiopia and Angola, we worked under the policy favoring maximum cooperation with the Gorbachev regime in the Soviet Union to solve regional problems. In Sudan, we were covered by the desire of our political leadership to demonstrate maximum concern for one of the most famine-devastated countries on earth.

That left Mozambique, where the civil war between the government and the RENAMO rebel movement was having an impact similar to the one in the Sudan. Over a million refugees had fled Mozambique and an equal number were internally displaced. The humanitarian situation, which was always in crisis, was receiving US assistance worth $100 million per year. No compelling policy reason argued for us to intervene in the Mozambique conflict, because the country had never really been an element in US–Soviet competition, despite its earlier Marxist regime and considerable Soviet military assistance. Nevertheless, the government there had been helpful to us with South Africa, serving as an important communications channel during the Namibian independence negotiations. We therefore wanted to be of help to them.

During 1987 and 1988, conservatives in the Reagan administration had sought to stimulate support for the RENAMO rebels in Mozambique as anticommunist "freedom fighters" but were unable to make much progress against Chester Crocker's and my resistance. Moreover, Reagan had developed friendly relations with Mozambican President Samora Machel, as well as with Foreign Minister Joaquim Chissano, who became president after Machel's death in an airplane crash in 1986. We were therefore pleased when conflict resolution efforts in Mozambique began in 1989 under Italian leadership. In 1991, we moved from a position of interested bystander to one of deep involvement after the Portuguese government prevailed upon Secretary Baker to back Lisbon's participation in the Mozambican peace process. In this case, our relations with a NATO ally provided the backing we needed to become more heavily involved.

Juggling several conflicts at one time

Since each conflict had its own "personality," we could not employ any single approach to all. In Angola, for one, the government saw the United States as part of the problem, and sincerely felt that the war could be ended on their terms if the United States would stop helping the UNITA rebels. Since domestic US politics prevented us from stopping our assistance to UNITA, had we even wanted to, our approach in Angola, therefore, was to work indirectly through the neighboring heads of state to stimulate a peace process.

In Ethiopia, we were able to exercise leverage directly on the regime because of their desire to replace declining Soviet interest and assistance with something else. That "something else" turned out to be a scheme to reach out to the Israelis for arms and technical assistance, working through the United States. We were able to take advantage of this scenario to exercise considerable influence on the protagonists.

In the Sudan, we were working with a democratically elected regime that lacked the competence to deal simultaneously with a major famine and a civil war. The regime was anxious to have a dialogue with the United States in the search for solutions. Normally, in African civil wars, the regime insists on its own legitimacy, as opposed to the "illegitimacy" of the insurgent forces. The regime's first approach to the problem is usually to ask the international community to help suppress the "illegitimate" rebels or "bandits." In the Sudan, the situation was reversed. Our biggest problem was in persuading the insurgents to get into a dialogue with the government, because they did not want to "legitimize" the regime despite its having been elected democratically. For its part, the regime was quite happy to recognize the "Sudanese character" of the rebels and would have been pleased to welcome them back to full participation in the "democratic process." When the democratic regime was replaced by an Islamic military dictatorship early in the game, the situation became more complicated, with the rebels being even less willing to enter into dialogue.

In Mozambique, the head of state fully understood the need for negotiations to end an unwinnable war, but his power structure bitterly opposed dialogue. They saw the rebels as creatures of the *apartheid* regime in South Africa. For them, a solution to the Mozambican war lay in the ending of minority rule in South Africa. With that formidable barrier to negotiations, our entry point into conflict resolution in Mozambique was to encourage the head of state to use the power and prestige of the US presidency to influence his own policy team. President Chissano twice brought his hard-line teams into the White House to listen to successive American presidents (Reagan and Bush) insist on the need for negotiations with rebels who, after all, were Mozambicans, not aliens from outer space.

The civil wars in Angola, Ethiopia, the Sudan, and Mozambique had been going on for a long time when Bush assumed the presidency and could be considered "mature" wars. The approaches to conflict resolution in those countries necessarily differed from our approaches to the three new wars that erupted during the Bush administration – in Liberia, Rwanda, and Somalia. In none of these countries could we invoke a broader, "extra-African" policy umbrella that would give us political cover for playing a role as a third party intervenor. We nevertheless became involved in all three, based mainly on the momentum of our work in the first four. Acting as a third party intervenor in Africa had become a critical part of the US policy environment fairly early in the administration.

The "mature" wars could be the subjects of slow reflection and deliberate, step-by-step approaches over lengthy periods of time, but the new wars presented the challenge of "crisis management." When a new conflagration breaks out, even if it first appears only as a hundred guerrillas running around the forested border areas of Liberia, there is little time to think about strategy. One wants to jump in and help achieve a negotiated settlement before major damage is done.

In Liberia, we jumped in quickly on the basis of the close historic relationship between Liberia and the United States. We were the big brother who was expected to restore order in the family. We sought to be mediators and power brokers along the lines of President Reagan's actions a few years earlier in the Philippines, where we had a similar historical relationship. It was not to be.

At the working level in the Bureau of African Affairs, we formulated detailed plans to effect a peaceful regime change in Liberia and were ready to try implementing it in the spring of 1990. Unfortunately, these plans were vetoed at higher levels. As a result, we became marginal players as the crisis unfolded. In the Philippines we had important naval and air facilities, at Subic Bay and Clark Field, that made our involvement in crisis management there imperative. Similarly, in Liberia we had $400 million in supposedly "essential" national security facilities. But when it came to making choices, Liberia was not considered sufficiently important for the United States to take charge.

In Rwanda and Somalia, others intervened before we did, and we were happy to play secondary roles. It was probably no coincidence, however, that here, where our interventions in the early stages were the least aggressive, the conflicts turned out to have the most tragic consequences of all. Our approaches were timid and tardy, leading to costly interventions later to deal with humanitarian catastrophes. There was also probable cause and effect between our refusal to intervene in Liberia and its total collapse as both a state and a society.

Clearly, for a variety of reasons both tactical and political, our interventions in the "mature" wars were more productive than those in the newborn wars.

Organizational style and some policy principles

Coopting the bureaucracy

While we did not seek a formal interagency consensus for a presidential policy decision regarding conflict interventions in Africa, the Bureau of African Affairs considered it vital to bring the national security community into the process at virtually every step of the way. We did this through a combination of formal and informal procedures.

We were fortunate in being able to convene interagency meetings without seeking the approval of higher authority. Our main mechanism was the Policy Coordinating Committee (PCC) for Africa, the formal multiagency body I chaired within the NSC system. We convened this body rather frequently on specific African conflict situations, including those where there was no civil war in process, such as in Zaire, South Africa, and Kenya. This practice had several objectives.

We wanted to identify potential impediments in the bureaucracy to our acting as intervenor – a big problem, as it turned out, in the case of Somalia. We also found the PCC a major source of information and insight. Each agency did research and prepared its representative for the meetings, which normally began with a briefing by a pair of analysts from the Central Intelligence Agency and the Defense Intelligence Agency. This practice set the factual scene for the ensuing debate and usually led to the development of ideas on the role of third party intervention, if any. At the end of these discussions we generally had a clear idea of how the United States might make a contribution to conflict resolution. The jump to actually taking an initiative from that point was both small and logical. Finally, these meetings simultaneously gave each agency, including the National Security Council staff, a stake in the process and reinforced State Department leadership.[3]

Informal small group meetings dealt with specific problems. We met weekly, for example, with the head of the CIA Operations Directorate for Africa. Small, ad hoc working groups focused on specific countries. These usually involved Defense Department Africa expert James L. Woods, NSC Africa Director Walter Kansteiner, Bureau of Intelligence and Research Africa Director Vincent Farley, the director of AID's Office of Foreign Disaster Assistance, Andrew Natsios, and the assistant legal advisor for Africa, John Byerly. Depending on the problem at hand, USIA, Treasury, and other State Department bureaus, especially the Bureau of International Organization (meaning United Nations) Affairs, would be brought in.

Decentralizing the Bureau of African Affairs

Within the State Department Bureau of African Affairs, the main role in our conflict resolution effort was played by the individual office directorates. It was there that we conceptualized specific country approaches and developed and carried out our day-to-day tactics. The office directorates were in direct touch with our embassies, both in the countries concerned and in neighboring countries with a keen interest in the evolution of the wars. Deputy assistant secretaries having subregional oversight responsibilities provided higher-level supervision. For example, Deputy Assistant Secretary Irvin Hicks worked directly with East Africa Director Jack Davison and his staff on Ethiopia and the Sudan. Principal Deputy Assistant Secretary Jeff Davidow supported Southern Africa Director Robert Perito and his staff on Mozambique and Angola. The country directorates were also in regular contact with other agencies and other State Department bureaus and prepared both the formal and informal interagency consultations.

My role as assistant secretary was to provide policy impetus to the entire process, keep the political levels informed, consult with appropriate congressional players, and deal with higher-level counterparts in other agencies to keep them interested and supportive. I also spent a significant amount of time stroking counterparts in other governments to keep them happy and supportive of our efforts or encourage them to take initiatives.

Above all, I was a deployable asset. The country directors frequently asked me to go to certain capitals, or appear at certain negotiations, in order to achieve specific short-term goals. To economize on both time and money, we would try to combine travel missions. The deputy assistant secretaries and I planned every trip to Africa or to Western Europe by any one of us to include a conflict resolution element of some sort. If I was going to a bilateral meeting in Paris, for example, I would be asked to travel to Brussels to meet with UNITA rebel leader Jonas Savimbi or the Angolan foreign minister who might be traveling in Europe at the same time. At the Namibia independence celebrations in March 1990, I took advantage of the presence of Kenyan President Daniel arap Moi to discuss Mozambique in an effort to stimulate a peace process there. Moi had become the mentor of the chief of the RENAMO rebels, Afonso Dhlakama, a relationship forged through Protestant church connections. During every African trip, I tried to visit at least two additional countries, even when there was no special business to transact, just to brief the heads of state and senior officials on what we were doing. I would seek their ideas and try to give them the feeling they were participating as stakeholders in the building of peace. While traveling, I made myself available to the United States Information Service as much as possible, to send appropriate messages via the press. In Washington I met extensively with a steady stream of visitors from governments and the private sector interested in the peace process of one or another African country.

Making use of the large US government talent pool

One of the principal advantages of keeping other agencies and State Department bureaus involved in our conflict resolution activities was the availability of the many talents in those organizations. The unsung heroes of several conflict negotiations, including those where the United States was not in charge, were the military experts and legal wordsmiths who came from within the US bureaucracy to sit patiently with apprehensive African negotiators in the search for "win-win" compromises. Military cease-fires, redeployments, troop encampments, and demobilizations are complex issues that carry implications for security and power. US military experts from the Pentagon or from attaché offices in places like Lisbon, Maputo, Addis Ababa, or Luanda played a vital role in bringing a number of peace agreements to fruition through both the negotiation and implementation stages. The State Department assistant legal advisor for Africa, John Byerly, and his team of lawyers also distinguished themselves with their contributions to successful negotiations, especially in Angola and Mozambique.

Coopting the other agencies also paid off in creative ideas. For example, conducting a free and fair election in October 1992 in Angola, which had lost most of its infrastructure during fifteen years of civil war, was a daunting prospect. How were the election workers going to be transported around such a large country along with the necessary supplies like ballot boxes? The Pentagon came up with a creative solution: Ask the Arizona Air National Guard to hold its annual exercise in Angola instead of somewhere in the United States. Thus in July and August 1992, Guard units encamped at the Luanda airport and flew daily missions transporting election workers or redeployed troops, meanwhile achieving their training objectives in real Third World conditions. Similarly, USAID found creative ways to provide relief food to encamped soldiers by feeding their families, who found ways to share with their soldier fathers and husbands.

Following a policy of talking to everybody

One tactical policy we adopted early on was that of avoiding fights over who was legitimate and who illegitimate among parties to a civil conflict in Africa. We decided to talk to everyone and not worry about who might be offended, either in the country concerned or among the ideologues in Washington who closely followed events.

I made this policy somewhat inadvertently during my confirmation hearings in April 1989, when I was pressed by Senator Jesse Helms to open a dialogue with the RENAMO insurgents in Mozambique. Until that moment, we had followed a policy of refusing to talk to RENAMO in view of their unsavory reputation for cruelty and human rights violations against civilians. I told Helms that it would be my policy to talk to anyone if it could contribute to peace. I was immediately slapped on the wrist for "making policy during confirmation hearings," but there it was, and we adhered to that policy throughout the Bush administration.

In addition to opening a dialogue with RENAMO, which offended both the Mozambican government and the American ideological left, we talked regularly to the "Marxist" insurgents in Ethiopia, which offended the ideological right. For ideological and historical reasons, we did not have formal diplomatic relations with the Marxist government of Angola, but dealt with them nevertheless as the legitimate power, much to the displeasure of our UNITA friends and their conservative backers in Washington. In 1990 and 1991, we maintained an active dialogue with various Somali insurgent groups, thereby making our close "ally" President Mohammed Siad Barre nervous. Overall, we decided that fighting legitimacy battles was a waste of time and that, as a superpower, we did not have to worry about offending anybody. We kept our eye on the prize of conflict resolution, which took precedence over diplomatic niceties.

No magic formulas for negotiations

We tried to avoid routine formulas for negotiations. We did not believe in standardized road maps to peace. In particular, we were not fanatics about cease-fires. Though they are an important element of peace, cease-fires are essentially elements of the bargaining process. When there is a war going on, the side that wants a cease-fire is almost always the one that happens to be at a temporary disadvantage on the battle-field. The side that has a temporary advantage wants something in exchange for the cease-fire. Our experience was that the most fruitful negotiations are achieved in the absence of a cease-fire, callous as that may seem.

We were also not fanatics about constitutional reform as part of the peace process, although it was clear that no rebel group could be expected to accept being integrated into a "status quo" power structure after having fought that power structure for a long period. If the UNITA rebels in Angola, for example, had accepted integration into the existing power structure in 1989, as proposed by the regional heads of state, we would not have been upset. Nevertheless, when UNITA said they preferred to keep fighting in order to force negotiations for "free and fair elections," we expressed understanding for that point of view as well.

We did not condone the refusal by any side to a conflict to enter into dialogue, nor the setting of preconditions for talks by one or both sides. Like the question of legitimacy, we considered negotiating preconditions to talks to be another waste of time. Likewise, we had little patience for lengthy negotiations about procedures for talks. For example, negotiations between the Ethiopian government and the Eritrean People's Liberation Front, which began in 1989 under the mediation of former president Jimmy Carter, foundered on the rocks of procedural wrangles. When we took charge of those negotiations, we plunged immediately into substance and ignored procedures. Procedural negotiations, such as the "shape of the table" talks on Vietnam, are essentially prenegotiation jockeying for advantage that we attempted to avoid.

In late 1992, toward the end of the Bush administration, with our Somali intervention still in progress and all the other experiences still fresh in our psyches, we decided that it would be "untidy" to leave office without having established a formal policy covering what we had actually done. Consequently, I initiated a process within the Policy Coordinating Committee for Africa to write a comprehensive US policy toward Africa. This process was completed in December 1992, with a cleared interagency policy document sent to the White House. That document formalized our key policy initiatives for the previous four years, emphasizing development based on economic reforms and free markets, democratization and good governance, and conflict management. On conflict, the new policy emphasized less of the US third party intervention that had been the case since 1989 and more support for Africa's own initiatives in the Organization of African Unity.

President Bush signed the policy document in January 1993 as one of his last foreign policy acts before leaving office.[4] We later learned, with much pride, that the Clinton administration reviewed the policy directive signed by President Bush and adopted it as its own.

*   *   *

Against this basic backdrop, the seven case studies that follow recount what actually happened in the "real world." In the end, our work as third party intervenors in these seven African conflicts taught us a great deal in terms of pragmatic approaches. We knew a lot more after the four Bush administration years about what does and does not work in conflict management in Africa.

Most notable was that the United States, as the sole remaining super-power, carries particular weight as an intervenor in Africa. Its involve-ment conveys certain intangibles – moral authority, a sense of security, confidence in the neutrality of US proposals, to name a few – that tend to create a positive environment for negotiations. That special status also gives the United States special responsibilities regarding African civil conflict. In effect, Washington's decisions to intervene, or not to intervene, diplomatically can greatly influence the prospects for peace and stability in Africa.

2
Ethiopia: Ending a Thirty-Year War

From a purely diplomatic point of view, the United States appeared unlikely to accomplish much in Ethiopia. Although we participated actively in famine relief, our diplomatic relations with Ethiopia's Mengistu regime between 1974 and 1989 were basically unproductive. We had very little to say to each other. Mengistu and his cohorts were such unreconstructed Stalinists that American conservatives put them in the same pariah category as Castro's Cuba. Yet, from my first days as assistant secretary for African affairs, Ethiopia loomed larger and larger on my radar screen. Both domestic and foreign policy reasons compelled our involvement.

US domestic imperatives: Jews and hunger

Prior to my Senate confirmation hearings in April 1989, I discovered that the issue of Ethiopian Jewry was quite hot in the Congress. Ethiopia's approximately 20 000 Jews had expressed the desire to emigrate to Israel, and the Ethiopian government was refusing to let them go. Republican senator Rudy Boschwitz of Minnesota was particularly vehement on the issue of the "Falashas," as the Ethiopian Jews were commonly called.[1] The two principal organizations maintaining pressure on the American and Israeli governments on the Falashas' behalf – the North American Conference on Ethiopian Jewry and the American Association of Ethiopian Jewry (AAEJ) – let me know that they were ready to support any diplomatic initiatives I might undertake.[2] AAEJ Executive Secretary Will Recant, a regular visitor to the Africa Bureau, kept the issue alive and brought us excellent information about events in Ethiopia.

Hunger in the Horn of Africa was another bipartisan burning issue. Civil wars in Ethiopia, the Sudan, and Somalia threatened millions of people with starvation. All three countries suffered regularly from drought conditions, and the wars prevented food production even during periods of good rainfall. The result was a need for massive external assistance. The United States had been the leading supplier of humanitarian assistance to the region and would continue to play a major role. Nevertheless, the Congress and the community of nongovernmental organizations were concerned that humanitarian relief efforts might flag. Because the Ethiopian and Sudanese governments used hunger as a weapon against rebels, continuing diplomatic pressure was required to assure free movement for relief convoys.

Within the Congress, the Joint Committee on Hunger, chaired by Representative Tony Hall, held hearings and spoke out forcefully about the Horn of Africa. In early 1989, advocates made a special effort to persuade the new Bush administration of the importance of the hunger problem. Deputy Secretary of State Eagleburger, impressed by the level of congressional interest, instructed me early on to give hunger high priority. He directed me to visit the Horn on my first trip to show our concern.

Bush's priority: work with the Soviets

Domestic concerns about Ethiopian Jewry and hunger in the Horn of Africa complemented Bush's overarching policy of collaborating with the Soviets to solve regional problems. In Africa, the Soviets had made their strongest Cold War commitments in Ethiopia and Angola and would certainly want our support to find graceful exits from both. In view of these domestic and foreign policy imperatives, it was not surprising that during my first overseas travel as assistant secretary I met with Soviet Vice-Minister Anatoly Adamishin in Rome, on 1 June 1989, to discuss possible US-Soviet collaboration on Africa. As recounted in Chapter 1, Adamishin and I agreed that joint efforts to end the war in Angola would be a natural follow-on to our earlier collaboration on Namibia.

Ethiopia was another story. The US government's cool relations with Ethiopia dated to Secretary Kissinger's 1974 decision to terminate our long-term arms supply relationship, citing the regime's abysmal human rights record. No US assistant secretary of state had visited Addis Ababa for fifteen years. From mid-1980 we were represented only at the level of chargé d'affaires, not ambassador. Despite our substantial humanitarian assistance, we had no real leverage with Ethiopia's Stalinist regime.

Adamishin was nevertheless more interested in Ethiopia than in Angola, and refused to be discouraged. He told me the Ethiopians wanted US friendship and asked if I would accept an invitation to visit Addis. I laughed, saying I would make that decision when the invitation arrived. I had to be careful, because a visit to Marxist Ethiopia by a high official in a Republican administration required political approval.

Sure enough, an official invitation for me to visit Ethiopia was delivered to US chargé d'affaires Robert Houdek in early June. My very capable East Africa director, John Davison, believed Ethiopia was becoming ripe for change. A visit at the assistant secretary level would be opportune, he advised, if only to listen and obtain a sense of the direction of change. Under Secretary Kimmitt agreed to request political clearance on the basis of the president's desire to enhance US–Soviet cooperation. The invitation was accepted, and a date set for 4–6 August 1989. From that point, I knew Ethiopia would be important in my overall plan for vigorous conflict resolution in Africa.

Many players, many agendas

In the US government view, ending Ethiopia's civil wars was the best way to assure the delivery of relief supplies to the starving and arrange the departure of 20 000 Ethiopian Jews. But terminating these long-running wars was not a viable possibility in the short term. Thus we had to adopt a multifaceted approach, pursuing a peace strategy while exercising every possible lever to achieve specific objectives. To this end we had to choreograph a complex diplomatic ballet among a large array of players.

The Ethiopian government

In mid-1989 the Government of the People's Democratic Republic of Ethiopia (GPDRE), was considered one of the world's most hardened Marxist regimes. *Perestroyka* à la Gorbachev had no place on its agenda. The dictatorial President Mengistu Haile Mariam had come to power in 1974 through a military coup that overthrew Emperor Haile Selassie, Africa's senior statesman and good friend of the United States.[3]

Ethiopia's change of government was particularly irksome to the United States for two reasons. First, the new regime was pro-Soviet and repressive. Second, we lost our important communications facility, Kagnew Station, in the Eritrean highlands near Asmara. After having been a major Cold War ally of the United States, Ethiopia swung

180 degrees in the other direction. It accepted a large Soviet military aid presence, granted them a naval facility in the Dhalak Islands in the Red Sea, and invited Cuba to send troops to help defend Ethiopia against military aggression from neighboring Somalia. Indeed, the projection of Soviet and Cuban power into Ethiopia and Angola in 1974–75 was the principal reason President Gerald Ford declared the end of détente between the United States and the Soviet Union shortly thereafter.[4]

At the outset of the Bush administration, Ethiopia was entangled in two major antigovernment insurgencies and several little ones. When Mengistu took power in 1974, he had inherited a twelve-year-old insurgency by Eritrean nationalists fighting for independence for their province on the Red Sea coast. In 1952 the United Nations had confederated Eritrea, a former Italian colony, with Ethiopia, without a referendum of the Eritrean people. The repressive regime in Addis Ababa also triggered a second big insurgency in the northern province of Tigray. Young Tigrean revolutionaries sought Mengistu's overthrow and a change of political system. The insurgents in both provinces called themselves Marxists, making it impossible for us to consider providing assistance to them, even though such political-military activity was both fashionable and politically acceptable in Washington at the time.

In 1989, the Ethiopian government was on notice that their Soviet mentors were tired and wanted to see movement toward peace. The Soviets advised President Mengistu to turn to the United States for assistance. When he invited us to become involved, we saw our role as helping to achieve a negotiated peace between the government and its internal enemies. As we later discovered, that was not Mengistu's agenda. What he wanted was to find a substitute for Soviet military support in the form of a trilateral anti-Arab alliance grouping Ethiopia, the United States, and Israel. Until the very end in May 1991, Mengistu's overriding aim was to win military victories in his unwinnable internal wars.

The Soviet Union

As our Soviet interlocutors explained with little subtlety, their interest was to disengage from Ethiopia with dignity. Besides the financial drain of arms shipments, the Soviets were supplying famine relief of 250 000 tons of grain per year at a time when they themselves were net importers of cereals. They also had a thousand military advisors in Ethiopia, some with frontline units. To make matters worse, Eritrean rebels had captured three of their military, and the Soviets hoped we could arrange their release. Finally, the Soviets reciprocated the US desire to demonstrate that the two superpowers could cooperate in solving regional problems. We wanted the reformist Gorbachev regime to look good, a concept the Soviets found appealing.[5]

Israel

Prior to 1974 the Israelis had friendly relationships with Emperor Haile Selassie's government. As a Christian society surrounded by Muslim Arab nations, Ethiopia considered Israel a natural ally. Israel wanted to remain close to Ethiopia because of Ethiopia's strategic position at the back door to the Middle East. Many Ethiopians had studied in Israel, and the existence in Gonder Province of an ancient colony of Ethiopian Jews dating back to biblical days fascinated the Israelis. The fascination was reciprocal, because Ethiopian lore teaches that their nation began with the love affair between their Queen of Sheba and the Hebrews' King Solomon, producing Ethiopia's first monarch, Menelik I.

The 1974 Mengistu revolution shattered the Ethiopia–Israel relationship. In 1989, the Israelis told us their priority in Ethiopia was the departure of the Ethiopian Jews. At the same time, we suspected they hoped to regain Ethiopia as an ally against the Arabs. That made sense considering how alliances had changed between 1974 and 1989. Both the Sudan and Iran had shifted from friendliness toward Israel to outright hostility.

The Ethiopian insurgents

There were many anti-Mengistu groups, both within Ethiopia and in exile communities throughout Europe, North America, and the Middle East. Of these, three were conducting serious military insurgencies that were keeping 200 000 government troops and the bulk of the country's resources tied down fighting a major civil war.

The Eritrean People's Liberation Front (EPLF)

EPLF began their war of national liberation in 1962, after Emperor Haile Selassie unilaterally abrogated the 1952 UN-mandated confederation between Eritrea and Ethiopia. Within the confederation, Eritrea had had considerable autonomy. The emperor's action reduced Eritrea to just another Ethiopian province under tight central government control. The EPLF's subsequent insurgency captured some mountain localities, but until late 1989 made little progress against Ethiopian defenses. The Eritrean diaspora, with thousands working in Middle East oil sheikdoms, contributed significant sums to the rebels.

The EPLF's war aim was to force a UN referendum giving the Eritrean people a choice between independence or remaining Ethiopian. Although the Ethiopian Army suffered significant casualties and the economic cost was significant, the Ethiopian people supported the GPDRE's determination to keep control of Eritrea. The national will to prevent Eritrean secession was in fact Mengistu's only political asset in an otherwise repressive environment.

Territorial integrity was also the only point of agreement between the American and Ethiopian governments. Although we sympathized with Eritrea's historical grievances, we were keen supporters of the cardinal principle of the Organization of African Unity – that colonial boundaries inherited by African states should be left intact to preclude demands for hundreds of ethnically based ministates.[6] At the time the United States considered the principle eminently sound. It discomfited me personally, however, because wherever I traveled for speaking engagements, Eritrean-Americans were there to protest. They were relentless picketers.

The Tigrean People's Liberation Front (TPLF)

TPLF, centered in Tigray Province, was dominated by the Tigrean ethnic group. Started in 1974, the TPLF had as its war aim not self-determination but the overthrow of Mengistu. In mid-1985, an internal power struggle led to the group's takeover by the Marxist-Leninist League of Tigray (MLLT). The MLLT's goal was to "combat all forms of revisionism, Maoism, Khrushchevism, Eurocommunism, Titoism, and Trotskyism." This was the TPLF's so-called "Albanian Model."

By mid-1989, the TPLF was a credible military force with roughly 65 000 soldiers capable of fighting in both conventional and guerrilla modes. Much of their equipment was captured from Ethiopians. In April 1988, a TPLF–EPLF agreement on military and political cooperation resulted in equipment swaps and coordinated military operations. But the TPLF's Marxist rhetoric made us leery. So whenever conservatives asked why we were not helping the insurgents against the hated Mengistu regime, we replied: "Those rebels are Marxist-Leninist-Albanians." Aggressive questioning stopped immediately.

The Ethiopian People's Revolutionary Democratic Front (EPRDF)

EPRDF emerged at the TPLF's Third Congress, held in Tigray 10–13 March 1989. The TPLF announced it was merging the TPLF and the

Ethiopian People's Democratic Movement (EPDM) to form the EPRDF . Although dominated by the TPLF, the EPRDF was an attempt to establish a nationwide political movement to demonstrate that the anti-Mengistu struggle was not confined to Tigray Province. The congress adopted a six-point peace plan: basic democratic freedoms, release of all political prisoners, establishment of a broadly based provisional government, self-determination for Eritrea, departure of all foreign military advisors, and dismantling of the regime's repressive security apparatus.

The Oromo Liberation Front (OLF)

OLF claimed to represent Ethiopia's largest ethnic group, the Oromo population in the southern and central regions, constituting between 40 and 50 per cent of all Ethiopians. The OLF was the weakest of the three insurgent movements and the least ideological. In our regular contacts with them through our embassy in Khartoum, they informed us the OLF was seeking self-determination, which they defined as freedom to practice and teach the Oromo language and pursue Oromo religious activities.[7] This objective was understandable, as the Oromos experienced linguistic, educational, and social discrimination from the more powerful Amhara ethnic group that dominated both the Haile Selassie and Mengistu regimes. While the OLF did not pose much of a military threat, they were qualified to claim a role in any effort to make peace.

The Ethiopian exiles

The Ethiopian exiles fled Mengistu's repression, with its overlay of human rights violations, between 1974 and 1989. Approximately 100 000, in a variety of professional and occupational categories, lived in the United States. They were hard-working, serious people trying to better themselves and provide good opportunities for their children. Passionate about their motherland, they reflected the different political tendencies at home, including Eritrean separatism. The one objective that united all the exiles was getting rid of Mengistu, but major differences would emerge after the war ended in 1991. Once the United States involved itself with Ethiopia in mid-1989, the Bureau of African Affairs became the object of much lobbying from exile organizations.

Bearding the wounded lion in his den

I visited Addis Ababa 4–6 August 1989, the first American assistant secretary of state to go there in fifteen years. I was accompanied by

Deputy Assistant Secretary Irvin Hicks. Robert Houdek, our very capable chargé d'affaires in Addis, guided us.

The Ethiopians provided sumptuous hospitality and major media attention. Their interest in resuming the close bilateral relationship of yore was clear.[8] The cold, damp weather reflected the morose atmosphere pervading Ethiopian society after fifteen years of repressive rule. Feelings of gloom and doom were palpable. An abortive military coup three months earlier, followed by bloody repression, added to the general paranoia.

A worrisome military situation heightened internal political tensions. Through a series of well-planned attacks, the TPLF had driven Ethiopian forces completely out of Tigray Province and also threatened Gonder, Welo, and Shewa provinces. The regime received notice from the Soviets that military support would diminish after the expiration of the arms supply agreement in 1991.[9] The only good news was the endorsement by the Shengo (parliament) on 5 June 1989 of Mengistu's six-point peace initiative. The plan accepted the EPLF demand for unconditional negotiations in the presence of mutually agreed upon neutral observers. Unfortunately, it did not include the TPLF, who were eventually brought in on a separate track.

I met with Mengistu the morning of 5 August. He was relaxed and informal, chain-smoking Marlboro cigarettes. I was particularly struck by the Star of David motif on the ceiling. Because the visit was the first for a long time, Mengistu felt the need to review the history of his regime, including the circumstances of his taking power ("I had no choice, the country was in a state of chaos"). He asked what it would take to improve relations between Ethiopia and the United States.

I was prepared with a checklist:

- *Human rights* – The regime held thousands of political prisoners under appalling circumstances.
- *Economic policy* – The Marxist economic system had driven the economy so far down that the World Bank classified Ethiopia as the world's poorest nation.
- *The unwinnable wars* – Despite major Soviet arms deliveries, the government had not defeated the insurgencies in Eritrea and Tigray. On the contrary, the rebels appeared to hold the military advantage in both provinces, although the GPDRE was far from desperate. I recommended early negotiations, and urged Mengistu to accept Jimmy Carter's offer to mediate between the GPDRE and the EPLF.

- *Ethiopian Jewry* – Without mentioning the "Falashas" specifically, I advised Mengistu of the strong feeling in the United States about Ethiopia's restrictive emigration policy. I noted we had been tough with the Soviets on this issue and would apply the same policy toward Ethiopia. He responded, "I know what you are referring to, and we will do something about it."

Mengistu listened calmly, promising progress on all issues. On economic questions, his government was preparing new laws designed to open the door to private investment. He pledged to bring in Jimmy Carter to mediate the wars and predicted early results. He hoped that we could resume normal diplomatic ties with an exchange of ambassadors. I said we would respond positively to concrete actions. Afterwards, at Bob Houdek's residence, speculating on what had caused Mengistu to swallow his pride and act like a pussycat, we concluded that Soviet pressure left him no choice.

Within days of our departure, we saw real evidence of Mengistu's determination to improve relations. On 7 August, an aircraft carrying Democratic Congressman Mickey Leland of Texas on a famine-related fact-finding mission, crashed in Ethiopia's mountains. Our request for permission to send a US Air Force search and rescue mission was granted with lightning speed, and our planes were allowed to fly wherever they wanted. The GPDRE's excellent cooperation would previously have been unavailable. Sadly, the aircraft was found with no survivors.[10]

During the second half of 1989, the GPDRE took several positive actions. Jimmy Carter presided over the first round of peace talks with the Eritrean insurgents in Atlanta, Georgia, 9–19 September, which were devoted to procedural issues. There was no agreement on selecting Carter's cochair, the list of outside observers, or the composition of a secretariat. Despite lack of progress, they all agreed to meet again in Nairobi later in the year.

Also in September, the GPDRE released 907 political prisoners, including three grandsons of the late Emperor Haile Selassie.[11] On 3 November, Ethiopia announced the resumption of diplomatic ties with Israel and authorized an Israeli consulate that would process Falasha departures.[12] On 4 November, procedural talks between the TPLF and Ethiopia began in Rome under Italian government auspices. As with the EPLF talks in Atlanta, the Rome talks were inconclusive. The Soviets were understandably interested and hopeful regarding both rounds. They sent a diplomat to Atlanta to be near the EPLF negotiations, despite our admonition that it could be harmful. The United States, while intensely interested, assumed a relaxed, arm's-length posture.

Mengistu's duplicity emerges

With the opening of peace talks, the establishment of relations with Israel, the release of prisoners, and the introduction of economic reforms, by the close of 1989 we saw grounds for optimism. We also saw disturbing signs that the GPDRE was playing games.

After the first round of talks in Atlanta, both heads of delegation visited us, each complaining of the other side's inflexibility. EPLF Secretary General Isaias Afwerki claimed he was negotiating in good faith. To prevent the GPDRE from reneging, however, he wanted the United States to be the guarantor of any accord. He said the Ethiopians were inflexible and only looking to buy time. The head of the GPDRE negotiating team, Ashagre Yigletu, chairman of the international committee of the Workers' Party of Ethiopia (WPE), said the same thing about the EPLF. While we were not surprised at the initial lack of progress, the Soviets became nervous. Supporting the GPDRE, Ambassador Dubinin urged Under Secretary Kimmitt to apply US pressure on the EPLF to be more flexible.

The next talks took place in Nairobi 20–29 November for the EPLF, and in Rome 12–18 December for the TPLF. They were equally unproductive. Our analysis was that the Ethiopians were not serious, and as Isaias said, were merely buying time. But for what purpose? We started looking for a possible weapons deal between the GPDRE and the Israelis in return for Jewish emigration.

Jimmy Carter's efforts finally foundered over the role of the United Nations as an observer. The EPLF wanted a UN presence as a reminder of the 1952 UN decision to establish a loose confederation between Eritrea and Ethiopia, which Addis had unilaterally and illegally abrogated in 1962. The GPDRE did not want the UN for fear of "internationalizing" the Eritrea problem. While the GPDRE did not actually veto the UN as an observer, it achieved its purpose by refusing to send the appropriate request to the UN secretary-general. Isaias correctly saw the GPDRE's position as a sign of bad faith, as did we.

The Rome talks with the TPLF also failed. There the procedural hurdle was not observers but the agenda. The TPLF, who wanted to discuss democracy and national politics, selected representatives of all provinces to sit with them. The government, which wanted to limit the negotiation to the "rebellion in Tigray Province" and "regional issues," refused non-Tigrean negotiators.

As 1989 ended, both insurgency movements became disillusioned. Isaias Afwerki was as angry with Jimmy Carter as with the Ethiopians, because Carter condoned the blocking of a UN observer. Nevertheless, neither group was ready to call it quits. They both assured us they wanted to continue negotiations.

In Washington, our policy of engaging with the Ethiopians did not draw as much criticism as I had feared. On 11 October 1989, Republican Representative Toby Roth of Wisconsin criticized us for considering upgrading US relations with Mengistu and warned us not to "squander our influence brokering truces between rival Ethiopian Communist factions."[13] Apart from such pinpricks, we had bipartisan support because our objectives were noble: peace in Ethiopia and the emigration of Ethiopia's Jews.

1990: Both war and diplomacy intensify

The year 1990 was decisive for Ethiopia's transition from war to peace. It was marked by the government's trying to play catch-up ball between military action and negotiations. In effect, the GPDRE began to make concessions that would have been more valuable to their interests in 1989 but in 1990 were too little and too late.

The course of the war

Both the EPLF and TPLF were less than enthusiastic about two rounds of unproductive talks bogged down in procedural disagreements. The GPDRE not only remained intransigent on procedures; they also refused confidence-building measures, such as the proposal by Jimmy Carter and ourselves for a cease-fire while talks continued. Addis said "verification would be too difficult." It was thus not surprising that both wars intensified in early 1990.

On 8 February, the EPLF launched an offensive that resulted in the capture of the strategic Red Sea port of Massawa (or Mits'iwa).[14] This dealt a major blow both to the GPDRE's capacity to import arms and commodities and to the humanitarian community's plans to use the port as its principal entry point for emergency food relief. As the wars expanded, so too did the need for emergency food relief. The capture of Massawa isolated the inland provincial capital, Asmara, effectively placing it under siege. The government army in Asmara could only be resupplied by air, escalating the war's cost. After Massawa was lost, the GPDRE bombed it continuously to prevent its use by the EPLF. Though the bombing was inaccurate and did little damage to facilities, it made the port too dangerous for shipping. We therefore used our leverage as mediators to persuade the GPDRE to stop the bombing so that relief shipments could be unloaded.

In the Tigrean war, the TPLF's offensive continued to prosper. By 4 March, the TPLF had captured key towns in Gonder province and were threatening the major Ethiopian air base at Bahir Dar. Their successes emboldened the TPLF to call upon Mengistu to transfer power to a broad-based interim government that would draft a constitution and hold internationally supervised elections.

Instead of intensifying negotiations, the GPDRE reacted to their military setbacks by stepping up the war effort. Press gangs began rounding up sixteen-year-old boys, sending them for thirty days of combat training, then off to the front. Needless to say, this did not improve national morale. At the same time, Mengistu was combing the world for arms, traveling to North Korea, Israel, East Germany, and the Soviet Union. On 19 April, government forces suffered heavy losses in an unsuccessful attempt to recapture Massawa.

An added feature of the Eritrean war was the harassment of shipping in the Red Sea by EPLF attack boats, targeting mainly Soviet bloc vessels. With three Soviet military advisors already in EPLF custody, these attacks on shipping added insult to injury.

By the summer of 1990, both wars had returned to a military stalemate of sorts, but with government forces much worse off than a year earlier. The TPLF had broken out of their Tigrean redoubt and penetrated Gonder, Welo, and Gojam provinces, all on the road to Addis Ababa. The EPLF had cut off Asmara from resupply by road and deprived the government of the port of Massawa. Nevertheless, one could not yet say that the government had lost the war.

A fresh US assessment

On 14 August at a meeting of the African Policy Coordinating Committee (PCC), the US team reviewed the state of play to determine if our approach was still valid. The PCC group reached consensus on the inevitability of Mengistu's downfall. We believed he was not capable of serious negotiations and would continue on a steady downward path toward military defeat. Until then, however, we would continue "limited relations" with the regime in pursuit of our humanitarian objectives (food for the hungry and Falasha emigration), advance the peace process "such as it was," enhance our cooperation with the Soviets, and position ourselves to change course when the time arrived.

We envisaged increased rather than diminished requirements for humanitarian relief immediately after a regime change and included that in our contingency planning. Despite our assumption that any successor regime would probably be an improvement, we would link US support and good relations to the emergence of "democratic values and practices."[15]

The PCC considered that a nonnegotiated change of regime might confront the United States "with a self-liberated Eritrea which has declared itself independent." We thus refined our policy on Eritrea as follows:

> Our current policy is in support of a unified Ethiopia with recognition that Eritrea's right to significant autonomy within the UN-approved federation was illegally abrogated by the Ethiopian Government in 1962. As we view the prospect of *de facto* independence for Eritrea as the result of military victory by the EPLF, we should keep our policy options open and avoid staking out legal positions unnecessarily. The possibility of US recognition of an independent Eritrea should be used to leverage both the EPLF and the successor Ethiopian regime.

The PCC also took note of Ethiopia's strategic location on the Red Sea, but did not propose to seek renewed military access there.[16] In general, the PCC review did not change our day-to-day policy, but it did anticipate some important new policy positions to occur when the regime actually did change.

The sluggish peace process

Despite an emphasis on military activity during the first half of 1990, the negotiating process was not dead. Jimmy Carter, the Italian Foreign Ministry, and the Soviets encouraged the parties not to give up.[17] A Carter Center press release had predicted that substantive talks would take place early in 1990. The same document disingenuously disposed of the UN observer issue by saying "a seventh invitation was issued to the United Nations, which declined to serve"; but the UN had declined to serve because they had not been invited by the Government of Ethiopia according to established procedures.[18]

Because we sympathized with the EPLF's bitter feelings about the UN observer issue, we did our best to bring the UN into the picture. I took advantage of the UN Special Session on Apartheid to meet with Secretary-General Javier Pérez de Cuéllar in New York on 12 December. I asked him if there might be a creative way the UN could find authority to send an observer to the EPLF–GPDRE negotiations. He said he had received a letter from EPLF chief Isaias Afwerki predicting that if a UN observer were not approved, war would start again. However, the General Assembly had given him authority to work on internal disputes in Afghanistan and Central America but not Ethiopia. While Carter and the EPLF had requested UN observers, the Government of Ethiopia had specifically said no. His hands, he said, were tied.

My last attempt on the UN observer issue was made in March 1990 at the Namibian independence celebrations in a meeting with Ethiopian Foreign Minister Tesfaye Dinka. I argued that Ethiopia was throwing away a good opportunity to engage in real dialogue with the EPLF before it was too late. I could tell he understood my point but was under firm instructions not to cave in. For Mengistu, a UN presence at the talks would lead directly to EPLF demands for a return to the UN-sponsored confederation of 1952. As Tesfaye Dinka told me several years later, when both of us were no longer employed by our respective governments, Mengistu could not give away what his predecessor Haile Selassie had seized.

On 27 March, Isaias Afwerki informed us that the UN observer issue had to be resolved to the EPLF's satisfaction before talks could be resumed. On 14 April, Mengistu told Carter he would not send a delegation to Nairobi to meet with the EPLF as long as the latter insisted on a UN observer. At that point Carter's mediation was effectively over.

The TPLF negotiations were not progressing either. A third round of "preliminary peace talks" took place in Rome 20–29 March 1990. The round ended in stalemate in the absence of agreement on the TPLF's demand that national and not just regional issues be discussed.

In our desire to try anything, we thought the United States and the Soviet Union might jointly propose UN Security Council action on the grounds that a humanitarian disaster was in the making. We tested this idea during US–Soviet ministerial consultations in Washington on 23 February, which fortunately included Soviet UN Permanent Representative Belogonov for the discussions on Ethiopia. Belogonov declared our idea a nonstarter. Ethiopia was sitting on the Security Council, he said, and could rally support from the other nonaligned members to prevent our getting the required nine votes to inscribe the item on the agenda. So much for the power of the superpowers.

US–Ethiopian relations in 1990

Despite our disappointment at GPDRE rigidity, we continued "constructive engagement." Our two major policy objectives were still relevant – assuring delivery of humanitarian relief, and arranging for the departure of the Ethiopian Jews. Moreover, an unexpected international event made the Ethiopian regime more important to us than we had previously thought possible. The Iraqis invaded Kuwait on 2 August 1990, and Ethiopia was a member of the UN Security Council.

GPDRE objectives did not change either. They wanted to raise our diplomatic relations to ambassadorial level, they wanted us to continue supporting Ethiopian territorial integrity, and above all they wanted us to acquiesce in Israel's replacing the Soviets as their major source of arms.

On 20 April, Democratic Representative Gary Ackerman of New York went to Ethiopia to check on the status of the Falashas awaiting exit visas. At the instigation of the American support organizations, 20 000 Falashas had left their homes in Gonder Province and crowded into a shanty town in Addis Ababa. The idea had been that outward processing of the Falashas would be facilitated if they were all in Addis near the Israeli Embassy and the international airport. But visa issuance was slow, and very few Falsashas were departing.[19]

Mengistu used the congressman's visit to propose a deal. He would release the Falashas rapidly in return for two concessions: (1) an exchange of ambassadors with the United States and (2) a US decision to "allow" Israel to give him more generous military assistance. Mengistu's proposal had the virtue of forcing us to consider how we would have to reward him. In a game of carrots and sticks, we had to decide when to give some carrots. Since only the White House could make a decision on ambassadorial exchanges, we recommended to Baker, who agreed, that President Bush acknowledge Mengistu's proposal with a pledge to exchange ambassadors once all of the Falashas had departed, the bombing of Massawa had ceased, and ships had begun unloading.

Next, on 16 June, our UN permanent representative, Ambassador Thomas Pickering, paid a visit to Addis. Mengistu told Pickering that his government would request the World Food Program to draw up a plan for shipping food relief through Massawa and would accelerate the departure of the Falashas – but discreetly, so as not to enrage the Arabs. In addition, Mengistu said he had changed his mind and would be willing to accept a UN observer at the peace talks with the EPLF. The negotiating situation began to improve because Mengistu's military situation was deteriorating.

Tesfaye Dinka came to Washington 25–26 July with new ideas. Since the GPDRE had taken steps to permit the opening of the Port of Massawa and had increased the number of Falasha departures, he was rewarded with a call on Acting Secretary Eagleburger. The secretary expressed satisfaction with the improvements on Massawa and the

Falashas, but informed Tesfaye that we would object strenuously to any deal with the Israelis to trade Jews for weapons.

In his meeting with me, Tesfaye asked for US assistance "behind the scenes" in restoring the Carter peace process. He asked us to inform the EPLF that the GPDRE was willing to consider an agreement that would afford Eritrea "very substantial autonomy" within a loose confederation. In addition, the GPDRE would be willing to accept the TPLF's proposal that the Rome talks discuss "the future of Ethiopia." If only they had made these concessions a year earlier.

Iraq's aggression against Kuwait on 2 August 1990 provided another opportunity for Ethiopia to demonstrate goodwill toward the United States. Within days of the invasion, the Ethiopian delegation on the UN Security Council began several months of close cooperation with the United States in an effort to apply maximum pressure on Iraq to withdraw from its conquest. At the UN General Assembly on 26 September, Tesfaye Dinka had a meeting with Secretary Baker, who thanked him for the strong support against Iraq. He told Tesfaye that as soon as Ethiopia was ready to table a firm proposal for Eritrean autonomy, we would be happy to host a trilateral meeting with the EPLF.

The trilateral meeting took place on 4 October in Washington with me presiding. The talks did not progress beyond a repetition of previous generalizations, but there appeared to be mutual interest in more dialogue. Tesfaye Dinka gave an oral presentation describing a new constitution in which Eritrea would have autonomous powers within a united Ethiopia. John Davison commented that the proposed arrangement would give Eritrea less power than any of the 50 American states. The EPLF still demanded a referendum, with secession as one option. What Tesfaye Dinka read to them, without leaving a written document, did not stimulate enthusiasm, because all power would continue to be lodged in the central government. In a memorandum to Under Secretary Kimmitt the following day, I wrote:

> One can discern agreement on one thing: both sides' desire to involve the US more directly. Addis wants to restart the Carter process with the US and USSR added to the observers already named. The EPLF probably would prefer to continue trilateral meetings, and would have great trouble with any Soviet involvement. (The EPLF is reluctant to renew the Carter initiative.) The sides asked me to propose a date, venue, and structure for the next meeting. While we want to escape a procedural morass, I agreed to volunteer some ideas. Our options include bringing Jimmy Carter back

into the process, continuing alone, or establishing some new structure (with the USG in the chair) that draws on procedures agreed in
the Carter talks.[20]

In early November, President Bush decided we should seek a Security
Council Resolution that would authorize the use of force against Iraq
if it failed to withdraw from Kuwait. We were concerned that the nonaligned nations in the Security Council might prevent the resolution
from receiving the required nine of fifteen votes. The three African
votes on the Council – Côte d'Ivoire, Ethiopia, and Zaire – were therefore crucial. Secretary Baker decided on a course of personal diplomacy
and asked me to set up a meeting with the three African foreign
ministers. It was arranged for 17 November in Geneva.

Baker met separately with each foreign minister for about thirty
minutes. In addition to myself, Under Secretary for Political Affairs
Kimmitt and Counselor Robert Zoellick were present. Zaire's foreign
minister Mushobekwa needed no persuasion. He listened to Baker's
pitch and said, "President Mobutu has always supported the United
States and will not fail to do so in this instance." Tesfaye Dinka was
accompanied by his UN permanent representative Tesfaye Tedesse.
Dinka pledged full Ethiopian support. He told Baker that Tedesse was
an expert on international law and would help draft the resolution.
In addition, Ethiopia would also help recruit the other nonaligned
countries, especially Ecuador, which was not enthusiastic about declaring war on Iraq. Côte d'Ivoire's Foreign Minister Simeon Ake was unable
to offer support on the spot. He needed authorization from President
Félix Houphouet-Boigny, which came within a week. The Bureau of
African Affairs had delivered three out of three votes.

In return for Ethiopian support, Tesfaye Dinka asked Baker for two
favors. First, he asked that we pressure the EPLF to return to the negotiating table and enlist the help of the Swedes and the Italians, "who
have influence" on the EPLF. He reiterated that the GPDRE "accepts a
federal system for Eritrea." Baker agreed to contact the Swedes and the
Italians. Second, Dinka asked Baker to tell the World Bank to make
its decisions on starting structural adjustment programs in Ethiopia on
strictly economic grounds. Bank officials were telling the GPDRE that
its "shareholders were discouraging structural adjustment projects" for
political reasons. Baker said, "We will send appropriate signals to the
World Bank."[21]

After the last foreign minister left the American mission, I was waiting
with Kimmitt and Zoellick while Baker escorted our visitor to his car.

Reacting to Tesfaye Dinka's enthusiastic support for our UN initiative, Zoellick said to me, "Your constructive engagement policy with Ethiopia has really paid off. We never told you about all those protest calls we received from conservatives about your visit to Ethiopia and your meeting with Mengistu. We did not want you to get discouraged." Well, as they say, what you don't know can't hurt you. In view of the GPDRE's assistance at the UN, it was clear that we had to take charge of the EPLF negotiation and generate some progress.

Whither the Falashas?

One reason we placed strong emphasis on the Falasha issue was the president's strong personal interest. In 1984–85, then vice president Bush was instrumental in the evacuation of approximately 10 000 Falashas in two airlift operations. Severe drought and civil war drove these Falashas from their homes in Gonder Province during 1984. For the most part, they walked into the Sudan. Our good relations with Sudan at the time helped us coordinate two Israeli airlifts from a remote airstrip there.

The establishment of diplomatic relations between Ethiopia and Israel in November 1989 started a movement of remaining Falashas toward Israel in early 1990, but in a trickle, not a torrent. By mid-1990, the Falashas waiting in Addis for departure numbered about 20 000. Medical, nutritional, and educational support were provided by the American Joint Distribution Committee with volunteer Jewish doctors, nurses, and counselors.

During 1990, Mengistu was clearly playing games with Falasha emigration, as its pace fluctuated with changing bureaucratic procedures. During one period the Ethiopians insisted that each application for an exit visa be accompanied by detailed support documentation from the "separated family members" in Israel. This requirement helped parry Arab criticism, showing Ethiopia was only uniting families, not supporting a "new wave" of Jewish emigration. It also helped squeeze the Israelis for military assistance. During 1990, the number of monthly Falasha departures ranged from a low of 30 to a high of 600. The total for all of 1990 was 3500. At that unacceptable rate, it would have taken at least another five years to clear the camps.[22]

For Mengistu, the name of the game was Israeli arms in exchange for Ethiopian Jews. This created a trilateral tension between Washington, Addis Ababa, and Jerusalem. Though the GPDRE knew we could not openly acquiesce in Israeli arms deliveries, they expected a wink and a nod indicating we would not protest if Jerusalem opened the arms faucet. But the United States drew the line at arms deliveries. We told both Addis and Jerusalem that we were totally opposed to their developing an arms relationship. Both Baker and Eagleburger said this to Ethiopian visitors, as did US Ambassador William Brown to the Israeli foreign and defense ministers. With Washington leaking like a sieve, we wanted to be sure that the cables and memoranda of conversation were unambiguous on this point.

In reality, we knew that Israel would dangle some military assistance before the Ethiopians to accelerate the Falasha exodus, and they knew that we were watching closely via our intelligence assets. Their method of dealing with this "tension" was to set up a smokescreen of information about what they were doing in the military field as a way of deflecting our gaze from activities that would annoy us. So, instead of denying any bilateral military activity with Ethiopia, the Israelis told us about deliveries of "nonlethal" equipment such as uniforms, boots, and medical supplies. They also told us about training Ethiopian military technicians in Israeli schools. Occasionally, the Israelis would lower their voices and say something like, "We've just delivered 25 000 obsolete old rifles and a few grenades." None of that bothered us, and the Israelis knew it.

What really worried us was the possible secret delivery of highly destructive weapons such as cluster bombs. Since we found none, we had no reason to protest. Unable to deliver the weapons Mengistu wanted, the Israelis were punished with a slowdown of Falasha departures. At the end of October 1990, visiting Israeli Foreign Ministry Director General Reuven Merhav proposed a trilateral Israel–US–Ethiopia meeting "to sort out all the contradictions on the Falasha issue." The Israelis had appointed Ambassador Uri Lubrani to take charge of the Falasha issue, and the trilateral meeting would mark his arrival on the Ethiopian scene. Naturally, we agreed to attend the meeting in Addis Ababa on 12–13 November.

The venue for the meeting, with Kassa Kebede, Uri Lubrani, and myself, was the headquarters of the Worker's Party of Ethiopia. Lubrani's main responsibility in Israel was Lebanon, which left little time for Ethiopia. But he had been ambassador in Addis prior to the break in diplomatic relations and knew the country well. Kassa had studied in Israel and spoke fluent Hebrew, hence his assignment to deal with the Falashas.

The meeting was informal and friendly. Probably its main value was that it took place. It was an opportunity for the Ethiopians to demonstrate they still had influence with important international players. That was supposed to be a fillip for flagging popular morale. Both we and the Israelis could demonstrate our perseverance on the Falasha problem. We all knew in advance that the result had to be an improved emigration rate.

I took advantage of a three-hour break in the meeting the first afternoon to visit the Falashas' camp. I found them living in difficult circumstances but with good support from American organizations. This was my first contact ever with Ethiopian Jews, whom I found to be no different in appearance from other Ethiopians. I was told by support workers that the long wait for emigration was taking its toll on morale, especially among the men, who were depressed because they could not work to support their families.

When the meeting reconvened, Kassa Kebede asked for my impression. I told him and Lubrani that I found the Falashas to be in relatively good shape and still upbeat as they awaited exit visas. On the other hand, I said, "They don't look Jewish to me." Lubrani found that amusing, but Kassa remained stone-faced. Very seriously he said, "But that is what we have been trying to tell you. All Ethiopians are Jewish. So why have the Falashas received all that special attention?"

As previously agreed with Lubrani, I made clear to Kassa the US view that Ethiopia had yet to put into practice its commitment to free emigration. I said the Falasha issue was an urgent question of basic human rights, and we would not be satisfied until all of them were in Israel. Since we had become the *de facto* mediator between the GPDRE and the EPLF and were under pressure to call an early new negotiating round, I felt confident that we would see some improvement. Sure enough, the emigration rate increased to 1000 per month starting in January 1991. At that rate, all the Falashas could be out within 20 months. That was not unreasonable.

The Soviets in 1990 – nobody loves us

With their persistent signals of retrenched support, the Soviets steadily lost influence with Mengistu. At the same time, they were unable to communicate with the insurgents. We were their only interlocutors on Ethiopia. Since US–Soviet cooperation was a White House priority, we tried hard to appear helpful and sympathetic.

The Soviets faced a growing problem with public opinion as *perestroyka* resulted in a more aggressive press. On 29 March 1990, for example, the Soviet daily *Izvestiya* criticized Soviet support for Mengistu. It noted that Soviet assistance was supposed to help repel external aggression. Since the conflict had become purely internal, why was assistance continuing, especially after the Cuban troops departed?[23] The three

Soviet prisoners in EPLF hands since 1988 made matters even worse. We asked the EPLF to be compassionate and release the prisoners but received a tough response. They said the prisoners would remain until the Soviets stopped supporting the GPDRE's defense of Asmara and withdrew their warships from the GPDRE naval facility on Dhalak Island opposite Massawa.

Between June and December 1990, the United States and the Soviet Union very visibly attempted to collaborate on food relief and peace issues. A new initiative was approved at the US–Soviet ministerial meeting in Moscow on 2 June 1990. The plan was for American food to be transported to blockaded Asmara in Soviet cargo planes. In addition, the superpowers would jointly sponsor a regional peace conference among governments in the region under UN auspices. This initiative, with which the Bureau of African Affairs had little involvement, was designed mainly to demonstrate US–Soviet collaboration, and less to affect the situation on the ground.[24]

The plan could not be implemented for two reasons. First, the EPLF warned that the relief aircraft would be targets in Asmara. The Soviets therefore decided not to take any chances.[25] Secondly, the proposed UN conference was never convened because there was no agreement on the terms of reference.

By the end of 1990, the Soviet presence in Ethiopia had been drawn down to a shadow of its former self. All dependents had departed, and only about 350 military assistance personnel remained, with instructions to avoid combat areas. That number was down from a 1989 total of 1500 advisors. Probably the best indicator of the Soviet decline was the military delivery statistic for 1990. Ten thousand metric tons of cargo – mostly munitions to support military operations – were delivered during the year, a two-thirds decline from 1989. "Socialist solidarity" was clearly on the wane.[26]

Taking charge of negotiations

After Secretary Baker promised Tesfaye Dinka in Geneva in November that we would encourage the EPLF to resume talks, we needed to take concrete steps. The EPLF's earlier loss of confidence in Jimmy Carter over the UN observer issue raised the possibility of further US–Soviet collaboration. On 5 October 1990, I had already recommended to Under Secretary Kimmitt that we become more directly involved in the talks, and that we sound out the Soviets about cosponsorship.[27] Kimmitt, a relatively young under secretary blessed with wisdom and perspective, responded, "Approve in principle, but check with the EPLF first."

In effect, Kimmitt was saying thanks for thinking about US–Soviet collaboration, but achieving negotiations should take priority. If the EPLF does not want the Soviets, don't insist. Kimmitt's instincts were right on target. A few days later, I received a letter from EPLF leader Isaias Afwerki indicating willingness to resume negotiations, but "with your involvement only."[28]

In taking over the Eritrean peace process, we could not just passively convene negotiating rounds, we believed, but should instead become fully involved in the substance of the conflict. We began with a review of the constitutional issues. John Byerly, assistant legal advisor for African affairs, undertook to research my fundamental question, "Would it be constitutionally defensible to restore the confederation that existed between Ethiopia and Eritrea from 1952 to 1962?"

Eritrea's grievance – self-government snuffed out

When the British Army liberated Ethiopia and Eritrea in 1942 from Italian occupation, Ethiopia reverted immediately to its previous state of sovereign independence. Eritrea, which had been an Italian colonial possession for half a century, became a ward of the international community, a responsibility assumed by the United Nations after 1945.

A UN commission sent investigators to the region for consultations with governments and with the inhabitants of Eritrea. On the basis of the commission's recommendations, the UN General Assembly decided on 2 December 1950 to confederate Ethiopia and Eritrea. The arrangement gave Eritrea considerable self-government and autonomy, with its own legislature, police, and taxation powers. The confederal government controlled only foreign affairs, defense, the currency, and the ports. As the UN resolution made clear, the new federal arrangement represented a compromise between "the wishes and welfare of the inhabitants of Eritrea, the interests of peace and security in East Africa, and the rights and claims of Ethiopia, in particular Ethiopia's legitimate need for adequate access to the sea." Without the two Eritrean ports of Asab and Massawa, Ethiopia would have been landlocked.[29] The confederation became operational in 1952 and worked well for ten years.

In 1962, the confederation disappeared with Ethiopia's formal incorporation of Eritrea as a province of Ethiopia. The autonomous government of Eritrea ceased to exist. The Ethiopians claimed the amalgamation was legally approved by the Eritrean parliament. Most observers, including the American consulate in Asmara, saw it as a unilateral coercive takeover by the Ethiopian regime. It had all the trappings of a Stalinist operation, with troops surrounding the building while parliament was in session. In any event, the action triggered the war that was still raging thirty years later. The Ethiopian government was not happy with the United States at the time of the merger, and its foreign minister expressed dismay to the American ambassador at the US failure to extend congratulations on the occasion of Ethiopia's unification.[30]

In retrospect, it was disgraceful that the United States did not protest the emperor's unilateral abrogation of the 1952 UN trusteeship decision. But political and military imperatives made it convenient for the United States to bite its tongue in 1962. The US communications base outside Asmara remained important for military and diplomatic traffic, and the emperor was still a strong US ally.

Now, our juridical review pointed to a return to the pre-1962 confederation. After thirty years of war, the EPLF was demanding the right to self-determination, with a secession option. The GPDRE's bottom line, with which we agreed, was the maintenance of Ethiopia's territorial integrity. Therefore, the only solution compatible with both demands was a return to confederation, without a secession option. The EPLF could accept nothing less.

The issue of territorial integrity: a principle at risk

A negotiated solution was not necessarily the only possible outcome. We also had to prepare for the contingency of an EPLF military victory. Our Policy Coordinating Committee meeting of the previous August had considered such a possibility real. We might be faced with a declaration of independence by an EPLF in full control of Eritrean territory, though the EPLF denied it was fighting for independence, only for the right of self-determination. Let the people decide their own constitutional future. Self-determination is like apple pie and motherhood. Who can be against it?

The territorial integrity of states is not to be taken lightly in any situation. It was especially important for our Africa policy, because the Organization of African Unity (OAU), the collective policy assembly of 53 African governments, had established the inviolability of colonial boundaries as a cardinal principle. African governments properly dread competing territorial claims and demands for self-determination by thousands of tribal groups. At the first OAU Conference of African Heads of State in Cairo in 1964, they "solemnly … pledged themselves to respect the frontiers existing on their achievement of national independence."[31]

US policy on territorial integrity was linked to that OAU principle. But Assistant Legal Advisor Byerly's study found that the colonial boundary paradigm did not quite fit the Eritrea–Ethiopia tandem. Ethiopia itself had never been a colony nor had it historically exercised hegemony over Eritrea. Eritrea, meanwhile, had been a colony but never achieved independence, going directly from colonial rule to confederation. Thus, it was hard to apply a literal interpretation of the colonial boundary principle to Eritrea. Nevertheless, the preservation of existing boundaries was so important to the OAU that we continued for the time being to advocate territorial integrity

The endgame: countdown to regime collapse

In December 1990, the United States tried zealously to set up a second round of trilateral US–EPLF–GPDRE talks. On 5 December, Secretary Baker signed letters to the foreign ministers of Sweden and Italy requesting them to encourage the EPLF to agree to new talks. Sweden sent a special emissary to London to confer with the EPLF representative. The Swedes' report back to Baker expressed disappointment at the EPLF's intransigence, noting EPLF bravado that "the war was going their way." In my own dialogue with Isaias Afwerki on 7 December, I urged the EPLF not to reject negotiations.

On 27 December, an EPLF delegation visited Stockholm to meet with Deputy Foreign Minister Pierre Schori. They told Schori that talks in Washington on 7 December had cleared up their "misgivings" about US policy on self-determination and satisfied them about the role and intentions of the United States. They were willing to sit down again with the GPDRE, but demanded "new and concrete proposals in writing."

Beyond negotiations, we were also working on a potential peace agreement. To this end, John Davison and Robert Frasure, NSC Africa director, went to Khartoum and Addis in October 1990 to discuss substance. They carried a "nonpaper" – a description of the kinds of issues on which the two sides need to engage in order to settle their differences by negotiation. It contained five points:

- The overarching concept of self-government for Eritrea.
- A negotiated structure spelling out the relationships (federal or confederal) between Eritrea and Ethiopia.
- An eventual act of choice for the Eritreans on the longer-term viability of the structure agreed upon.
- Enforcement guarantee mechanisms.
- Confidence-building measures.[32]

Our scenario had the EPLF making a major concession by accepting a deferred referendum and an interim federal system with substantial, guaranteed autonomy. For its part, the GPDRE would make a major concession by accepting an Eritrean self-determination referendum several years in the future. Presumably, the GPDRE would be so anxious to win a vote in favor of continued federal association that they would do everything to make the trial period succeed. A leap of faith was thus proposed to Addis as a substitute for guarantees of territorial integrity.

As of the end of 1990 both direct and indirect negotiations had essentially been a dialogue of the deaf. The EPLF wanted to talk only about self-determination, while the GPDRE wanted to talk only about federalism. What was needed was a reversal, with the EPLF conceding federalism and the GPDRE conceding choice. In discussing the five points with Davison and Frasure, both sides conveniently endorsed the concessions required of the other but failed to acknowledge those required of themselves. We were not surprised but remained hopeful, as both sides agreed to meet in London on 18 February. If nothing else, we had succeeded in clearing the table of Jimmy Carter's procedural headaches and plunged directly into substance.[33]

Tabling written proposals

Because of the Gulf War and terrorist threats, official US travel was discouraged. We therefore switched the meeting venue to Washington, thereby delaying the talks to 21 February.

Prior to the talks, Anne Reid, the veteran Africa analyst in State's Bureau of Intelligence and Research, suggested that the Ethiopians would not move beyond their previous proposal, essentially a weak federal system with most powers remaining in Addis. According to her analysis, Mengistu had interpreted US–Ethiopian collaboration against Iraq as the beginning of a grand anti-Arab alliance, including Israel, that would help him defeat the insurgents. Mengistu believed we had bought his argument that the EPLF was a stalking horse for an Arab takeover of Ethiopia.

We did not see it that way. Indeed, the EPLF was heavily Christian. Eritrean Muslims outside the EPLF had formed a number of smaller secessionist groups. Of these the best known was the Eritrean Liberation Front, a minor player at best. Nevertheless, Mengistu saw only two options. Either the EPLF accepted his brand of (pseudo) autonomy and the war would end in a peace deal; or the EPLF refused, at which point the United States would "allow" Israel to enter the war on Ethiopia's side.[34]

The talks began the afternoon of 21 February and ran through late the next afternoon. In addition to chairing the sessions, I hosted a cocktail reception the evening of 21 February at the Foreign Service Club, across the street from the State Department. The GPDRE delegation was headed by Ashagre Yigletu, who had led all previous delegations to negotiating sessions, with both the EPLF and the TPLF. The EPLF delegation was headed by Secretary-General Isaias Afwerki, whose presence was considered a mark of respect for the United States.

As requested, both sides tabled written proposals. The GPDRE presented a nicely printed booklet entitled *Proposal of the GPDRE on the Peaceful Resolution of the Problem of Eritrea*.[35] Though not as fancy, the EPLF's document laid out their position clearly. Referring to our "five-point paper," I began by emphasizing the need to compromise on the basic issues. All issues were interrelated, and agreement had to be reached on all. The main tradeoff, I said, was between "choice" and "association."

The GPDRE proposal was the same as the one Tesfaye Dinka had presented orally the previous October. Eritrea would be an autonomous region within an Ethiopian Federation, with its own legislature and taxation power. One interesting new feature was Eritrea's right to have its own police force. The proposal contained no act of ratification by the Eritrean people and generally gave the central government all the real power.

The EPLF proposal called for a cease-fire to be enforced by UN peacekeepers, an interim period of UN administration in Eritrea, and a UN-sponsored referendum in which the people of Eritrea would decide their future form of government, with independence one of the options.[36]

The two proposals did not stimulate much give and take. Ashagre commented that the EPLF offered nothing new and was unwilling to compromise. Isaias said the system of government was not the issue. The issue was the GPDRE's refusal to change its attitude, meaning its refusal to consider an act of self-determination for the Eritrean people. Almost the only thing the two sides agreed upon was to continue meeting under a US chairperson. They also agreed that the US "five-point paper" should serve as the basis for future discussions. Accordingly, we agreed to develop additional ideas and to set a date for the next round.[37] In conclusion, we issued a press statement, citing the exchange of proposals, the significant differences between the two sides, the US agreement to convene further meetings, and all sides' agreement on priority for relief activities.[38]

On 25 February, Secretary Baker sent a memorandum to President Bush emphasizing that both sides wanted us to continue our efforts. He also told Bush that, on the margins of the meeting, the EPLF had indicated their desire to release their three Soviet prisoners to the United States. The Soviets had met EPLF demands by removing their ships from Dhalak Island and terminating their airlift to Asmara. The prisoners were turned over to Ambassador James Cheek in Sudan in April 1991.

The last battles of the war

We also learned on the margins of the negotiating round that the EPLF was planning one more military offensive. They were thus really happy that the GPDRE had not proposed a bold new solution that would have given new life to the talks. Isaias also told Robert Frasure and UN Under Secretary James Jonah that the EPLF and the TPLF had agreed their primary objective was now Mengistu's overthrow. There was no way the EPLF would make a separate deal with Mengistu and leave the TPLF in the lurch.

The GPDRE did not believe the war was irretrievably lost, despite its 1990 setbacks. Indeed, during the second half of 1990, the Ethiopian army had some success in pushing the TPLF back in the northwest, the army's Asmara defenses were increasingly impenetrable, air bombing was becoming more accurate, and the army enjoyed an unlimited supply of raw recruits. Their main weakness northwest of Addis Ababa, where they had unseasoned troops and fluid defenses, was precisely where the TPLF chose to launch a major offensive within days of the Washington talks.

By the middle of March 1991, the TPLF had registered significant gains on the battlefield. They had cut the road from Addis to Gonder and controlled the key road junction of Bahir Dar and its airport, as well as the Gojam capital, Debre Markos. These developments led US chargé d'affaires Robert Houdek to establish a military warning point at the town of Ambo on the Omo River, 50 miles from Addis. If the TPLF captured Ambo, embassy dependents and nonessential personnel would be evacuated to safehavens. In Eritrea, the EPLF, while not attacking, exerted sufficient pressure to discourage the transfer of government troops to the TPLF front.

The TPLF's military success between February and mid-April had two major repercussions. First, the GPDRE increased its blackmail on the Israelis. "Give us arms or there will be no further Falasha departures." Second, the GPDRE suddenly became interested in offering unprecedented major concessions.

Growing panic in Addis

With the northwestern front rapidly falling apart, reasonable advisors pressed Mengistu to accept a more realistic policy. The result was an extraordinary meeting of the "rubber stamp" Ethiopian parliament, the Shengo, on 22 April. After a short debate, the Shengo issued a declaration that effectively accepted the TPLF preconditions for a cease-fire. The statement offered a roundtable negotiation with all Ethiopian parties to formulate a new democratic order. During the discussions, Ethiopia would be under a caretaker regime.

The only Shengo precondition was that the "unity of Ethiopia not be compromised." In effect, Mengistu had accepted the TPLF demand for a transitional government during negotiations. Unfortunately, the TPLF and the EPLF had to reject the declaration because it precluded a referendum in Eritrea. Even on this question, however, Tesfaye Dinka told Bob Houdek that "unity" was not an absolute precondition. It was negotiable, just like everything else. In other words, the regime was desperate.[39]

Squeezing the Falashas

Simultaneously with the TPLF's military successes the exodus of Falashas stopped cold, in contrast to the rate of 1000 departures per month in January and February 1991. On 7 March, Uri Lubrani told US Ambassador William Brown in Tel Aviv that the GPDRE was increasing the pressure on Israel to provide lethal weapons. Prime Minister Shamir was holding to his policy of allowing only nonlethal deliveries, but the situation was becoming difficult. Lubrani asked us to step up the pressure on Mengistu to allow the departures to resume.

In Washington, we examined several options to help the Falashas waiting in Addis with two months' worth of supplies in case combat reached the city. We were reluctant to send special messages or emissaries because we had nothing to offer in exchange. We too could be blackmailed. It was only after the Shengo issued its 22 April declaration that we knew we had a lever. With the GPDRE offering to hold unconditional talks and accept a caretaker regime during a roundtable conference, it was clear that we controlled the only promising negotiating framework. Indeed, the Shengo declaration was only hours old when Tesfaye Dinka began exhorting Bob Houdek to organize the next round of talks.

We and the Israelis knew that if the Falashas were going to escape before Addis became a battleground, they had to get out fast. Haggling over numbers per month was no longer relevant. During a visit to

Washington in April, Uri Lubrani told me the Israelis had put into place the capacity to airlift 18 000 Falashas from Addis to Tel Aviv over a period of four to five days. Undoubtedly, we agreed, the GPDRE would exact a financial price. Lubrani said any payment had to be open and "believable," not an outright ransom payment.

After further brainstorming, we concluded that the best method was to reimburse Ethiopian Airlines for revenues lost because Israeli aircraft would now carry the exodus. The 4000 Falashas who had already emigrated had all flown Ethiopian Airlines from Addis to Rome, transferring there to Israeli charters. Although the Falashas all flew one way, the Israelis had to buy them roundtrip tickets. A quick calculation covering 18 000 travelers added up to a price tag of about $35 million. Lubrani asked if the United States might be helpful in this respect. I said I did not think we would allow that amount of money to stand in the way. Shortly thereafter an amendment was added to the Defense Department appropriations bill allocating up to $15 million to the Office of Humanitarian Assistance for "immediate emergency airlift assistance."[40] The Falasha lobby had done its work well.

On 25 April, the town of Ambo was captured, triggering "ordered departure" for embassy dependents and nonessential personnel. We and the Israelis agreed that the way to exert pressure on Mengistu over the Falasha issue was to send a special high-level emissary. The White House agreed, selecting former Senator Rudy Boschwitz, the American politician with the most experience in the Falasha movement who had lost his reelection bid in November 1990.

Boschwitz arrived in Addis on 27 April, accompanied by Deputy Assistant Secretary Irvin Hicks and Bob Frasure, and met with Mengistu the following day. With two politicians bargaining, a deal was reached fairly easily. Mengistu agreed that the Falasha departures should be rapid because he wanted it over with. He did not want long-term trouble from the Arabs. For the same reason, Mengistu wanted the departure to be secret, which was not feasible. He also insisted that the United States "supply the financial assets to cover costs." We all knew what that meant. Finally, Mengistu wanted the United States to take charge of the peace process pursuant to the Shengo's declaration.

Mengistu promised to show flexibility on every issue except the unity of Ethiopia, which could not be compromised. Boschwitz agreed to all of the demands, offering to host an all-parties roundtable on Ethiopia's future in London within two weeks. The immediate objective would be a transition to democratic elections and a new political system.

After the Boschwitz visit, Hicks and Frasure briefed the TPLF and the EPLF in Khartoum and urged them to come to London. Both agreed to participate, and both assured us there would be no military attack on Addis Ababa while negotiations for a new political system were in progress. Hicks and Frasure warned the EPLF that no country would recognize a unilateral Eritrean declaration of independence, so they should refrain from precipitous action. Within days we received assurances from Isaias that such a declaration was out of the question. He understood the need for international legality.

On the basis of these consultations, we invited the parties to meet in London on 15 May. Our plan of action contained the following features:

- A transitional government would be composed of all political groups, including exiles.
- Free elections would be held within one year.
- A general cease-fire would prevail.
- All parties would support emergency relief activities.
- All existing administrative controls, whether government or insurgent, would remain in place.
- The Eritrea issue would be postponed.

The first two weeks of May were hectic, to say the least. When the Falasha airlift had not yet begun by 10 May, we postponed the London conference from 15 May to 20 May to increase pressure on the GPDRE to get cracking. At the same time, the TPLF continued its military offensive. We received a message from Meles Zenawi, the TPLF secretary general, that he would attend the London conference. The military offensive, he said, was designed not to undermine the conference but to pressure the GPDRE to go through with it. In Addis on 9 May, Uri Lubrani told Bob Houdek that he believed Mengistu wanted to get enough money from the Falasha departures to buy the weapons needed to launch yet another counteroffensive and that Mengistu hoped to prolong the conference while the army prepared to regain the initiative.

On 11 May, I sent a message to Tesfaye Dinka that we could not hold the London conference on 20 May unless we saw some movement on the Falasha question. On 14 May, Lubrani was still in Addis trying to bring the Falasha issue to closure. He told Houdek the two sides were still haggling over an "explainable" price for transportation costs. Because of continued nonperformance on the Falashas, we postponed the London conference yet again to 27 May. In the meantime, Mengistu appointed Tesfaye Dinka prime minister, while the insurgent offensive continued, cutting the relief road from Addis to Tigray.

On 19 May, I met Lubrani in London. He had left Addis with the Falasha negotiations still in deadlock. He told me he had bargained down the GPDRE asking price from $100 million to $58 million and wondered if an additional American gesture might be helpful. For example, President Bush could write Mengistu expressing continued support for Ethiopian territorial integrity. In any event, he asked us not to "pull the rug" out from under the London talks until 24 May in the hope that a deal could be made in time for a 25–26 May airlift.

Under the pressure of military developments, sentiment was growing that we should delink the London conference from the Falasha question. Bob Frasure felt strongly about this. With an insurgent victory virtually assured, he believed we should work with the rebels to make sure the war ended with a "soft landing." In other words, the GPDRE was finished in any event, so we should concentrate on influencing the victors to initiate the democratic transition we had hoped to negotiate. The London conference should proceed even if the Falashas did not get out in time. Their exodus could always be negotiated with the new regime. I took the opposing side, arguing that President Bush felt strongly about the issue and we had a commitment to the Israelis. In any event, I refused to be stampeded. It was a decision we could make at the last minute. I denied Frasure's recommendation that we inform the Israelis of a delinkage.

Mengistu's departure: the logjam breaks

We had known for some time that Mengistu had contingency plans in the event of a worst case military scenario. During 1990, we heard from Zimbabwe that Mengistu had purchased a farm outside Harare, and in 1991 he sent his wife and children to live there. Zimbabwe owed Mengistu a favor. He had provided substantial assistance to the ruling ZANU party during their successful guerrilla war against the white Rhodesian regime between 1975 and 1980.

On the morning of 21 May Vice President Tesfaye Gebre-Kidan informed the government ministers that Mengistu had fled the country. The president took off as scheduled on a flight to southern Ethiopia that morning to meet with new army recruits. But when the flight was about midway, he ordered the pilot to fly to Nairobi. Thus ended the rule of one of the world's last Stalinists.[41]

One of Acting President Gebre-Kidan's first acts after taking power was to inform Bob Houdek that the "the Falasha issue can be quickly and easily resolved." The GPDRE would accept a payment of $35 million and would allow a 48-hour airlift if President Bush would send him a personal appeal. A presidential letter requesting the immediate departure of the Falashas was cabled to Addis on 22 May. Bush pledged to encourage the TPLF to observe a cease-fire, said we remained committed to the London conference, and that we were deeply appreciative for such an act of generosity. Gebre-Kidan also directed Tesfaye Dinka to head the Ethiopian delegation to London to negotiate the details of a transitional government, including all political entities, both combatant and noncombatant.

On 24 May, the Israelis informed us the airlift was under way and recommended that we ask the TPLF to refrain from attacking Addis while the mission was in progress. That same day, the White House issued a statement announcing the beginning of the airlift of 18 000 Ethiopian Jews from Addis Ababa to Israel. In a gesture to the GPDRE, the statement said:

> We want to express our appreciation to Acting President Tesfaye Gebre-Kidan of Ethiopia. We understand that the Ethiopian decision to allow the Falashas to depart the country was taken in response to a letter from President Bush on May 22. Our initiative in this humanitarian operation commenced with the visit of Senator Rudy Boschwitz to Addis Ababa as a special emissary of the President on April 26–27.
>
> The United States will be hosting a conference in London starting May 27 to help facilitate an end to the tragic war in Ethiopia. We hope at that time to see the establishment of a provisional government and agreement on a plan for a political transition leading to peace and democracy.
>
> Israeli Prime Minister Shamir called President Bush at about 11 a.m. aboard Air Force One to thank him for the American role in the release of the Falashas....[42]

The airlift was completed without complications in a magnificent display of logistical coordination. Among the passengers in the last plane out was Ethiopia's chief negotiator Kassa Kebede, who decided he had no future in Ethiopia. The London conference was still on track. With the Falasha issue out of the way, we could concentrate on bringing an end to the Ethiopian civil war with a "soft landing."[43]

The London conference

The US negotiating team arrived in London on 26 May, the Sunday of Memorial Day weekend. My group included former senator Rudy Boschwitz, Deputy Assistant Secretary Irvin Hicks, East Africa Director

John Davison, NSC Africa Director Robert Frasure, and Ethiopia desk officer John Hall. Our Africa watcher at the American Embassy, Michael McKinley, who had been one of Chester Crocker's strong right arms in the tripartite negotiations for Namibian independence, made all the arrangements. We stayed at the Berkeley Hotel just off Oxford Street, about five minutes' walk from the American Embassy. The British government kindly made available one of their large conference rooms for the actual talks.

Is Addis burning?

Shortly after we arrived, a telephone call from Bob Houdek reported a deteriorating security situation in Addis. Acting President Gebre-Kidan had told Houdek that he was losing control of the capital. Retreating Ethiopian troops from the northwestern front were in total disarray, fully armed, and becoming dangerous to civil order. Something needed to be done to prevent destruction and civilian hardship.

We considered options and agreed that the conduct of the TPLF army to date had been reasonably good. Over the previous eighteen months, the TPLF had occupied many cities and towns outside their native Tigray with virtually no reports of raping, looting, or pillaging, and they appeared to be well disciplined. It seemed to us that the only way to restore order in Addis was for the TPLF to enter the city before, rather than after, the peace conference.

I asked to see TPLF Secretary General Meles Zenawi, who had received the same alarming reports. Although he had pledged not to enter Addis until after the London conference, I said, we would have no objection to the TPLF's moving in and restoring security for the population. Meles agreed. I told him that I would make a statement on the Voice of America (VOA) and the BBC informing the Ethiopian people that the US government had recommended this action, in the hope that the Addis inhabitants would not panic and flee. I made the statement over the VOA and the BBC in a sidewalk interview in front of the hotel.

The people did not panic, but I earned the enmity of many anti-TPLF Ethiopians, who accused me of "handing over the city of Addis to the TPLF's dictatorial rule." While most Ethiopians rejoiced at Mengistu's departure, the citizens of Addis did not rejoice at the arrival of the TPLF peasant army. They called the Tigreans *woyanes* in Amharic, roughly equivalent to "rednecks." The TPLF's action also changed the composition of the peace conference.

As soon as he heard the news, Prime Minister Tesfaye Dinka and his delegation came to see us. Dinka vigorously protested our decision to break the earlier agreement precluding a military entry into Addis. He had hoped that the conference itself would agree on a transitional regime including the GPDRE and thereby obviate the need for troops to occupy Addis at any time. From his perspective, once the insurgents entered Addis the possibility evaporated of a broadly based transitional government charting a negotiated new course.

After hearing the background to our decision, Dinka left to call his acting president. Upon returning he stated that Gebre-Kidan denied suggesting that we invite the TPLF to restore order. In view of our action, Dinka said, he would denounce the conference as a farce and walk out. We were thus left with a conference of military victors, but that did not mean there was nothing left to discuss. On the contrary, Ethiopia's political and economic future was at stake.[44]

Charting a new course for Ethiopia/Eritrea

We held our bilateral consultations with the three "insurgent" delegations on Sunday 26 May in the Berkeley Hotel.

The EPLF, led by Secretary General Isaias Afwerki, decided the main element of the discussions would be the establishment of a provisional government in Eritrea. The future of Ethiopia did not concern them. We argued that decisions made concerning Eritrea could not fail to have an impact on the future of Ethiopia and that the EPLF should act reasonably. The EPLF should not declare independence immediately despite the fact that the Ethiopian Army in Eritrea had surrendered. If that happened, the major industrial powers would not grant recognition.

Isaias said he understood perfectly. Independence would mean nothing without international legitimacy. It was important to have a referendum duly supervised and certified by the United Nations. To avoid causing psychological problems in post-Mengistu Ethiopia, the EPLF would wait three years before holding a referendum.

Isaias requested US endorsement of this approach. The request created a dilemma. We had been telling everyone until the last minute that we supported Ethiopia's territorial integrity. Changing our policy might incur the wrath of the Organization of African Unity. After some discussion, I decided to endorse the referendum because Eritrea was historically a "special case," as explained in the legal opinion we had received the year before. We did not want to undermine the transitional package being put together in London. A self-determination referendum was clearly a key element of that package.

Meles Zenawi and the TPLF could not have been happier. With respect to Eritrea, he said, it was sad that a separation was necessary, but why fight reality? In any event, it should be possible to maintain close economic links, with eventual political ties being forged after the healing passage of time. Meles said that it was not the TPLF's intention to impose its program on Ethiopia just because it had taken over in Addis. He pledged a transitional government representing all points of view. Only after the adoption of a new constitution and the holding of an election could a new regime implement a program.

I chided Meles about reports that he had once described the TPLF as "Albanian Marxists." If he intended to replicate the Albanian experience, then Ethiopia was doomed to a fate worse than under Mengistu. Meles told me not to worry. His use of the term "Albanian" was meant to describe his movement as being totally independent of all outside influence, just as communist Albania rejected ideological guidance from the Soviets, Chinese, and Yugoslavs. Otherwise, the TPLF rejected the disastrous Albanian model.

The delegation of the Oromo Liberation Front (OLF) was headed by Yohannes Lata Wagayo. Since the OLF had done little of the fighting, their position was weaker than those of the EPLF and TPLF. Nevertheless, the two major groups treated Lata as an equal, at least in public. Lata said the Oromo people, like the Eritreans, wanted to engage in an act of self-determination. However, there was no question of the Oromo people voting for independence. They wanted to remain Ethiopian. But for psychological reasons, it was important that they too have a referendum. I discouraged Lata from pursuing this policy objective, arguing that it was a nonstarter with the international community and could be traumatic for Ethiopia. I advised him to aim for a federal system which would give a measure of self-government to the Oromos.

The peace conference began the morning of 27 May in the conference room provided by the British Foreign Office, whose East Africa director Richard Edis sat in. I opened the meeting with a statement urging the parties to work out a transition to a democratic form of government and to maintain a single economy of Ethiopia and Eritrea. I also urged them to do everything possible to facilitate international relief efforts. I stressed the importance of guaranteeing fundamental human rights to all ethnic groups, in effect serving notice that the international community would not tolerate the substitution of a new dictatorship for the old one.

After my statement, the three parties decided to continue on their own without a mediator now that their common enemy, the GPDRE, no longer existed. They repaired to a private room for their own discussions, which produced a short public statement. After lunch, the parties asked me, and I agreed, to read their statement to the many press people waiting outside.

The statement said that a decision had been made to hold an all-parties conference in Addis Ababa no later than 1 July, at which time a transitional government would be debated and launched. Provisional governments in Ethiopia and Eritrea would work out temporary arrangements regarding roads and access to ports. I informed the reporters that I would provide more detail at a press conference the next morning at the American Embassy.

The United States caused it: the myth of the superpower

The staff of the United States Information Service arranged everything for the 28 May press conference at the spacious American Embassy auditorium. Senator Boschwitz and I presided. The auditorium over-flowed with local and international press. USIS employees who had been in London for several years told me they had never before seen as many television cameras in that room.

Boschwitz made the opening statement, congratulating the victors for agreeing to establish a transitional regime that would prepare democratic consultations, write a constitution, and hold free and fair elections. He also expressed appreciation for the safe departure of the Ethiopian Jews. I followed with a prepared statement summarizing our consultations with representatives of the outgoing government, the TPLF/EPRDF, the OLF, and the EPLF. I characterized my summary as "United States recommendations and observations."[45]

In making the statement I had several objectives: (a) to lock the military victors into a democratic path, (b) to delay Eritrean action on independence until passions could cool, (c) to warn the new rulers that human rights abuses and undemocratic practices would preclude for-eign assistance, and (d) to remind everyone that international relief remained a high priority.

My main political recommendations were:

- A transitional government should be quickly established and should assume all legal and political responsibility.
- The transitional government should be broadly representative of Ethiopian society, including diverse political groupings, and wher-ever appropriate should employ the existing civil administration.
- The primary responsibilities of the transitional government should be to prepare Ethiopia for free, democratic, internationally monitored

elections in nine to twelve months and to organize a constituent assembly to propose a new constitution.

• The new constitution should guarantee fundamental individual rights and should respect the identity and interests of the different peoples of Ethiopia.

• The transitional government should consider an appropriate amnesty or indemnity for past acts not constituting violations of the laws of war or human rights. Accused persons should be afforded due process of law.

I also emphasized the EPLF's decision to delay a referendum for three years, at which time the Eritrean people would choose between remaining in Ethiopia or becoming independent. In the meantime, both Ethiopia and Eritrea would have transitional governments that would work out cooperative arrangements regarding access to ports, cross-border trade, currency, telecommunications, civil aviation, and other issues.[46]

In the question period, considerable interest focused on two subjects: Why did the United States "authorize" the entry into Addis of the TPLF army? And, what was the US attitude toward Eritrean self-determination in view of our long-standing policy supporting the territorial integrity of African states?

On the issue of the TPLF entry into Addis, there was considerable misunderstanding about our decision. I depicted the early entry of the TPLF into Addis as a solution to the growing chaos in the city – a "soft landing" to save the city from needless destruction in a war that was already over. But some at the press conference refused to believe the American superpower would make such a decision on the basis of such a limited objective. From their conspiratorial point of view, the United States had decided to favor the ascendence to power of the TPLF/ EPRDF alliance, with all other political factions left out in the cold. They could not believe that we lacked the power to force the TPLF to stay out of the city indefinitely while a broad-based provisional government was constituted through negotiations. The TPLF, who waited patiently at the gates of Addis only as a courtesy to us, could have entered at any time without our permission.[47]

The issue of Eritrean self-determination also gave us problems. In my remarks, I had simply informed the press without comment about the decision to hold a referendum after three years. The press were naturally probing for an embarrassing policy reversal. Because the referendum after three years was a key element of the London peace package,

I decided to be very clear about our modified policy. Above all, I did not want to say anything that might cause the EPLF to panic and declare instant independence.

The question was: "Mr Cohen, American policy has consistently opposed the dismemberment of Ethiopia pursuant to OAU principles about colonial borders. What is your government's policy, therefore, with respect to Eritrea?"

I replied that the United States favored a self-determination referendum because the Eritrean people never had an opportunity to decide for themselves. This made Eritrea a special case. At the same time, it was our hope that the Eritrean people would opt to remain in Ethiopia, because we considered unity to be good for both.

Eritrea became the main news item. My statement caused tension among my superiors in Washington and among Ethiopian exile leaders in the United States. After the press conference, I went to Mike McKinley's office at the Embassy to peruse cables about the signing of the Angola peace accords in Lisbon, scheduled for 31 May. In my mind, our conflict intervention in Ethiopia was effectively over, and I was moving on.

Very soon after the opening of business in Washington, I received a call from Secretary Baker. This was unusual since Baker spent very little time worrying about Africa, essentially leaving policy to me. When I needed policy guidance or validation, I usually consulted Under Secretary Kimmitt. Baker expressed concern about my endorsement of self-determination in Eritrea, fearing that the Washington press corps could exploit it to cause problems. The German government, he explained, was exerting pressure on the United States to recognize the independence of Slovenia and Croatia. The United States was resisting because we feared that unilateral declarations of independence in Yugoslavia could lead to violence.[48] My support for a referendum in Eritrea could open the door to press accusations of policy inconsistency. If self-determination is good enough for Eritrea, why isn't it good enough for Croatia and Slovenia? I protested that consistency is not necessarily the best way to deal with specific country problems, an argument he found naive.

Fortunately for me, the Washington press corps did not harass Baker on Eritrea, so when he arrived in Lisbon on 30 May to witness the signature of the Angola peace accord, he had forgotten our phone conversation. He was all smiles over the double victory for US policy in Ethiopia and Angola in the space of one week, especially its highlighting of US–Soviet cooperation.

The impact of our Eritrean policy on Ethiopian politics did not fade away as easily, however. Many Ethiopians saw our statement on Eritrea for what it was, recognition of the realities of military conquest, along with an effort to help Eritrea's transition to independence remain nonviolent. Many others interpreted it as a US "giveaway" of Eritrea. We had legitimized Ethiopian dismemberment, for which they could never forgive us. In later conversations with Meles Zenawi, the TPLF secretary general who subsequently became prime minister of Ethiopia, I asked him about the strong sentiment regarding Eritrea. He called the subsequent secession of Eritrea unfortunate, but the maintenance of close economic ties made the breakup less traumatic. In any event, he doubted that all those nationalists who wanted to keep Eritrea would be willing to go to war.[49]

Postpartum depression: isn't anybody happy?

Between the London Conference and the all-parties conference in Addis scheduled for 1 July 1991, we witnessed an outpouring of gloom and doom from Ethiopian-Americans, numbering over a hundred thousand. They spanned the socioeconomic spectrum, from the garage attendants and taxi drivers of Washington, DC, to university professors, urban planners, and senior business executives. The Eritreans among them were unanimously happy, of course. Many others, however, expressed strong doubts about the future. In my naive way, I expected all Ethiopians to be ecstatic after Mengistu's downfall. But there was no dancing in the streets.

I don't think ten minutes had elapsed after the TPLF entered Addis before a large number of Ethiopian-Americans started deploring the usurpation of power by an "upstart and dangerous political movement" and blaming the United States. They bombarded their congressmen with letters demanding a judicious application of American power and influence to fix it. In effect, what they wanted us to do was pressure the provisional rulers of Ethiopia to hold the planned all-parties conference somewhere outside of Ethiopia under a neutral chairman, preferably a senior US official. This would effectively neutralize TPLF military power and start the new Ethiopian political process from square one. The TPLF military victory would thus be irrelevant, and all elements of Ethiopian politics would have an equal chance under a protective US umbrella.

Some members of Congress took the issue seriously enough to invite me to their offices to discuss it. I remember Senator David Boren, an Oklahoma Democrat, telling me his Ethiopian constituents were afraid to go to Addis. They feared the TPLF would incarcerate anyone who held differing views or had criticized the TPLF in the past. Some also played on the "Marxist" demon. How can the United States allow these Marxists to take power? That the TPLF and OLF had promised to establish a broadly based transitional government, had invited every-one to come to Addis with total guarantees of safety, and had allowed a free press to emerge did not impress anyone.

I told Senator Boren and others there was no basis for anticipating TPLF hostile acts against political opponents. We could not ignore the results of military conquest even if we wanted to, I argued, and could not in advance accuse the TPLF of dictatorial ambitions. I insisted we give the new leadership an opportunity to demonstrate their declared commitment to democracy.

At the all-parties conference in Addis on 1 July I led the US delega-tion. Because of strong emotions about our Eritrea policy, the State Department's Office of Security sent out a five-person protective team. My first experience of being encased in a full-time security envelope, it was not enjoyable. On the flight to Addis I did find some Ethiopians returning from exile with an attitude of "let's give these fellows a chance." But in general, the atmosphere in Washington had remained morose. I personally feared that early and vehement opposition to the military conquerors by many Ethiopians would become a self-fulfilling prophecy. The more they prejudged the leadership of the TPLF as dicta-tors likely to replicate the repressive rule of the Mengistu regime, the more they generated an atmosphere of fear and suspicion that could push the new rulers to employ authoritarian methods in dealing with opposition.

Years later, I continue to be questioned by Ethiopians about US policy in 1991. Some recall my statement at the London press confer-ence in response to a question about the link between aid to Ethiopia and democracy. I said, in French, "No democracy, no development assistance." Eight or so years later, they argue that Ethiopia has not democratized under TPLF/EPRDF rule. My response is that while Ethiopia has a long way to go before it has true democracy, the Ethiopian politi-cal system has become far more open and liberalized than under Mengistu. Democracy cannot be built in a day.

In late 1997 and early 1998, the Ethiopia–Eritrea relationsip began to develop tensions. The Eritreans, for example, issued their own new currency, which the Ethiopians refused to accept for cross-border trade. In May 1998, small territorial disputes over arable land along the border

between Eritrea and Ethiopia's Tigray Province erupted into armed violence involving military units on both sides. Instead of seeking dialogue between the old revolutionary allies ruling the two countries, the
EPRDF/TPLF leadership decided to confront Eritrea with an ultimatum
demanding that the Eritrean army immediately withdraw from captured territories or face the use of force by the Ethiopian military. The
Eritreans refused to admit they were the aggressors and rejected humiliation by ultimatum. This led to full-scale warfare along the border,
with large numbers of killed and wounded on both sides. As of late
1999, major mediation efforts by the United States and the Organization
of African Unity had failed to end the state of war between the two
neighbors.

Needless to say, those of us who had gotten to know and appreciate
both new Ethiopian and Eritrean leadership groups before, during, and
since the London conference were deeply distressed by the war that
none of us thought would ever happen. A number of theories as to the
reasons for the war and its ferocity have been advanced by citizens of
the two countries as well as by foreign political scientists. These range
from a clash of personalities, between Meles Zenawi and Isaias Afwerki,
to a profound desire by the people of Ethiopia to retrieve the lost
province of Eritrea. In one view, the deep animosities within Ethiopia
toward the EPRDF/TPLF ruling group that surfaced in 1991 and continued to exist as of late 1999 were a contributing factor, leading the
Ethiopian government to hope by its intransigeance in the conflict
to stimulate a unifying nationalism. Whatever the reason, this tragic
development reflects the fragility of transition from authoritarianism
to democracy in Africa and underscores the need for persistence in
conflict management.

Analysis: did the United States make a difference in Ethiopia?

The military conflict in Ethiopia ended through military victory by
insurgent forces, not through negotiations. Does that mean the US
intervention became irrelevant? There is no simple yes or no answer.

We were drawn into the Ethiopian conflict for reasons not directly
related to conflict resolution. Our political leaders wanted to collaborate openly with the Soviet Union to solve regional problems, and the
Soviets needed help in Ethiopia. Pressure from the US antihunger
lobby to ensure that people in the Horn of Africa did not starve
because of drought and war and political pressure to assure the safe

departure of 20 000 Ethiopian Jews also weighed heavily. Finally, we needed Ethiopia's support in the UN Security Council to authorize war against Iraq. The Africa Bureau interpreted these mandates broadly enough to address the root conflict causing Ethiopia's problems.

We did score well in accomplishing our immediate objectives. The Soviets were pleased with our support in Ethiopia, especially the release of their three nationals by the EPLF in April 1991.[50]

As for hunger, our status as advisors and mediators gave us leverage on both sides to open food corridors and the disputed Port of Massawa for the relief agencies. Major famine did not occur on our watch.

In dealing with Mengistu's duplicity, especially his determination to blackmail the United States and Israel over Jewish emigration, I believe we got the better of him. By exploiting his need to keep the United States engaged, we were able to force him to open up food corridors to enemy territory. And we took advantage of the chaotic final moments in Addis to leverage official cooperation on airlifting the Jews to Israel. Our decision to play along with Mengistu, rather than denounce him openly and thereby end the dialogue, was correct. All in all, we considered our main policy objectives to have been fulfilled. But could we claim an additional merit badge for conflict resolution?

We played a significant role in helping negotiations, such as they were, to occur, first under Jimmy Carter and the Italians, and then through State Department mediation. Mengistu unfortunately saw negotiations as another way of waging war, but we played along in order to achieve our own objectives.

The assorted discussions during negotiations, especially in the corridors, helped shape the peace that followed. The negotiating environment allowed us to establish parameters for the postconflict period, as when we put Isaias Afwerki on notice that an immediate Eritrean declaration of independence would not be recognized. We also exploited our special status to preach the virtues of an economic union between the separated states.

A further question concerns the impact of negotiations on the war itself. Years later, people who were in Ethiopia at the time told me that when we took over the negotiations in October 1990, the Ethiopian will to fight started to decline. As the negotiating round of February 1991 appeared promising, it was not hard for the Ethiopian soldiers to conclude that the war was almost over. No soldier wants to be the last to die before the armistice. It may not have been totally coincidental, therefore, that the Ethiopian army collapsed shortly after the February negotiating round. Although US involvement was certainly not the only reason for the collapse of morale, it may have been the final straw. The lesson here is that superpower involvement in a Third World conflict, even as a neutral party, can have unintended consequences. Or as the Africans say: "When the elephant walks by the village, the grass gets crushed."

The enormous attention paid to US policy illustrates above all the degree to which Africans are willing to believe that the superpower United States can play God and can accomplish anything in Africa provided it has the political will. That means the United States must be exceedingly prudent in its policy pronouncements. We may have limited short-term objectives, but our statements are subject to broader interpretation according to the aspirations and prejudices of those involved.

The London conference itself, which would not have happened without our persistence, produced some favorable impact despite the situation on the battlefield. As I testified before the House Foreign Affairs Subcommittee on Africa on 19 June 1991, the conference had helped:

- Avoid a bloody battle for Addis through our coordination of arrangements for the TPLF forces to enter the city.
- Persuade the TPLF/EPRDF that the transitional regime must be broadly based, with wide participation.
- Put off to a calmer time the final decision on the future of Eritrea.
- Put the new Ethiopian power structure on notice that there could be no return to the human rights abuses of the past.[51]

Would all of this have happened in any event, even if I had not gone to Addis in August 1989 in response to an official invitation? That is difficult to say. Though the Ethiopian army would probably have folded at some point, a "soft-landing" end to the war was by no means automatic. But the US intervention did, in the end, affect the course of the last days of the war and the postconflict process of recovery and rehabilitation.

3
Sudan: Total North–South Incompatibility

Although Angola had the highest priority on our African conflict agenda in early 1989, Sudan grabbed our attention first. An estimated 250 000 people had died of starvation in the southern third of Sudan during 1988. Television reports of emaciated mothers and dying babies stimulated a strong demand from the US public for action.

The cause of this massive death toll in southern Sudan was neither drought nor floods nor disease but civil war. Government and rebel forces had been fighting intermittently since the country's independence from Britain in 1956. The most recent phase of the war, which began in 1983 had greatly intensified by the beginning of 1989. The southern insurgents, fighting as the Southern People's Liberation Army (SPLA), demonstrated increasing ability to capture territory and confine government forces to the larger towns. Leading the SPLA was Colonel John Garang, an American-educated PhD in economics who had defected from the Sudanese national army.

Another tragic fallout of the war was population displacement. Two million southerners had fled to the region around the capital city of Khartoum in the north, where they lived as internal refugees in miserable shack encampments. Extensive international media coverage guaranteed significant political attention in the West.

What was the war all about? In early 1989 the question could not easily be answered. The government in power in Khartoum had been elected democratically in 1986. Civil society flourished, with powerful labor unions, professional societies, and a healthy free press. Yet, the government was unable to reach a democratic accommodation with the political leaders of the southern insurgency. Still unresolved was the problem of devising a political structure for Sudan that could accommodate the desires of both its Arab Muslim citizens of the north and its African Christian, or Animist, citizens of the south. The entire history of the Sudan, from colonial rule through thirty years of independence, illustrated the near impossibility for the two cultures to coexist within one state.[1]

Diplomacy driven by humanitarian concerns

Even before the Bush administration, there had been a rash of congressional hearings and press coverage on Sudan's humanitarian crisis. During the congressional recesses, a number of members had visited the south to see the devastation firsthand. They found hundreds of thousands of people with no means of livelihood, prevented by the war from growing food crops and keeping livestock and subsisting on help from aid organizations. It was a heart-rending human crisis.[2]

One of the main tasks Deputy Secretary of State Lawrence Eagleburger performed for Secretary James Baker was making sure that congressional concerns were addressed rapidly and comprehensively. His initial call to me when I had just begun as assistant secretary for Africa in April 1989 was about the Sudan. He described the steady stream of congressional letters and calls urging action to relieve the suffering there. Consequently, he wanted me to give the problem a high policy profile. As a gesture of US concern, I was to visit the Sudan early. The US government must demonstrate that it cared and was doing something.

My travel to East Africa during the period 20 May–4 June dovetailed with other meetings scheduled in Europe with the South African foreign minister and my Soviet counterpart Anatoly Adamishin. Prior to travel, I thoroughly reviewed events in the Sudan with my East Africa team – Deputy Assistant Secretary Irvin Hicks, office director John ("Jack") Davison, desk officer Jeff Lunstead, and Robin Sanders, my executive assistant, who had served in Khartoum.

Our review indicated that the situation as of April–May 1989 was actually improving, thanks in large measure to the public outcry. The Sudanese government and the United Nations had agreed during a special emergency relief conference 8–9 March to establish a new program called "Operation Lifeline Sudan" (OLS). Its objective was to open emergency relief corridors via air, sea, barge, and rail beginning 1 April 1989.

To make sure that OLS would work, the SPLA and the government agreed to a month-to-month cease-fire effective 1 May. In the previous six months, the SPLA had made significant gains on the ground. In addition to capturing a number of important market towns in the south, they were besieging the provincial capital city Juba, which housed the main government garrisons. The government welcomed a cease-fire, which stopped the SPLA advance and enabled the government to regroup for later fighting. The SPLA was ready for a cease-fire because food was badly needed.

On the political front in Khartoum, Prime Minister Sadiq el-Mahdi's coalition government was shaky. Sadiq had received a tough ultimatum from the military high command and the labor unions demanding a more broadly based government, a more balanced foreign policy to replace the pro-Libyan posture then in place, and a visible demonstration of his commitment to make peace with the SPLA.[3] The economy's near-collapse, with inflation running rampant and the government unable to service its loans, made peace essential. The United States was about to stop assistance because Sudan was more than a year behind on its loan repayments. But Libya remained important as the only country willing to supply arms to the regime.[4]

Sadiq took the ultimatum seriously. As a peace gesture to the SPLA, he "froze" (but did not revoke) Sharia law[5] and offered to hold a constitutional conference to establish a more representative democratic system. This caused the fundamentalist National Islamic Front party (NIF), headed by the renowned Islamic scholar Hasan al-Turabi, to quit the governing coalition in protest against the weakening of Islamic rule.

When Irv Hicks, Jack Davison, Robin Sanders, and I arrived in Khartoum on 23 May, there were grounds for optimism. Operation Lifeline Sudan had begun, and political détente was in effect, with both sides observing a cease-fire. Remembering my instructions from Larry Eagleburger, I decided to focus on fighting hunger by eliminating the many bureaucratic obstacles along the so-called "humanitarian corridors."[6]

My conversations with Prime Minister Sadiq and his ministers were cordial, even though we were phasing out both military and economic aid. Sadiq complained about SPLA leader John Garang. The Sudan was a democracy. Garang wanted a democratic solution. Why not work within the system instead of making war? Sadiq also told me that no government in Khartoum could ever repeal Sharia law and expect to get reelected. However, he had now stopped implementing criminal amputations and was allowing non-Islamic provinces to opt out of Sharia. He could not understand, therefore, why Garang did not accept these actions as gestures of peaceful intent. Sadiq also had unkind words for Egypt, which he accused of constantly meddling in Sudanese politics.

Dodging stray bullets, we flew to the southern provincial capital of Juba in a Red Cross relief airplane. Juba seemed more typically African, in contrast to Khartoum, which seemed more like the Middle East. In Juba I saw hundreds of thousands of internally displaced people living in camps run by international relief organizations. The southerners I met distrusted both Khartoum and the SPLA, although negative feelings toward "the Arabs" were much stronger. People just wanted the war to end so they could get on with their lives. Juba was in dreadful shape because it could be supplied only by air. The Christian churches active in the south placed blame for the tragedy squarely on Khartoum.

In meetings and in my public statements in the Sudan, I stressed the following:

- The cease-fire should continue because it was vital for both the relief effort and the peace process.
- The United States would condemn the first side to break the cease-fire.
- The government's decisions to freeze Sharia law and to organize a national political consultation, in accordance with SPLA wishes, formed a good basis for negotiations. I congratulated the government and encouraged the SPLA to react positively.
- The United States did not support either side in the war. We supported the peace process and the efficient delivery of relief.
- The United States did not want to take over the peace process. The two sides were communicating and did not need a mediator.

The visit made me relatively optimistic that the OLS relief program would succeed. Both the government and the SPLA seemed ready for serious dialogue. Clearly, the humanitarian problem could not be solved without ending the war and resuming normal political life. Programs like OLS provided only temporary solutions. Nevertheless, for the moment I was pleased that we had been able to contribute to the relief of the hungry and that a political solution appeared possible. We did not seek a peacemaker role. Despite its democratic beginnings, the regime worried us because of its tendency toward vacillation and ineptitude and its close ties to Libya. As for the SPLA, we sympathized with their aspirations but worried about their reported human rights violations.

Our first opportunity to meet SPLA leader John Garang arose in June, when he sought support for his cause in New York, Washington, and Iowa (where he visited Grinnell College, his alma mater). Like many men of the Dinka ethnic group, Garang is quite tall. But unlike many of the others, including journalist and leading southern intellectual Bona Malwal, traveling with him, Garang is not characteristically thin. On the contrary, he looked like a football lineman, and his demeanor was frank and self-confident with Americans.

Garang's main objective was to disabuse us of any optimism about the regime's pledges to sustain a humanitarian relief effort or negotiate a fair peace settlement. He described Sadiq's close relationship with Libya and his unwillingness to revoke the Sharia laws as telltale signs of his true political feelings. Sadiq was determined to govern Sudan as an Arab Islamic state to the detriment of the "majority of Sudanese, who are not Arabs." Under Sadiq, the impoverished south had no hope of gaining a fair share of resources. He could not be trusted. Later, I commented to my colleagues, "Garang appears to be waiting for the next coup."

On 28 June 1989, I chaired an Africa Policy Coordinating Committee (PCC) discussion on Sudan policy. Rumors persisted of a military coup in preparation in Khartoum. We agreed on humanitarian relief as the highest priority, along with encouragement to both Khartoum and the insurgents to negotiate seriously. The regime evoked little enthusiasm among the agencies, despite its democratic origins. USAID, Treasury, and OMB called the regime's economic management hopeless and recommended that we continue winding down US aid.

Andrew Natsios, the energetic and capable director of USAID's Office of Foreign Disaster Assistance (OFDA), expressed strong doubts about the willingness and ability of the regime to carry out its side of the bargain in implementing OLS. He recommended allowing our relief officials to go into rebel-held areas with or without Khartoum's permission.

The military representatives from the Joint Chiefs of Staff emphasized Sudan's strategic location along the Red Sea facing Saudi Arabia. We had prepositioned military equipment and supplies in Port Sudan for use in the Persian Gulf in the event US fighting personnel had to be deployed there. The US Central Command (CENTCOM), responsible for US defense interests in the Middle East, believed we should stay close to the Sudanese military no matter how negative we felt about the civilian regime. They recommended that we therefore continue supplying arms to Sudan. Although they did not actually say so, the JCS representatives gave me the impression that they would not be unhappy to see a military coup in Khartoum.

Paradoxically, we faced a democratically elected regime that was unable to elicit much sympathy from any of the interested agencies. Our highest priority had to be the successful implementation of OLS, and the government's cooperation was vital. We therefore did not want to phase out economic assistance more rapidly than the eighteen-month period required by regulations.[7]

Sudan's strategic location and our need to keep friendly contacts within the Sudanese military were not contested. But the delivery of lethal equipment with the hope it would not be used in the south against the insurgents was politically unsustainable, given the strong feelings in the United States about the war and the famine. We compromised, therefore, by deciding to continue "nonlethal" assistance to the Sudanese military during the overall winding down period. I also told Andrew Natsios that for the time being I would not allow US aid personnel to go anywhere in the Sudan without the Sudanese government's permission.

The military returns to power: how "green" was this coup?

On 30 June 1989, only two days after our interagency consultation, the military deposed Sadiq in a bloodless coup. Brigadier General Omar Hassan Ahmed el-Bashir headed a newly established Revolutionary Command Council (RCC), composed largely of devout Muslim officers and a few token southerners. An audible sigh of relief rippled through the Africanist community in the US government, welcoming the departure of Sadiq's hopelessly inept regime. With the army in charge, we expected to distribute humanitarian relief with fewer bureaucratic hassles, as well as establish a military-to-military dialogue between army and rebels.[8]

I feared that our agreements with both the Sadiq regime and the SPLA for OLS implementation might be in jeopardy and hoped I would not have to persuade the RCC to confirm its support for OLS. I therefore returned to Khartoum 4–6 August to tell the new leadership at the highest level about America's concern for the humanitarian problem in the south. But before going to Khartoum for a second time, I took the advice of our ambassador to Egypt, Frank Wisner, and visited Cairo for consultations with the Egyptians. No other government more intensively followed events inside Sudan than Egypt, and Wisner thought their insights would be valuable. I agreed.

In Cairo, I had general exchanges on Africa at the Foreign Ministry with Deputy Prime Minister Boutros Boutros-Ghali and his staff. But to discuss Sudan, Ambassador Wisner took me to see the head of Egyptian Intelligence, General Amin Namr. The giant neighbor straddling the

Nile waters upstream from Egypt was obviously too strategic to be entrusted solely to diplomats.

General Namr was upbeat about the coup. He predicted it would be good for Sudan, for Egypt, and for "Western interests." The Sadiq regime had been too close to Libya and totally incapable of making peace. The new military rulers were well and favorably known to Egypt, and good things would happen. Just wait and see. After that pep talk, I looked forward to visiting Khartoum. I was troubled, however, by the absence of any Egyptian concern for the southern Sudanese insurgents.

I was struck by Namr's characterization of the SPLA leader. "John Garang is looking for power in Khartoum," he said. "He will never have power in Khartoum. He must understand that fact before peace can be achieved." In other words, Garang should not be under any illusion that the Sudanese people would support his objective to make Sudan a secular democracy. He must look instead for a solution that would allow the south to coexist with the Arab north in some type of federal system, but under overall Arab control.

I arrived in Khartoum 6 August, not long after our new ambassador, James Cheek, who had come from two years in Ethiopia. Cheek was a veteran of several diplomatic hot spots, including Afghanistan and Central America. In Ethiopia he had had direct contacts with the southern Sudanese rebel leaders. So he arrived in Khartoum with considerable understanding of Sudan and much experience with regimes under siege.

In another among several ironies, we had to temper our enthusiasm for the new regime by terminating aid pursuant to Section 508 of the Foreign Assistance Act, which ends assistance to any regime arising from a military coup against a democratically elected government. The Sudanese coup fit that description perfectly, although no one mourned the previous regime.

My meeting with Bashir was friendly. As he sat manipulating his Muslim prayer beads, he told me (in Arabic through an interpreter) that the RCC's highest priority was to end the war in the south. He pointed to the 27 July announcement that the RCC and the SPLA had agreed to begin peace talks in August as a sign of their sincerity. He saw no reason why an agreement could not be reached rapidly. The regime did not intend to force any Sudanese to accept Islam against their will. It planned to restore democracy soon via a national dialogue. Bashir also promised to cooperate in the implementation of OLS. In short, he told me everything I wanted to hear.[9]

After the meeting, negative feedback about the regime began to pour in. On the way back to the Embassy, Jim Cheek told me that Bashir was surrounded by some of National Islamic Front leader Hasan al-Turabi's fundamentalist militants, who appeared to be telling him what to say. Later, at the ambassador's reception in our honor, Sudanese guests from various professions were unanimous in warning me that the new regime was bad news. The RCC officers were not the professional Western-oriented military we had known in the past but extremists determined to Islamicize and Arabize the south and impose a theocratic regime on Sudan. I was advised not to be fooled by the imprisonment of Turabi along with Sadiq and the other political leaders. Turabi was described as the person "pulling the strings" from behind the scenes. I was also warned about growing Sudanese cooperation with terrorist groups.

In a brainstorming session with Jim Cheek and his staff the next day, I posed the following question. "Let's assume the new regime is fundamentalist. Does that automatically mean we could not work with it to achieve our two main objectives – implementation of OLS and the beginning of a peace process in the south?" They responded that we should not assume a fundamentalist regime would automatically be uncooperative. Give them the benefit of the doubt, but call their bluff. In short, don't panic. My upbeat attitude was called into question during my flight from Khartoum to London, when I asked the outgoing British ambassador for his prognosis. He expressed great concern about the most recent developments in Sudan, saying, "I am especially concerned that you Americans are not worried."[10]

Between August and year's end, ominous reports from Khartoum increased. Women magistrates, senior civil servants, and other professionals were being forced into unemployment. Freedom of the press, independent newspapers, political parties, labor unions, and student organizations were abolished. Women were discarding Western dress in favor of veils and floor-length robes. Islamic green was appearing on all buildings. Nonetheless, I was fixated on US objectives, determined to push these as far as I could, fundamentalism notwithstanding. The resulting policy of "constructive engagement" toward the military regime required us to maintain a useful dialogue. I found, however, that as time passed, this policy ran afoul of the human rights and hunger lobbies, not to mention the friends of John Garang. All were demanding to know why we were not openly condemning the Sudanese regime.

A flurry of abortive peace efforts

Peace talks in Addis Ababa 19–20 August made virtually no progress. The SPLA's nonnegotiable demand was for a completely secular state, with Sharia law applied only for Muslim family matters. Like its predecessor, the military government felt it could not survive politically if it accepted this ultimatum.

In response to the SPLA's tough position, the government on 8 September asked a hastily assembled "National Dialogue on Peace" to develop peace proposals. Although invited, the SPLA boycotted the conference, which was composed of prominent individuals rather than civil society organizations, most of which had been abolished or banned. While Garang undertook a high-profile diplomatic offensive in southern Africa, the conference in Khartoum was discussing a democratic, federal system with "local option" on Sharia law. Its recommendations were promulgated 21 October. A week later, the SPLA broke the cease-fire by capturing the town of Kurmuk in Blue Nile Province, 400 miles south of Khartoum.

The resumption of hostilities rekindled concerns for the relief program in the south. The 1989 Operation Lifeline Sudan program had avoided famine, thanks to the cease-fire, the efficient work of the UN and the relief organizations, and US pressure. The new program for 1990, called OLS II, was clearly in jeopardy. The regime was bombing SPLA towns and halting food flights from Kenya and Uganda, charging, without basis, that the aircraft were carrying arms for the rebels. In mid-November, government bombing was extended to northern Uganda, where the SPLA had some supply camps.

We were becoming quite jaded, with a "plague-on-both-their-houses" attitude emerging. We were upset with Garang for his rigidity on the Sharia issue and with the regime for its bombing of villages and deliberate interruption of relief shipments as an element in its war-fighting strategy. The regime was effectively saying, "OK, Garang, if you refuse to negotiate a reasonable peace deal, you will see how rough life can become."

In mid-November, former president Jimmy Carter, who was mediating the war between the Ethiopian government and the Eritrean separatists, decided to take a stab at providing good offices for the Sudanese protagonists as well. The two wars were linked: Three major Ethiopian rebel groups were receiving arms via Sudanese routes under RCC protection, while the Sudanese rebels were receiving arms from the Ethiopian regime.[11] Although Carter was able to bring the two sides together for talks in Nairobi on 1 December, they made no progress. He cited Sharia law as the major stumbling block. Nevertheless, as a glimmer of hope, Carter cited the two parties' agreement to include the recommendations of the National Dialogue on Peace as one of the bases for discussion at an eventual constitutional conference.

Because peace negotiations were stalled, we had to shift our focus from good offices to renewed pressure on the parties to facilitate the free passage of humanitarian relief. For General Bashir we inaugurated a presidential correspondence, with letters from President Bush in November 1989 and again in January 1990. The second letter to Bashir said:

> I understand that your government is currently reviewing Operation Lifeline Sudan and its principles and that you are currently making crucial decisions on critical aspects of the relief effort, including the resumption of relief flights, the role of nongovernmental relief agencies, and financial arrangements, including the exchange rate to be used for relief activities. Time is growing short, and I trust that you will expedite these decisions and that you will be as forthcoming as before. As I noted in my previous letter, the world will applaud Sudan's humanitarian generosity.
>
> I know that you are disappointed, as we are, that peace negotiations have not produced a cease-fire, nevertheless, I urge you to persist in those negotiations. We are urging the SPLA to do likewise. In the meantime, however, it is vital that the relief effort resume, with or without a cease-fire.[12]

When Sudan desk officer Jeff Lunstead drafted the presidential letters, he faced a classic dilemma of US policy. Can we deal with a foreign leader on issues of interest to the United States while ignoring the nasty things that same leader is perpetrating in his own country? This particular Sudanese regime was cut from a different cloth than its predecessors. While some previous regimes had been dictatorial and undemocratic, this one was unusually ruthless and lethal, showing zero tolerance for opponents. It was assassinating internal enemies, using live ammunition against student demonstrators, executing convicted currency traffickers, and sentencing strike leaders to death.

Internal repression notwithstanding, hunger in the south and the need for governmental support for OLS II remained our main priority. Nor were we about to give up on a possible peace process. Hence, Bush credited Bashir for being sincere about negotiations – after all,

John Garang was the party refusing to negotiate seriously – and between January 1990 and July 1991 we resisted congressional pressure to condemn the regime in public so that we could broker peace talks.

The Sudanese leadership was well aware of our dilemma and did everything possible to keep on our good side diplomatically. When Jim Cheek delivered Bush's letter urging support of OLS II, Bashir replied, "No problem. I have made a decision and it will be done." In a press interview, Bashir declared. "The American administration is now convinced that the present regime in Sudan is better than its predecessor."[13] And, on 20 February the Sudanese chief justice announced that all prisoners awaiting corporal punishment (such as amputations) under suspended Islamic law provisions (*Huddud*) would have their sentences commuted to ordinary prison terms.

In a letter to President Bush in mid-March 1990, President Bashir was pleased to report that he had convened a national peace conference in Khartoum in which people from all walks of life had participated. Although the SPLA had been invited, it had declined to attend. Bashir further reported that the conference had adopted a framework for peace negotiations with the SPLA movement, which the absentee SPLA had accepted at the Nairobi talks. Bashir also told President Bush that he supported Operation Lifeline Sudan, which was our overriding concern at the time, and invited the United States to continue its good offices. In our zeal for peacemaking, letters like that one made our juices flow.

Enter Francis Deng through the side door

In early 1990, fighting in the south was heavy. Despite daily SPLA shelling of Juba, the regime continued the search for a negotiating formula that Garang might accept. In the absence of direct contacts with Garang, the RCC quite intelligently sought the help of Dr Francis Deng, a highly respected southern Sudanese working in Washington, DC, as director of Africa studies for the Brookings Institution. A former Sudanese ambassador to the United States, Deng was close to John Garang. In addition, he spoke Arabic and knew his way around Khartoum. We found this development intriguing because of reliable intelligence that some leading northern Islamists favored allowing the south to secede. At that point, the war was a quagmire, and the option of cutting loose the "pagan" region increasingly attracted some.

Deng met secretly in London in late January 1990 with two RCC members – Colonel Martin Malwal Arap, and Lieutenant-Colonel

Bakri Hassan Salih. They asked Deng's advice on how to persuade Garang that the regime genuinely desired peace. Deng consulted the State Department before responding. An old friend of the Bureau of African Affairs, Deng visited me and the East Africa team on 6 February 1990. In his view, the two RCC members spoke for Bashir but not necessarily for the entire RCC, which was probably divided on the southern question.

Deng conceded that the SPLA's "vision of a rigidly secular Sudan" was understandably unacceptable to the north. In his view, the most viable solution lay in a "loose federal arrangement with considerable provincial autonomy under an umbrella of unity." He believed such a solution inevitable and thus better achieved through negotiations than warfare. He suggested a meeting built around this theme, with "participants attending as individuals rather than as representatives of their respective sides, and in the presence of objective observers."[14]

It was noteworthy that Deng had embraced some of the RCC's public statements. Beyond the exemption of the southern provinces from Sharia law, however, the RCC had not yet addressed provincial autonomy. How was Deng's idea to be launched? Deng insisted only the United States could convincingly lay out the options for the Sudanese regime – "either accept loose unity by agreement, or be faced with de facto secession by force."[15]

We were skeptical that more proposals for roundtable conferences could advance the peace process. With the regime's ruthless behavior toward its own Arab citizens well known, it would take more than a conference invitation to convince the SPLA of the regime's seriousness. A "dramatic gesture on the part of the government is needed," I told Deng. "What would happen," I asked, "if the regime pulled the army out of the south completely?" I then answered my own question: "They would be conceding the reality that they could not control the south by military force. The SPLA would have to be persuaded to reciprocate by pledging not to declare an independent south. A constitutional convention would follow. Bashir might even find some resonance on his right among NIF militants who were advocating allowing the south to run itself." Deng asked for time to reflect.[16]

After his London and Washington talks, Deng met in Khartoum with Bashir and former Nigerian President Olusegun Obasanjo to examine peace options. Bashir's message was consistent: "Tell Garang we want to discuss peace." Deng returned to the view that only the United States could make a peace process happen. He encouraged us to present our proposals directly to Bashir and Garang. He and Obasanjo had raised with Bashir the idea of the government military's evacuating the south, but Bashir considered the idea politically impossible.

The beginning of a diplomatic shuttle

At that point we decided to advance some possible icebreakers. The idea of a government military withdrawal from the south had sounded nice and dramatic initially but was dead on arrival. We therefore looked for some intermediate steps that would encourage talks. With the SPLA doing well on the battlefield, Garang would resist our peacemaking lest he lose his military momentum. Unsurprisingly, the losing side was more inclined to accept a cease-fire than the side registering successes.

As the SPLA captured towns, Garang became the main target of the Congressional Hunger Caucus in early 1990. The more territory he captured, the more hungry mouths and transportation corridors Garang was responsible for. On 13 February, Representatives Frank Wolf and Gary Ackerman and Senator Gordon J. Humphrey pleaded with Garang to do something about the "tens of thousands of southern Sudanese who have been effectively cut off from urgently needed resupply efforts" as the result of SPLA's gains and its blockade of Juba. Garang henceforth shared with Khartoum responsibility for the humanitarian impact of war.[17] Moreover, Garang's reluctance to talk to Bashir began to hurt his image. Bashir was depicted as the man anxious to talk peace at the drop of a hat. He made it sound simple, telling visitors, "All that is needed is for Bashir and Garang to sit down together, and we can work out a solution."

At the end of February, Kenyan president Daniel arap Moi invited Bashir and Garang to Nakuru, the presidential retreat 80 miles from Nairobi. The meeting was set for 27 February. Although both had accepted Moi's invitation, only Bashir showed up. At the last minute Garang had decided not to go. Instead, he went to Addis Ababa to see his old friend Robert Frasure, the US chargé d'affaires. Moi was not amused.

Garang told Frasure he was committed to a political solution. He knew that a military victory was impossible. He was ready for negotiations at several levels, but he refused to start at the summit in a private meeting with Bashir. He liked my proposal for a northern troop evacuation, which he characterized as "constructive disengagement within a united Sudan," as a prelude to serious negotiations. He promised to support OLS II and said he was open to ideas about relieving the siege of Juba so that the hungry could be fed. He appeared to be nostalgic for the deposed Sadiq regime, as opposed to the Bashir/Turabi crowd, whom he called pan-Arabist. For Garang, the bottom line was "a multiracial, multireligious, secular Sudan." Frasure told him, as a friend, that he should focus on ways of making a deal to end the war and not try to remake the Sudan.[18]

Our uncomplicated proposal was geared to politicomilitary realities. Government forces were encircled in the towns. The SPLA ruled the countryside. The city of Juba was being resupplied by air for both military and civilian needs. Our proposal called for the government to thin its troop strength by 50 percent. In return, the SPLA would withdraw its forces 15 kilometers from the besieged towns. Both sides would cooperate in the delivery of humanitarian aid. External monitors would enforce their commitments, including a cease-fire. This was supposed to build confidence as a backdrop to a "constitutional conference." The basis for discussion would be general acceptance of a "federal system." The participants would be "self-selected" from a broad spectrum of interest groups, including the banned political parties.

I decided to take this plan to the two parties. En route to Khartoum, I stopped in Cairo 2–4 March to get an update on Egyptian views of Bashir. Intelligence Director Namr told me they were still favorable. He predicted my peace proposal would find a friendly reception in Khartoum. The Egyptians liked the plan. As for Garang, he still needed to end his obsession with gaining power in Khartoum.

While I was in Cairo, Bashir was visiting Tripoli, where he signed a document agreeing to the "integration" of Sudan and Libya within four years. I presented my proposal to him in Khartoum on 9 March. He did not react negatively and agreed to study it carefully. A few days later, Ambassador Smith Hempstone presented the proposal to John Garang in Nairobi, who denounced it as a "cease-fire favoring the government." He said he preferred our original idea of a total government evacuation of the south. Because the SPLA was doing well in combat, Garang wanted a bigger price for a cease-fire than the mere thinning out of government forces. Khartoum's response came on 2 April. They were willing to "roll back" their forces but not to withdraw, meaning they rejected "thinning out."

Back in Washington, I was asked to testify on Sudan policy on 15 March before the House Africa Subcommittee sitting jointly with the Select Committee on Hunger. The purpose was to call attention to the deteriorating food security situation in the south and to apply pressure to all parties to support OLS II. Subcommittee chairman Howard Wolpe wanted a full airing of the bad human rights situation in the

Sudan, including an explanation for the administration's failure to denounce the regime in a "campaign of public diplomacy." I made a balanced presentation, calling attention to human rights violations and the regime's failure to cooperate with OLS II. However, I also mentioned improvements in the human rights area, especially the release of some political prisoners. I discussed the proposals of the "National Peace Dialogue," characterizing them as a valid basis for negotiation. I also characterized as encouraging Bashir's promises about the food security situation.[19]

The hearing made clear that the Congress was becoming impatient with all of the parties to the conflict and would soon become impatient with the administration if there were no improvement. I reminded the committees that legislation had required us to stop virtually all US assistance, leaving us with little leverage.[20]

Needless to say, the controlled Sudanese press took everything out of context, emphasizing my favorable statements about the regime (human rights are improving in some areas), my unfavorable statements about the SPLA (they broke the cease-fire in October 1989), and my positive view of the recommendations of the National Peace Dialogue.[21]

On 18 May I met with Garang in Nairobi in a new effort to move the peace process forward. Garang had lost interest in the issue of troop dispositions. He was concentrating instead on the constitutional conference that was supposed to deliver a political solution. Garang was suspicious of Bashir's offer to "sit down man-to-man" and work out a settlement. He called that proposal totally unacceptable because of its undemocratic nature. "Neither Bashir nor I represent many Sudanese," Garang said modestly. "Who are we to make decisions for the entire nation?" Garang said he would accept only a conference that included representatives of all civil society, including the banned political parties and labor unions. In effect, he would be willing to grant a military cease-fire, interrupting the SPLA's favorable military momentum, in return for a representative conference. Ironically, Garang was demanding a return to the political system existing under the previous Sudanese government he had detested.

I considered Garang's position reasonable, especially his willingness to accept a cease-fire at a time he held a winning military hand. I could also understand why Garang would not want to negotiate one-on-one with Bashir. What guarantees would the SPLA have that the regime would not renege on any bilateral agreement a few years later? It had happened before with the regime of President Gaafar el-Nimeiry (1969–85), who reneged on a 1972 agreement to exempt the south from Islamic law. Garang wanted a solution that had the endorsement of the entire spectrum of Sudanese society. He also saw himself as the leader of the "non-Arab majority." As my Egyptian interlocutor had told me, "Garang wants power in Khartoum." While I understood Garang's position, I told him he was wrong to refuse dialogue with Bashir, who was occupying the high ground. The RCC regime could always justify escalation of the war as long as Garang rejected Bashir's offer to talk.

I sent Bashir a message indicating my belief in the reasonableness of Garang's proposal for an all-parties conference and the attractiveness of his cease-fire offer. On 26 May Bashir told Jim Cheek that he could not accept, at least in the first phase, an all-parties meeting. In the first instance, only government and SPLA military representatives should talk. Bashir naturally focused on suspending a conflict he was losing, while Garang concentrated on achieving political objectives while he was ahead. On 4 June the Sudanese government officially rejected our proposal.

While disappointed, we saw the mutual rejection of our proposal as just the opening exchange of a long negotiation. We were not about to give up. But the eruption of the Gulf War in August 1990 had a negative impact on our Sudanese mediation.

War in the Gulf brings out the regime's true colors

Even before Iraq's invasion of Kuwait in August 1990, pressures against our "constructive engagement" policy toward the Sudanese parties began to mount. In June, the *New York Times* blasted our policy:

> What does it take to get the United States Government to express revulsion and horror? Washington has expressed only perfunctory concern about the Sudan...where a wave of political terror has claimed doctors, lawyers, journalists, poets and trade unionists. Hundreds have been detained and scores executed for the crime of dissent. With the connivance of Colonel Qaddafi of Libya, an Islamic fundamentalist regime now foments civil war and tribal massacres. Washington has yet to find words to condemn this lurch into darkness.[22]

The growing press furor was fed by the NGO network, especially Human Rights Watch, which had excellent internal Sudanese sources.

Concurrently with the press drumbeat, the regime grew nastier. Restrictions on US diplomats traveling outside Khartoum were tightened. On 10 June, Sudan formally protested US initiatives in the UN General

Assembly to repeal Resolution 3379 ("Zionism is racism"). National Islamic Front "security officers" joined Sudanese embassies to infiltrate opposition groups in exile.

At about the same time, the Egyptians realized that falling in love with Bashir had been a mistake. In mid-July, President Mubarak received Garang in Cairo and demonstrated "extreme hostility" toward Bashir, according to Garang's readout. Garang was encouraged to make an alliance with the outlawed northern political parties, and the intelligence chief who had provided a favorable prognosis about Bashir was shipped off as an ambassador.

Iraq's August conquest of Kuwait was the catalyst that brought Sudan's radical Islamism fully to the surface for the first time. August in Khartoum was filled with anti-American demonstrations and rabid anti-Western media propaganda. On 17 August, an influential NIF extremist, Hag al-Nur, told a US embassy officer that the NIF considered our policy a blatant US attempt to "become master of the Arab world." Saudi and Egyptian support for US policy did not matter, since these Arab governments were "un-Islamic and corrupt." As radical Islam saw things, the Iraq–Kuwait war was part of the fight against corrupt Western culture in the Middle East. The majority UN view that strong countries like Iraq should not be allowed to gobble up weak neighbors like Kuwait, was totally irrelevant. The hard-line Turabi wing of the NIF was clearly in the ascendancy.[23]

On 19 August, US–Sudanese relations were further inflamed when the US Navy intercepted the Sudanese vessel *Dongola* carrying chemicals to Iraqi-occupied Kuwait. The action was taken pursuant to Security Council Resolution 661 imposing a blockade on Iraq. Sudanese media called the action "illegal and an act of piracy and barbarism."[24] At the end of August, the Arab League voted to condemn Iraq, with only the Sudan and Mauritania voting against. Needless to say, my efforts in Washington in support of a constructive dialogue with Khartoum were greatly undermined.

Between the congressional hearings in March and the October session of the UN General Assembly, the internal situation in the Sudan had also deteriorated. The regime was impeding the work of OLS II, harassing relief flights, delaying rail and barge shipments, and again bombing southern towns. It also forced internal refugees to leave the Khartoum area, bulldozed squatter shacks, and moved the displaced to the desert without piped water or schools.

On 1 October at the United Nations in New York, I had a tough meeting with Sudanese Foreign Minister Ali Ahmad Sahloul. He explained that the regime was serious about a "new democratic political structure." He rejected criticism of its treatment of OLS II, arguing that the relief organizations were flouting Sudanese sovereignty by flying around the country without authorization. He also refuted reports of forced displacement of internal refugees and urged us to continue encouraging both the government and Garang to move forward in a peace process. I replied that it was difficult for us to maintain a constructive dialogue "in view of the terrible things happening in the Sudan." And, since both Bashir and Garang had rejected our proposal, I had no immediate plans for further travel.

On 24 October Libya's Muammar Qaddafi presided over the formal end of the Sudanese "national dialogue." On 15 November Garang came to Washington and met with me and Robert Frasure, now director for African affairs on the National Security Council staff. Garang described Libya's support for the government as ominous, requiring a tough external response. We urged Garang to accept Bashir's invitation for direct talks. Frasure said, "Don't wait for Bashir to be overthrown. The follow-on regime might really be fundamentalist." But Garang was unmoved. For him, the regime was ultrafundamentalist, and he would not legitimate Bashir by meeting with him. As in the case of Sadiq el-Mahdi, Garang had decided to wait for the next coup. An indication of this was Garang's decision to link the SPLA with a group of retired northern generals running a Cairo-based antiregime movement called the "Legitimate High Command."

Bashir tarnished his image even further in December, when he visited Iran seeking oil, arms, and economic assistance. During the visit, the Iranians declared the southern Sudanese rebels "anti-Islamic." Bashir declared that Sudan would implement Islamic Sharia law under a new "federal" system, with the predominantly non-Muslim southern states excluded from religious punishments.[25]

At the Senate Foreign Relations Africa Subcommittee hearings on Sudan, chaired by Paul Simon on 27 November, the Bashir government received massive criticism. Witnesses deplored the regime's interference with humanitarian relief, its human rights violations, and its support for Iraq. In my testimony on our efforts to engage the government and the SPLA in a dialogue on restarting the peace process, I criticized both sides for the lack of progress:

> The US Government has...suggested to both sides that a military disengagement and partial withdrawal, followed by political talks could be a fruitful procedure. Unfortunately, the two sides were

unable to agree on the parameters of a disengagement/withdrawal. On the political side, they disagree on who should participate in political talks. The government insists that it and the SPLA only should take part. The SPLA, on the other hand, insists that other Sudanese political forces, the trade unions, [and others], should also participate. In truth, we have seen little evidence that either side is willing to make the difficult concessions that will be necessary to make peace possible.[26]

When US forces began military action against Iraq on 17 January 1991, Islamic radicals in Khartoum became hysterical. Hundreds of thousands of Iraq supporters marched through the streets. Anti-American rhetoric was fierce.[27] In Washington, that was enough for us. We ordered the US Embassy shut down and all Americans to leave temporarily until the end of the Gulf War. The Sudanese–American dialogue fell silent.

After Desert Storm: a new round of hope and deception

Immediately after Iraq's defeat in Operation Desert Storm, Sudan was isolated from its once good Middle Eastern friends such as Egypt, Saudi Arabia, Kuwait, and the Emirates. All were unforgiving toward Saddam's supporters. The Bashir regime thus tried to normalize relations with the United States, beginning with Ambassador Cheek, who returned to Khartoum in March 1991 to restart embassy operations.

Foreign Minister Sahloul told Cheek that Sudan was seeking a "regional solution" to the Gulf crisis via an "all-Arab conference." Unfortunately, most Arab countries disagreed, and some were actively hostile to Sudan, especially Egypt. He accused Kuwait and Saudi Arabia of sending arms to the SPLA, and Egypt of sponsoring the "Legitimate High Command" group of former Sudanese military officers.[28]

On the internal conflict, Sahloul said the regime wanted to reopen negotiations with John Garang despite "considerable unrest and dissent" within the SPLA. Cheek welcomed the change of attitude, expressing a desire to cooperate with the regime in relief aid matters. Sahloul earnestly promised to facilitate US–Sudanese cooperation on relief programs, adding, "but even beyond that, we want to cooperate politically as well."[29]

Cheek's analysis was optimistic. The regime clearly recognized that backing Saddam Hussein had been a mistake. It was looking to the United States to help normalize its relations in the Middle East.

Cheek proposed to take advantage of that to leverage improvements in the humanitarian relief program, which he called "the "bellwether" of the relationship.[30] Indeed, worsening hunger had been severely aggravated by drought.

US media were again providing dramatic coverage. The *Washington Post*, in a typical story, reported: "In the face of a drought for the second consecutive year, Sudan has rebuffed Western efforts to launch a relief program."[31] In March, we warned that 15 million people in Ethiopia and Sudan faced starvation.[32] But a glimmer of hope emerged from the signing of a new Sudan–UN agreement for a major new relief effort. Cheek's strategy was working.

Also in March the dynamic new secretary-general of the Organization of African Unity, Salim Ahmed Salim, volunteered his good offices to restart a peace process in the Sudan.[33] For the OAU, this was an unprecedented move marking the beginning of a new proactive approach to civil conflict, hitherto considered purely internal affairs not subject to external interference.[34]

Against this background of multiple initiatives, I received a visit in April from Sudanese national security advisor Fatih Irwa. I gave him ample time because he was an integral member of the regime's core power structure. Like the foreign minister before him, Irwa stressed improved US–Sudanese relations as vital to problem resolution in the region and within Sudan. He argued that the Sudanese government had been falsely accused of extremism. They were ready to participate in a peace process and wanted US help. They wanted to negotiate with Garang in good faith, but he was constantly moving the goalposts. He asked that I return to Khartoum to give the US–Sudanese dialogue a fresh start.[35]

I told Irwa that we supported OAU Secretary-General Salim's peace initiative. We had given Salim our earlier proposals, all of which we considered still relevant. We had also informed Salim that despite all our disagreements with the regime, we respected Bashir's willingness to talk to Garang. However, US–Sudanese relations would go nowhere if Sudan did not cooperate on relief in all provinces. For two years, every time we were about to launch a peace initiative, relief problems disrupted our relations. Finally, I declined to visit Khartoum in the immediate future because of Sudan's continuing pro-Iraq image in Washington. In sum, though the meeting was friendly, Irwa should have received a clear impression that any chance for better US–Sudanese relations would depend on Sudan's own actions, in particular its actions regarding relief.[36]

The following month, May 1991, turned out to be a watershed for the Sudanese civil war and for US–Sudanese relations. Two key inter-related developments occurred.

First, the thirty-year civil war in Ethiopia ended with the victory of insurgent forces over the Mengistu regime (see Chapter 2). Mengistu's defeat struck a major blow to John Garang and the SPLA, which had received much of their arms from the Mengistu regime and used Ethiopian territory for safehavens and training camps. The victorious EPRDF party in Ethiopia was grateful to Khartoum for its wartime support. Consequently, as soon as they assumed power, the EPRDF stopped the arms flow to the SPLA and closed their camps.

Second, Foreign Minister Sahloul's passing comment to Jim Cheek in March about "unrest and dissent within the SPLA" proved prophetic as the movement started to split. Ethnic rivalries exacerbated deep personal and philosophical differences among the top leaders. One of the most formidable military leaders in the movement, Riak Machar, led the anti-Garang dissidents. Fighting erupted between the different factions, resulting in the deaths of some important movement personal-ities and even greater hardships for southerners caught in the crossfire.

Because of the SPLA's internal split and loss of Ethiopian support, the regime abandoned negotiations as the main path to peace. Military vic-tory had suddenly become an option. Unsurprisingly, Garang dropped his previous preconditions for negotiations and expressed willingness to accept Bashir's proposal for face-to-face talks. Equally unsurprisingly, Bashir was no longer disposed to open the dialogue with Garang and proposed lower-level talks to start the process.

On 1 July 1991, I attended an Ethiopian all-parties constitutional conference in Addis Ababa as an observer. The Sudanese also sent a delegation. During the conference, RCC member Colonel Mohamed al-Amin Khalifa sought me out and delivered a simple message. American mediation in the Sudan conflict was no longer necessary. The Sudanese would work with Nigerian head of state Ibrahim Babangida, then chair-man of the OAU, to set up a "ministerial-level" meeting with the SPLA, after which the OAU would also be dismissed. So, one month after begging us to resume conflict resolution, the regime told us to stay out.

A few weeks later, we received another signal that the regime was not that sincere about improving US–Sudanese relations. On 17 July while embassy officers were visiting the University of Khartoum, a nonvio-lent student demonstration began. The security forces responded in a decidedly unpeaceful manner, aiming live automatic gunfire at the demonstrators. Before they could leave, the embassy officers were detained and roughed up, despite their diplomatic identification.[37]

On 16 July, during one of my periodic reviews of African developments with Egyptian ambassador Sayed el-Reedy, I analyzed the situation in the Sudan as of that moment. Despite the activity related to negotiations and democratization, I told him, "the Sudanese Government seems convinced it can win militarily, and a major Sudanese military offensive is underway, although preliminary reports suggest it is bogging down. Garang is down but not out. He still gets considerable help from Zimbabwe and other sub-Saharan states. The war is likely to drag on."[38]

The only bright spot as of July 1991 was the improved cooperation between the regime and the United Nations, which was slowly making headway in delivering humanitarian relief. But the regime's escalation of the war, in the mistaken belief it could win a military victory, complicated efforts to move supplies through combat areas.

1991 to 1996: slow descent into regional war

With the United States mediating role in the Sudan essentially over, we concentrated our efforts on humanitarian relief, even though these efforts could not really succeed without an end to the war. Our best hope was to minimize the number of deaths from starvation and disease from one rainy season to the next. As the conflict dragged along, certain basic realities became clear:

- *SPLA splits* – The regime played a hand in the interfactional animosity and fighting in the south. It was clearly financing and arming Riak Machar's group, whose units facilitated much of the gains made by the Sudanese army between July 1991 and mid-1993.[39]
- *Radical Islam takes total control* – Any existing influential moderate elements in the regime when it came to power in 1989 were either gone or suppressed by 1991. By then, radical Islamists, with close ties to Iran, were clearly in command.
- *Sudan becomes a regional problem* – Most radical revolutionary regimes have an irrepressible compulsion to export revolution to their neighbors. The Khartoum junta was no different. Reliable sources in 1992–93 informed us that Sudan was sending arms to Algerian Islamic fighters, Egyptian guerrillas, and antiregime elements in northern Uganda.[40]

African efforts to mediate were enthusiastic but inconclusive. Nigerian mediation on behalf of the OAU faded by the end of 1991.

The Nigerians were succeeded in 1992 by the Intergovernmental Authority on Drought and Desertification (IGADD), a regional grouping in the Horn of Africa of Sudan, Kenya, Uganda, Ethiopia, Eritrea, and Djibouti. IGADD was able to bring the regime and the SPLA together for occasional talks but without tangible results.

As evidence of Sudan's growing external subversion mounted, the United States grew increasingly hostile. We sponsored anti-Sudan resolutions in both the UN Human Rights Commission and the General Assembly. We placed Sudan on our official list of terrorist nations and opposed World Bank and IMF loans. We flirted with the idea of providing assistance to the SPLA but backed away because of the interfactional fighting and the SPLA's reported human rights violations.

In June 1992, I visited Uganda for the annual meeting of the Global Coalition for Africa. In a private conversation, Ugandan President Yoweri Museveni requested US military assistance, especially antiarmor weapons such as vehicle-mounted or helicopter-mounted TOW missiles. He expected Sudanese tanks to cross the border to assist northern Ugandan Islamic rebels. While sympathetic to Museveni's anxieties, I told him that Sudanese assistance to Ugandan rebels would most probably take the form of money and light arms, with an outright invasion by Sudanese military units unlikely. Most significant was Museveni's view of Sudan as an aggressive regional menace.

In December 1992, the United States led a UN military operation in Somalia designed to save hundreds of thousands of Somalis from starvation (see Chapter 8). Shortly after US forces arrived in Somalia, I made a rapid tour of the Horn of Africa to assure the availability of airports and other logistical facilities as needed by our troops. During my visit to Khartoum, Ambassador Donald Petterson took me on an intensive round of calls on key Sudanese security officials, including my old interlocutor Fatih Irwa.

The Sudanese internal situation was tense. Petterson told me of horrible human rights violations. In November, two Sudanese employees of USAID in Juba had been picked up for alleged "subversive activities," tried by a military court, found guilty, and executed. Petterson was not about to continue a normal relationship after that horror.[41] I also received detailed information about the many locations throughout Khartoum of safe houses for Middle Eastern terrorist organizations such as Hamas, PFLP, Abu Nidal, and Black September. They were all there. Despite the unfolding tragedy, I was amused by Fatih Irwa's opening question. "Secretary Cohen, now that you have invaded Somalia, are we next?" I assured him we were not about to invade Sudan but kicked myself later for not sowing some doubt.

In March 1993, in one of my last acts as assistant secretary, I testified before the House Africa Subcommittee. It was my sad duty to report our failure as conflict intervenors in Sudan over four years.[42] Toward the end of 1994 and throughout 1995, Sudan managed to alienate both Eritrea and Ethiopia, despite their gratitude for Sudan's assistance during the war of liberation against the Mengistu regime. Hard evidence revealed that Eritrean and Ethiopian nationals of the Muslim faith were receiving military training in Sudan to run guerrilla operations against their own governments. By the end of 1995, both governments were sending commandos into Sudan to attack training camps. By early 1996, the Eritreans were openly hosting anti-Khartoum political meetings, and the SPLA was again receiving military assistance from Sudan's neighbors.

By mid-1996, Riak Machar's faction had faded militarily, Garang and the SPLA were again on the offensive, and Khartoum was facing the unanimous enmity of its neighbors. The overall consensus of the region favored the overthrow of the Sudanese regime. With northern Arab Sudanese rebels having new physical access to Sudan via Eritrea, the regime faced growing external military dangers as well as internal ones from the SPLA.

In April 1996, I met John Garang again in Washington, at the home of his good friend Ted Dagne, an Africa specialist with the Congressional Research Service. Garang was clearly in an upbeat mood. His forces were marching again, and the Bashir regime's pariah status was unambiguous. While the United States was still uncomfortable with the thought of providing Garang direct assistance, it had apparently opted for indirect assistance through the neighboring "frontline" countries, Uganda, Ethiopia, and Eritrea. From my historical perspective, what I found most interesting about Garang was his continued aspiration to exercise power in Khartoum in a united Sudan, despite growing signs of the total incompatibility of the north and south.

Postmortem: did naiveté lead US astray?

From the start we were never sanguine about our ability to help Sudan. The conflict appeared intractable, and we had higher priorities in Ethiopia and Angola related to US–Soviet relations. Nonetheless, domestic pressure required our visible engagement.

Humanitarian aid versus conflict management

We maintained a high-profile approach to humanitarian relief and a low profile on conflict resolution. Was our approach too unbalanced?

And did we miss opportunities for peace as a result? With the Sadiq and Bashir regimes, we probably focused too much on relief, but they controlled the barges, railways, and air traffic systems. We had a certain ideological sympathy for the SPLA and were thus probably too diffident with them. Ironically, while the humanitarian crisis was directly linked to the war, our efforts to work both issues at a high level were probably incompatible. We could have limited ourselves to the humanitarian side and left conflict resolution to others such as the UN or the OAU. Or we could have worked only the conflict resolution side, leaving the humanitarian issues to the multilateral agencies and the NGOs.

We could probably have accomplished more if we had deployed an aggressive, high-level approach to conflict, especially before the 31 July 1989 coup. The humanitarian problem was being aggressively and effectively addressed in any event by some courageous multilateral leaders such as the late James Grant, then director-general of UNICEF, and James Priestley of the UN Development Program.

Were we too soft on radical Islam?

We can't say we weren't warned about the nature of the July coup. The signs of radical Islam were all there, but we decided to give the regime the benefit of the doubt. Until we saw human rights violations, support for terrorism, and the export of revolution to neighboring states, we maintained a normal diplomatic posture. We also gave weight to opinions from Egypt, which was taken in by Bashir's apparently reasonable approach until the Gulf War revealed his true colors. In retrospect, I do not regret our "constructive engagement," which at least helped the protagonists define the issues and develop their respective positions.

How useful were the tactics?

At the outset, we found the two sides in a state of denial. Sadiq el-Mahdi's regime said, "Tell those rebels to join our democracy. What is there to discuss?" John Garang said, "Tell those guys in power they need to stop thinking like Arabs and accept that we are all Sudanese." I found similar attitudes in virtually every African conflict we addressed.

Our initial approach was thus the classic one. Convince both sides that legitimate issues need to be discussed and clarified, such as the form of government, the relationship between the provinces and the central government, the place of religious law in the constitutional regime, and the role of civil society. In this phase of our approach, I found the northern Arabs more amenable to suggestions than John Garang, who was generally more rigid and unyielding. The Arab northerners were more likely to say, "Yes, the SPLA are Sudanese who should be at the table." Garang shrank from negotiations lest he bestow legitimacy on the illegitimate. In short, he tended to wait for the next coup.

We opted for an incremental approach, with proposals to lighten the military pressure on the south by thinning out the forces and loosening the blockade of cities and towns, as a prelude to serious talks. Our approach foundered on disagreements about the structure of the talks. We should have been tougher with Garang at this stage. He wanted the structure of the talks to reflect his view of the new Sudan, thus imposing his vision even before the talks started. We were seduced by Garang's demand to include all of civil society in the talks, which fell nicely within our definition of democracy and was therefore "reasonable." In retrospect, we should have insisted more strongly that Garang accept Bashir's offer of direct government-to-SPLA negotiations.

We also violated our own rule that we talk to everybody. We should have spent more time with Hasan al-Turabi, who radicalized the military coup in his own fashion. This physically slight religious fanatic with university degrees from both France and England never projected evil when he received visitors. He was all smiles and unthreatening as he discoursed on the importance of a pan-Arab reawakening that would reject Western cultural influence. The man we saw essentially as a harmless intellectual was in reality the mastermind of a dangerous web of terrorism and subversion.

Déja vu all over again

Five years later, in July 1998, at a joint hearing of the House Foreign Affairs Subcommittees on Africa and Human Rights, the subject was Sudan. It was exactly as if time had stood still. Representatives Frank Wolf and Tony Hall were still describing starvation and human tragedy in southern Sudan. The assistant secretary of state for African affairs, Susan Rice, spoke about US efforts to make Operation Lifeline Sudan succeed for yet another year. Sudanese-sponsored rebels continued to commit atrocities in northern Uganda. John Garang's forces were still capturing and losing towns but were no closer to victory than in 1993. IGADD was still holding sporadic negotiating sessions with no progress. Riak Machar, dropping all pretense of being a rebel, had moved to government employment in Khartoum.

Some changes had occurred over five years, however. Where we pursued a policy of constructive engagement toward the Bashir regime, the Clinton administration applied economic sanctions, closed our embassy in Khartoum, and pursued a policy of isolation. Ironically, while I was castigated for our friendly dialogue with the regime, Assistant Secretary Rice was criticized for not talking to the regime to promote humanitarian relief and peace negotiations.

Furthermore, the continuing IGADD negotiating process, while still far from a resolution, had stimulated some interesting exchanges on a referendum that would offer southerners the options of secession, federation, or unity. By the end of 1998, IGADD mediators had achieved agreement on the tough issue of what constituted Sudan's geographic "south" for referendum purposes. Large proven oil reserves in south-central Sudan will probably be shared in the event of a final divorce between the north and the south. As initial confidence-building measures during a transition to a referendum, the SPLA reintroduced the thinning out and separation of forces that we had proposed in 1990–91.

Toward the middle of 1998, seven years after the Khartoum government opted to try for a military victory over the SPLA, both sides apparently reached the point of mutually hurting stalemate. Working with anti-SPLA southerners had not borne fruit for the government, and collaborating with the former Sadiq el-Mahdi government in exile did not advance the SPLA's military fortunes. Thus, at the beginning of 1999, there appeared to be hope that prolonging a cease-fire established for the movement of humanitarian relief might set the stage for full-scale peace discussions.

Those of us rendered cynical by decades of north–south conflict in Sudan were not yet ready to celebrate in early 1999, despite the optimistic signs. Behind the negotiations, we suspected the true intentions of both sides. The Bashir regime probably still wanted to divide, conquer, and "Arabize" the south, and John Garang probably had not abandoned his vision of a secular and democratic united Sudan. But the surprisingly effective mediating work of IGADD taught us that quiet, patient efforts over long periods of time are recommended for intervenors. In short, don't lose hope and don't give up.

4
Angola: From Euphoria to Tragedy

Angola headed our African agenda early in the Bush administration. US involvement in the Angolan civil war had begun in 1986 through "covert" assistance to Dr Jonas Savimbi and his UNITA insurgents.[1] It was a surrogate war between the Soviets and Cubans on one side and the United States and South Africa on the other. With President Bush and Secretary Baker placing a high priority on ending the Cold War, Angola was a logical place for superpower collaboration. Thus, we worked with the Soviets in Angola to solve what was euphemistically called "a regional problem." Together we witnessed a four-year saga of high drama and heady triumphs, followed by abject despair as it all came apart in the end.

For me, resolving the Angolan civil war was a natural follow-on to Chester Crocker's diplomatic triumph in southern Africa that culminated in the tripartite accords signed in New York on 22 December 1988. That agreement provided the framework for Namibia's independence and the total withdrawal of Cuban and South African troops from Angola. With external forces out of Angola, only the civil conflict remained.[2] American diplomacy was on a roll. Our prestige in Africa had never been higher. The atmosphere was ripe for conflict resolution in Angola.

The making of a game plan

In December 1988, Savimbi and his UNITA high command were feeling lonely. Their South African friends had already withdrawn their troops, and with the projected departure of Cuban troops, UNITA believed US interest in Angola would diminish. In addition, the scheduled transition of Namibia to independence under UN supervision between January 1989 and March 1990 would cut off one of UNITA's best supply routes. In his only public statement about the tripartite agreement, Savimbi expressed bitterness that Secretary Crocker had been either unable or unwilling to include an internal settlement in the package.[3]

At the end of 1988, I was finishing up my two-year stint as senior director for Africa on the National Security Council staff. To ensure that Angola was not being overlooked, I contacted President-elect Bush's staff to discuss the future of our Angolan policy. My worries were unfounded. Concern for UNITA's future was strong. Its lobbyists and their congressional allies had done their job well.

Bush's staff and I agreed that only the president-elect himself could reassure Savimbi. I drafted a letter for Bush reminding Savimbi that, while the United States was responsible for mediating Namibian independence and foreign troop departure from Angola, we were not a signatory to those accords and were not bound by their provisions.[4] Our support to UNITA would remain strong, and we would continue military aid until the Angolan government accepted "national reconciliation," meaning genuine negotiations leading to a legitimate political role for UNITA.

Bush sent the letter and released it to the press. It was his first foreign policy decision.[5] The letter reassured not only Savimbi but also his Washington supporters in both political parties. By contrast, liberal Democratic Africanists like Senator Paul Simon and Representatives Howard Wolpe and Mervyn Dymally and centrist Republican Senator Nancy Kassebaum were disappointed that Bush did not reach out evenhandedly to the Angolan government as well.

Further policy formulation had to await the actual arrival of the new foreign affairs team. I spent the waning days of the Reagan administration lobbying heavily for the job of assistant secretary of state for Africa. As the apparent (and ultimately successful) front-runner, I was invited to join a congressional delegation visiting east and southern Africa during the first week of January 1989. The visit's centerpiece was the annual meeting of the African American Institute (AAI) in Lusaka, Zambia.

Senator Paul Simon of Illinois, who chaired the Subcommittee on Africa, headed the delegation, which included Democratic Representatives Charles Rangel and Donald Payne of the Congressional Black Caucus. During 1987–88, when I kept the congressional Democrats briefed on the tripartite negotiations, I had developed relationships of confidence with them, despite their dislike for our "constructive engagement" policy toward *apartheid* South Africa.[6]

At the AAI conference, the legislators delivered a clear message to the Angolan government representatives, including Foreign Minister Pedro de Castro van Dunem, more popularly known as "Loy," his *nom de guerre*. Loy told them his government expected a major effort by friends in the Congress to prohibit further US assistance to UNITA. Both Simon and Payne emphasized their personal opposition to US support for UNITA but urged the Angolans to be realistic. Assistance to UNITA continued to have majority bipartisan congressional support, and there was little hope for a change in 1989. They both therefore urged the government to open negotiations with UNITA. I found our congressmen's performance quite impressive. For them, partisanship did stop at the water's edge.

After consultations on the Hill and with colleagues on Secretary of State James Baker's new team, I knew that a policy of aggressive conflict resolution in Angola would be welcome. It was an obvious place in Africa to pursue Baker's desire for collaboration with the Soviets in solving regional problems. Congressional conservatives had been reassured by Bush's letter that we would not sell out Savimbi's interests in our rush to befriend the Soviets. Congressional liberals wanted to undermine assistance to UNITA but agreed that negotiations were the only pragmatic option. At my confirmation hearing before the Senate Foreign Relations Committee on 3 May 1989, I used my opening statement to inform Congress, as well as my Africa Bureau team-in-waiting, that we would give priority to peace in Angola.[7]

March–September, 1989: nothing went right

Absent from Crocker's tripartite mediation, UNITA was anxious to get into the negotiating game. The New York agreement had greatly reduced their South African support, and American aid was insufficient for a military victory.[8] We were in constant contact with UNITA through their office in Washington.

Communicating with the MPLA government in Luanda, however, was another matter, with no diplomatic representatives in our respective capitals. While the Angolan government was willing to establish formal diplomatic relations, we had a firm policy of refusing recognition to any Angolan regime before the achievement of "national reconciliation."[9] Along with continued arms deliveries, our nonrecognition policy upheld UNITA's confidence and morale.

We urged UNITA to make statements calling for "national reconciliation" on its radio station inside Angola, called "VORGAN," or the "Voice of the Black Cockerel." On 13 March 1989, Savimbi broadcast a proposal for direct talks with the government. He also announced a four-month unilateral moratorium on major military actions and the release of prisoners.[10]

Despite the absence of diplomatic relations, we and the Angolan regime found ways to talk, visiting each other regularly. We also had good channels via the British embassy in Luanda and through the Joint Political Military Commission supervising the New York agreements. The commission members, Angola, South Africa, and Cuba, met quarterly to discuss implementation, with the United States and the Soviet Union as official observers. These meetings provided opportunities for bilateral US–Angolan discussions with both military and political officials. The personal relationships developed during the earlier tripartite negotiations facilitated the dialogue. In particular, the Angolans liked Colonel Charles Snyder, on detail to the Bureau of African Affairs from the Army, Deputy Assistant Secretary James Woods from the Office of the Secretary of Defense, and John Byerly, State's assistant legal advisor for Africa.

The Angolans' message was clear. Peace in Angola should begin with the cessation of all US assistance to the UNITA "bandits." Individual members of UNITA would be eligible for "amnesty" on a case-by-case basis. Otherwise, there was nothing to negotiate.

In view of the government's uncompromising posture, we decided to work through Angola's neighbors, who were bearing the burden of refugees and arms trafficking. We applied diplomatic pressure through our embassies in Brazzaville (Republic of the Congo), Libreville (Gabon), Lusaka (Zambia), and Kinshasa (then Zaire), asking our friends there to push the Angolan government toward meaningful negotiations. In late April, President Omar Bongo of Gabon responded by convening an informal meeting of regional heads of state to urge Angolan President José Eduardo dos Santos to open a substantive dialogue with UNITA.

Dos Santos reacted to this peer pressure by convening his own subregional summit meeting of eight heads of state, in Luanda on 16 May 1989, to present his own peace plan. It marked the first time the MPLA used the term "national reconciliation," a gesture to UNITA. The rest of the plan, however, was unrealistic. Dos Santos called for Savimbi's "exile," UNITA's integration into the ruling MPLA party, and UNITA's acceptance of the existing Constitution.[11] The leaders designated President Mobutu Sese Seko of Zaire, one of Savimbi's most trusted friends, to present the plan to UNITA.

Various statements between March and May 1989 had the virtue of defining the positions of the protagonists. Savimbi wanted dialogue between equals – UNITA and the ruling MPLA party. The two sides would agree on the terms of a cease-fire, set up an interim regime, and hold elections. The government, by contrast, wanted to continue the Marxist one-party state, maintain state control by the MPLA "vanguard party," and integrate UNITA into existing military and political entities. UNITA would receive dignified treatment through amnesty and power-sharing.

Although the two positions were far apart, we nevertheless saw a basis for serious negotiations. We decided early on not to specify what compromise solution might be either acceptable or unacceptable to the United States. We were comfortable with the prospect of supporting a reasonable accord between the two parties, brokered by Angola's neighbors. We wanted peace in Angola and a dignified exit for ourselves, a view shared by the Soviets.

We made rapid contact with Mobutu after the 16 May Luanda summit to compare notes. Mobutu told our ambassador in Kinshasa, William Harrop, that power-sharing was the key to peace in Angola. Negotiations would consist of putting all the top governmental and military jobs on the table and sharing them between the MPLA and UNITA. He said nothing about Savimbi's demand for elections or an interim government. That Mobutu did not embrace Savimbi's point of view despite their close relationship should have warned us that something was not right. But it was only later that we understood the problem.

We expected Mobutu would next begin confidential mediation to bridge the gap. Instead, he surprised us by convoking yet another summit conference with 18 African heads of state, on 22 June 1989 at his northern Zaire village retreat of Gbadolite. His objective was twofold: to give political validation to the Luanda peace plan, and bring dos Santos and Savimbi together for the first time to initiate "national reconciliation." When asked what he was trying to do, Mobutu explained that the summit would not preempt subsequent serious negotiations. An all-African guarantee for "national reconciliation" would be symbolized by a public dos Santos–Savimbi handshake. Power-sharing talks would then follow in a good atmosphere. A (tacit) side benefit would be a new Mobutu image as statesman and peacemaker.

News of the proposed Gbadolite summit greatly agitated Savimbi. It was hard to blame him. He faced the prospect of 18 heads of state ganging up on him to accept a peace plan that would submerge UNITA into a Marxist one-party state. Granted, UNITA would get top jobs in a power-sharing arrangement, but any prospect for a democratic system would disappear. On the other hand, his presence at the summit would give him the political legitimacy he craved. Dos Santos would be forced to recognize him. In follow-on talks, UNITA could argue for more than just a cease-fire and power-sharing.

We realized what was driving Mobutu and his fellow heads of state. Most of their countries were still one-party dictatorships at that time. The beginning of the African democratization trend was still two years away. Continuity of the dictatorial Angolan system appeared normal to its peer group. None were overjoyed at the prospect of an existing "legitimate" regime being forced to change as the result of armed insurgency or, God forbid, free elections. After all, rebel Savimbi would be recognized as a legitimate leader. His movement would be integrated into the existing power structure and would share the wealth. What more could he possibly want?

Preventive diplomacy to persuade the participants that more than just power-sharing was at stake might have been in order. After all, the Angolan war was also about democracy and elections, and too much blood had been shed to accept anything less. Nonetheless, while Savimbi was worried, he did not reject Mobutu's initiative outright. He was too beholden to Mobutu for logistical support and was inclined to trust Mobutu to protect his interests. The United States had no reason to abandon its earlier decision to accept any mutually acceptable solution. The prospect of power-sharing within the existing system did not shock us. The single-party state was still the rule in most of Africa in any event. If the MPLA and UNITA could negotiate a workable power-sharing deal, that was fine with us.

Instead of convincing Mobutu to modify the script for Gbadolite, we spent most of the period 1–22 June persuading Savimbi to attend. Mobutu told Ambassador Harrop he was counting on us to assure Savimbi's participation. It took quite a few telephone conversations to persuade Savimbi that Gbadolite would only be the start of a process and he should grab the opportunity to gain legitimacy as an Angolan political leader.[12] At the same time, dos Santos was not that enthusiastic to see Mobutu take over the process. After all, arms for UNITA transited Zairian territory. Nevertheless, he was persuaded to go to Gbadolite by his good friend Chief Antonio Fernandez, a wealthy Nigerian businessman and diplomat, who was always available to act as a quiet envoy for the United States in delicate situations.

The Gbadolite summit was a personal success for Mobutu but a disaster for Angola. There were no direct talks between dos Santos and Savimbi, and there was no written record of the general consensus. Each head of state felt free to give his own interpretation of what he had heard in executive session. There was, however, a written communiqué announcing three agreed principles:

1. Mutual desire to end the war and effect national reconciliation.
2. Proclamation of a cease-fire effective 24 June 1989.
3. Establishment of a mixed UNITA–MPLA commission, under Mobutu's mediation, to negotiate Angola's political future.[13]

If everyone had been faithful to the published communiqué, real negotiations might have been possible. But the government insisted there was an unpublished consensus on its own fundamental points – exile for Savimbi, integration of UNITA into the MPLA, and continuation of the existing one-party Marxist state. Zambian President Kenneth Kaunda increased the confusion by telling the press that Savimbi would be exiled temporarily.[14] UNITA categorically rejected all interpretations, insisting that the published communique represented the only agreements and that Angola's future remained to be negotiated. The cease-fire effective 24 June was not repudiated, but in the absence of a verification procedure it could not be enforced.

For a short while, Mobutu was hailed as a peacemaker in the international press. Savimbi's appearance before 18 heads of state as dos Santos's equal impressed the analysts.[15] A week later, Mobutu showed up in Washington for an official working visit, the first African leader so honored by President Bush. He came with visions of the Nobel Prize dancing in his head. He even had the temerity to tell a press conference that the Americans should end military assistance to UNITA since the cease-fire would be followed by negotiations and a political solution.[16]

Despite the confusion of Gbadolite, the parties made halfhearted efforts to continue the process. Between 22 June and 17 August, the Zairians convened four negotiating sessions in Kinshasa. Because of the acrimony over MPLA's call for Savimbi's exile and the MPLA's refusal to sit in the same room as UNITA, direct talks were impossible and indirect talks fruitless. The eight heads of state who had met in May in Luanda met again on 18 August in Harare, Zimbabwe, and reaffirmed the original MPLA peace plan, this time including Savimbi's exile. In the interim, I had visited Luanda on 7 July to argue against Savimbi's exile and for unconditional negotiations. I argued, to no avail, that implementation of an agreement would be easier with Savimbi inside Angola keeping his fighters under control.

During August 1989, I participated in a bipartisan congressional seminar on southern Africa held by the Aspen Foundation in the Swiss Alps.

I briefed the members of Congress about Angola and the abortive negotiations, reiterating support for national reconciliation and unconditional negotiations. The members expressed approval of our policy, although they disagreed among themselves on continued US support for UNITA. After the seminar, my wife Suzanne and I were to take a five-day Rhine River cruise from Basel to Amsterdam, but in Basel my office called to say that Dr Savimbi wanted to see me urgently and proposed meeting in Morocco. On 18 August I flew to Rabat and met with Savimbi in a Moroccan government villa.

Savimbi told me he had gone to Gbadolite in June reluctantly on my recommendation. Events since then had confirmed that Gbadolite was stacked against UNITA. That the MPLA delegation in Kinshasa refused even to sit in the same room with UNITA proved they were insincere about reconciliation. He had also lost confidence in Mobutu. There was no way UNITA could adhere to the cease-fire, he said. His generals would kill him first. He wanted me to know that more war was in the offing and he was counting on continued American support. He could not accept a power-sharing agreement that left the MPLA communist dictatorship intact. Free, democratic elections had to be the bottom line.

I told Savimbi we would not abandon UNITA and that his insistence on negotiations without preconditions was reasonable. In the end, it was UNITA, not the United States, that had to be comfortable with the peace process. I warned him, however, not to undermine his own reputation by being the first to repudiate negotiations. He should run out the negotiating string as far as possible before returning to combat. Savimbi said he understood that, but made no promises. He was happy to receive my reassurance of continued support. Then I flew back to Basel, hopped on a train to Heidelberg, and joined Suzanne on the cruise two days late.

To reinvigorate the negotiations, Mobutu convoked yet another meeting of the "Luanda Eight" in Kinshasa on 18 September. He also invited Savimbi. To avert another setback, I quickly rushed to Kinshasa and met Mobutu on 11 September. Mobutu assured me and Ambassador Harrop that if Savimbi attended, it would be possible to begin meaningful negotiations based on true power-sharing, with everything else negotiable. He asked me to convince Savimbi to participate for a second time.

Harrop and I flew to South Africa where the Foreign Ministry had offered their Pretoria guest house as a meeting venue. For the entire day on 13 September, we met there with Savimbi and Jeremias Chitunda, his vice president and former representative in Washington.

Savimbi was emotionally resistant to our arguments from the outset. We told him the MPLA had gotten his message about exile, which was now out of the question, and Angola's political future had to be on the table. We urged him to give the process one more chance.

Savimbi would have none of it. He and Chitunda told us they had lost confidence in Mobutu. He was just another member of the club of dictators. Yes, Mobutu had been a great help, but in the end he was just like all the rest, a dictator for life. At the end, Savimbi was gracious enough to say that he would consider it and would fly immediately to Jamba to confer with the UNITA Central Committee. At cocktail time, we were joined by South African Foreign Minister Pik Botha, who put his arm around Savimbi and urged him to go to Kinshasa "to give peace one more chance." Again, Savimbi said he would consider it.

When I returned to Washington on 15 September, a few days prior to the Kinshasa summit, I heard that Savimbi had traveled from Pretoria to Abidjan, not Jamba. I was not surprised, because Savimbi considered Côte d'Ivoire president Félix Houphouet-Boigny to be his adopted father and mentor. I had had many meetings with Savimbi since 1987 in Houphouet's residence, with the old man an active participant. I was also not surprised to learn that Savimbi had decided to avoid Kinshasa. Houphouet had undoubtedly confirmed Savimbi's view of the club of presidents who supported the status quo in Angola. I tried to reach Savimbi by phone, but he refused my calls. I did manage to reach Houphouet, who assured me he was urging Savimbi to go to Kinshasa, but I suspected just the opposite.

As a gesture to Mobutu, Savimbi sent a delegation to Kinshasa headed by Jorge Valentim, UNITA's chief negotiator. Without Savimbi, the delegation was rudely treated by the Zairois, who did not allow them to speak. The result was predictable. The original MPLA plan was endorsed once again, but peace was not in the cards until another round of fighting could clear the air. This time, the press understood that peace prospects were diminishing.[17]

On the weekend of 16 September as the Kinshasa meeting was convening, my team and I were in the State Department working the telephones to avert a result that might aggravate tensions in Angola. On Sunday afternoon, our political superiors directed us to modify our policy of approving any reasonable solution acceptable to both the MPLA and UNITA regardless of the contents. That afternoon, we found the department swarming with UNITA supporters, led by the lobbying firm Black, Manafort and Stone, and Sean Cleary, a South African diplomat seconded to UNITA. They were in Secretary Baker's office as well as the office of Under Secretary for Political Affairs Bob Kimmit. As a result, we were directed to issue an official statement insisting on nothing less than free and fair elections in Angola. Southern Africa director Bob Perito and I sat there shaking our heads. A new precondition for a settlement had been added to the conveniently vague concept of "national reconciliation."[18]

Needless to say, our statement hit the Kinshasa summit like a bomb. Mobutu saw a conspiracy between UNITA and the United States to undermine him and quickly responded. All transshipments of American supplies to UNITA through Zairian territory were suspended immediately and indefinitely. With South African lethal support having stopped in August 1989 and US deliveries newly suspended, UNITA's military outlook suddenly weakened.[19]

One more MPLA bash and then peace talks

The dry-season military offensive between June and November was a tradition in the Angolan conflict. About every other year, the Angolan army, the FAPLA (People's Armed Forces for the Liberation of Angola), took advantage of the dry terrain to move against UNITA forces south of the town of Cuito Cuanavale. Because of the diplomatic activity between May and September 1989, the FAPLA did not move against UNITA during the dry season that year. When it became clear, however, that UNITA would not adhere to the cease-fire signed at Gbadolite, FAPLA launched a wet-season offensive in December. As in previous years, the offensive was preceded by a major infusion of Soviet equipment, including armor and artillery.

Despite the unproductive summit conferences of June, August, and September, Mobutu continued his efforts. He made a new cease-fire proposal in November. In light of the ominous FAPLA buildup, UNITA accepted, proposing negotiations with no preconditions. This time, the government refused and began its offensive on 23 December along the Kuzumbia River between Cuito Cuanavale and Mavinga. The operation involved armored vehicles, tanks, and several thousand troops, with Soviet advisors providing hands-on support.[20]

When Mobutu stopped the transit of US supplies to UNITA in September, we searched for new supply routes, but could identify no diplomatically feasible or cost-effective alternatives. Our only option came down to a rapprochement between Mobutu and Savimbi. We sent a quick recommendation to the National Security Council staff that President Bush invite both Mobutu and Savimbi to Washington and work his magic. They accepted and came in the first week of October.

Each man spent about 45 minutes meeting separately with President Bush, with Savimbi going first. Savimbi expressed profound appreciation to Bush for his support. He wanted only democracy for Angola, he insisted, and fair treatment for his Ovimbundu people. He was deeply disappointed by Mobutu, who had cast his lot with dos Santos and the club of one-party dictatorships. Bush reaffirmed US support for UNITA and pledged continued assistance until national reconciliation was achieved. But he said Savimbi would have to meet Mobutu halfway to retrieve their former good relationship, despite the Gbadolite fiasco. Savimbi promised to follow Bush's advice.[21]

The meeting with Mobutu was less tense than expected. He was bitter about Savimbi's refusal to accept the Gbadolite process but felt it was still possible to rekindle the negotiations. Bush evoked their long-standing friendship. He argued that the United States and Zaire had come too far in the Angola peace process to stop just when success was on the horizon. He asked Mobutu to let bygones be bygones. Having been appropriately stroked and reassured of his importance to our African policy, Mobutu agreed to reconcile with Savimbi. He asked us to transmit an invitation to Savimbi to participate in his upcoming birthday party at his villa on the French Riviera. He also asked that I be present as a witness.

We arrived at Mobutu's italianate Cap Martin villa, on the heights overlooking the bay of Villefranche, at noon on Sunday, 15 October. Mobutu received us on the terrace under a brilliant Riviera sky. A US aircraft carrier was anchored in the bay. UNITA Vice President Jeremias Chitunda accompanied Savimbi, and Robert Perito, my director for southern African affairs, accompanied me. After ordering aperitifs, Mobutu asked that a screen be installed to block the view of the aircraft carrier. Forever the showman, he whispered to me, "I know the American military have listening devices on those ships."

Mobutu then apologized to Savimbi for what had happened. He admitted that personal ambition had gotten the better of him. He suggested they turn the page. He said, "in front of our American friend Cohen, I pledge to you that I will support you to the end." He offered his hand, and Savimbi took it. That was that. We then adjourned to the swimming pool terrace for the birthday party, with 250 guests and a jazz orchestra flown specially from Kinshasa for the occasion. Later, I shared a car to Nice Airport with Chitunda, who said, "You know, Mr Secretary, I am convinced that the guy is sincere." Who was I to refute his naive analysis?

After the reconciliation, we thought UNITA's supply problem had been solved. But the first flight in the resumed supply run on

27 November crashed on landing at the Jamba airstrip, killing the entire five-man crew.[22] Locating and outfitting a replacement aircraft would take another two months, leaving UNITA's stocks without replenishment between September and January. In view of the Soviet's major resupply of FAPLA, UNITA's future continued to look bleak. No wonder Savimbi was amenable to a cease-fire in November, in contrast to his refusal at Gbadolite in June.

Our official reaction to the FAPLA offensive was critical but not strident. We reserved our main pique for the Soviets, who were supporting war rather than peace. On 8 January 1990, with FAPLA advancing toward the Lomba River and Mavinga, we issued the following statement:

> We are very concerned about the dangerous escalation of offensive military action by the MPLA against UNITA-controlled territory in southeastern Angola. That this offensive action is receiving close support from a substantial number of Soviet military advisers at the front line is increasing our concern. These actions come at a time when UNITA is prepared to agree to a cease-fire and unconditional negotiations. We therefore urge Luanda and the Soviet Union to stop the offensive immediately and concentrate instead on the peace process.[23]

Conditions were ripe for one last FAPLA effort to defeat UNITA, or failing that, to marginalize them as a guerrilla force by confining them to the barren wastes of southeastern Angola. South African troop support for UNITA, as well as its deliveries of lethal equipment, had ended in 1988.[24] Cuban troop withdrawal was proceeding on schedule pursuant to the New York accords. Twenty-five thousand, or 50 per cent, had departed by 1 November 1989, and the remaining 25 000 had moved above the 13th parallel. That remaining force was useful in protecting FAPLA's rear areas from UNITA guerrilla attacks, but by mid-1990 most of those Cubans would also be gone. One last bash against UNITA, even in the rainy season, therefore made military sense.

The FAPLA offensive got off to a good start. The "ultimate assault" was advancing well. Four hundred FAPLA tanks were able to cross the Lomba River and reach the outskirts of Mavinga, the last UNITA stronghold on the road to their headquarters in Jamba. If FAPLA could take Mavinga and Jamba, UNITA would be reduced to scattered guerrilla bands without a logistical base. We and UNITA were worried. Hope for a negotiated settlement hung in the balance.

Shortly after the FAPLA offensive started in December, James L. Woods, the veteran deputy assistant secretary for African affairs in the Defense Department, asked to see me privately. He and I had gotten to know each other well during our many overseas trips for the 1997–98 tripartite negotiations, accompanying Chester Crocker, who valued Woods's judgment on political as well as military matters. As assistant secretary, I relied on him for a perspective on conflict issues different from those provided by my staff and our embassies. Our two staffs also worked well together.

Woods expressed uneasiness about the CIA's business-as-usual attitude toward Angola. He said there was unanimous agreement in the Pentagon that the FAPLA offensive was extremely serious and dangerous. The absence of the deadly accurate South African artillery, which had been so valuable in thwarting the 1987 offensive, rendered UNITA vulnerable to FAPLA's armor and superior troop strength. He said it was vital and urgent that deliveries be accelerated. In other words, deliver the goods when needed, not after it was too late. Woods and his colleagues from the Joint Chiefs of Staff promised to help find the necessary supplies and transport on a rush basis.

Jim Woods's strategy worked. The American "surge," particularly rapid deliveries of antitank weaponry, helped UNITA break the back of the FAPLA offensive in Mavinga itself. Soviet tanks rolling in formation were easy targets for UNITA gunners sneaking in from behind. In addition, FAPLA logistics failed in an area known as "the end of the world," between Cuito Cuanavale and Mavinga, where there was just nothing FAPLA could consume and where its lengthy supply lines were vulnerable to UNITA sabotage. By mid-February, it was clear that FAPLA's "ultimate assault" had failed, and UNITA was out of the woods. By advising dos Santos that he should not accept an invitation from his congressional friends to visit Washington, we also showed our loyalty to UNITA.[25]

Of growing political significance was a UNITA program to infiltrate special forces into government areas far from its own territory. Begun even before the FAPLA offensive, the program was accelerated in early 1990 in response to the Gbadolite fiasco. Failing to defeat UNITA in conventional war was bad enough, but UNITA's sabotage of utility lines in the big cities posed a real political problem for the regime. This program continued beyond the FAPLA offensive and helped stimulate negotiations.[26] In this respect, a positive signal emerged from the February 1990 Moscow ministerial meeting between the US and Soviet foreign ministers. The communiqué deplored the lagging peace process in Angola and called for a cessation of hostilities and negotiations.[27] The Soviets had finally agreed that military options were exhausted.

Toward the end of February 1990, we returned to planning for negotiations. Still the official mediator, Mobutu had devised a new plan based on reciprocal concessions and a cease-fire. The MPLA would abandon their demand for Savimbi's exile, and UNITA would drop their demand for multiparty elections.[28] We knew it would not work because UNITA was locked into a nonnegotiable demand for democracy. In any event, Mobutu was no longer able to handle a mediation that was bound to be far more complex than he thought. For its part, government rhetoric refused to admit failure in Mavinga, arguing they had accomplished their mission of "punishing" UNITA without recourse to Cuban support. They also found a convenient scapegoat in the surge of US arms deliveries.[29]

We decided to call for direct negotiations without preconditions. As opposed to Mobutu's approach of cease-fire first and negotiations second, we believed that Angola required the reverse. In Angola, the side that had the military advantage always refused a cease-fire, while the side that was in difficulty always wanted a cease-fire before negotiations. After the battle of Mavinga, a battlefield stalemate had set in. Thus, talks with no cease-fire and no preconditions might be acceptable.

Bob Perito and his team in the Directorate of Southern African Affairs reminded me that Namibian independence was set for 21 March 1990 in Windhoek and that Secretary Baker would lead the US delegation. As often happens in the conduct of foreign policy, special occasions provide an opening for high-level initiatives.

April–November 1990: negotiations and frustration

The eighteen-hour flight on Secretary Baker's air force plane from Washington to Windhoek provided an opportunity to discuss Angola and South Africa. To everyone's delight, Baker invited Chester Crocker, the man whose diplomatic skills had paved the way for Namibian independence, to join the delegation.

Airborne discussions led to a scenario for Baker's encounter with President dos Santos. There would be press photos to signal our recognition of Angolan government legitimacy, despite our continued refusal of formal diplomatic relations. Baker would say that it was time for direct talks with UNITA without preconditions and with everything on the table, including a cease-fire. Our assistance to UNITA was limited in volume and defensive in nature. We had no intention of seeking the demise of the government through military or any other means. However, our assistance to UNITA would continue until national reconciliation was achieved. If negotiations ended the fighting and initiated a democratic transition, the United States would open an interests section in Luanda, and Baker would recommend that President Bush invite dos Santos to Washington.

Dos Santos was friendly, listened to Baker carefully and agreed it was time for serious negotiations. However, he asked Baker how anyone could possibly trust Savimbi's word. Baker replied that any agreement would need appropriate controls and verification. Baker asked dos Santos to reflect and suggested he designate a senior official to meet separately with me to discuss next steps.

I followed up with Alphonso Pitra, an MPLA hard-line advisor on national security matters. As I expected, Pitra was unable to discuss details because the MPLA policy machine moved slowly. I was pleased, however, because I saw a resigned acceptance of inevitable direct MPLA–UNITA negotiations. I was also subjected to a torrent of bitter invective blaming UNITA, South Africa, and the United States for all of Angola's ills. Pitra demonstrated a sense of abandonment because of the Cuban troop departure and the Soviet decision to phase out their assistance. Talk of a possible mediator produced little. When I volunteered the United States, Pitra responded with the Portuguese equivalent of "It will be a cold day in hell." More important, because Mobutu had authorized resumed arms deliveries to UNITA the previous November, he too was ineligible.

After three days in South Africa, Baker stopped in Kinshasa, Zaire, en route back to Washington, to meet Jonas Savimbi. We sought his agreement for negotiations and wanted to buck up Mobutu's morale as a frustrated mediator. At the same time, Soviet Foreign Minister Eduard Shevardnadze traveled from Windhoek to Moscow via Luanda to put pressure on the MPLA. After the failed offensive, the Soviets had decided enough was enough.[30]

Needless to say, Savimbi was in a good mood. Heavy combat was still in progress near Mavinga, but he was confident the FAPLA had run out of steam. Government casualties were heavy, and FAPLA morale was low. UNITA had prevented FAPLA from taking the Mavinga airport, which they desparately needed as a logistics base. In addition UNITA sabotage efforts in the rest of Angola were embarrassing the regime. Savimbi had no problems with Baker's proposal. Negotiations without a cease-fire had been UNITA's main objective.[31]

We had a working lunch on Mobutu's river boat *Kamanyola*, which was furnished like a New Orleans bordello. Baker expressed appreciation for Mobutu's support for negotiations. He insisted that Mobutu was still the chief mediator and that we would be happy to proffer both support as cosponsors and technical assistance. Mobutu was relieved to hear he was still viewed as a regional statesman. I took leave of Baker at the airport as I had other business in Central Africa. Getting on the plane, Baker said, "You had better cut a deal on Angola fast, Hank, because time is running out on our ability to deliver assistance to UNITA. These Cold War programs are going out of style."

With both the MPLA and UNITA ready for negotiations, the big question in March–April 1990 was identification of a suitable mediator. On 7 April the presidents of Angola, Gabon, Congo, and São Tomé and Príncipe met in Santo Antonio, Príncipe, to discuss the peace process. Mobutu's absence for the first time was dos Santos's effort to circumvent him.[32] During the 4–6 April US–Soviet ministerial conference in Washington, Baker and Shevardnadze agreed to cosponsor confidential direct talks between the MPLA and UNITA at a neutral site in Europe. The proposal was transmitted to both parties and Mobutu via diplomatic channels. Savimbi and Mobutu accepted, but the MPLA refused. Fear of superpower collusion stimulated the MPLA to approach the Portuguese as an alternative. UNITA agreed to Portugal, provided Mobutu could remain the official mediator.

Portugal made sense. Lisbon had major political, economic, and emotional interests in Angola. For that reason, we always kept the Portuguese fully briefed about our activities. The young state secretary for foreign affairs, Jose Durão Barroso, could think of no higher calling than to midwife a negotiated settlement. Angola and Mozambique were politically important in Portugal, because very few voters did not have ties to the former colonies.

The Angolan government trusted the centrist Social Democratic government in Lisbon, which was friendly to the MPLA. Lisbon considered the MPLA more qualified to manage the country than UNITA. By contrast, UNITA had close ties to the leftist Portuguese Socialist Party led by State President Mario Soares. Soares had been heavily influenced by Socialist International colleague Leopold Senghor of Senegal, who considered Savimbi the true representative of Angola's "black majority."[33]

State Secretary Durão Barroso moved quickly to bring the parties together for secret "talks about talks" 24–25 April at Evora, Portugal. A second round in Oeiras, Portugal, 16–18 June, addressed basic political principles. Flush with satisfaction from the MPLA's agreement to sit in the same room for the first time, UNITA took the high ground with four unilateral concessions:

- UNITA recognized the Angolan state and its president.
- UNITA recognized the MPLA as a legitimate political party.
- UNITA withdrew its demand for a transitional government. The incumbent MPLA regime would govern Angola until elections.
- UNITA offered a three-month truce to build confidence.

There was basic agreement on a verifiable cease-fire and army unification. However, the MPLA refused to accept either recognition of UNITA as a political party or multiparty democracy. Their negotiators claimed that the Angolan constitution called for a single-party, Marxist state, which they could not negotiate away. The MPLA's main demand was for an immediate cease-fire, the integration of some UNITA forces into the Angolan army, and demobilization of the rest. In five negotiating sessions, the UNITA recognition question emerged as the main obstacle.

We maintained an active dialogue with Savimbi each step of the way, encouraging him to remain firm on recognition as a tradeoff for a cease-fire. In September, Durão Barroso asked us to persuade Savimbi to accept a parallel negotiation on cease-fire modalities while talks about principles continued. Savimbi agreed, with the understanding that a cease-fire document would be signed simultaneously with an agreement on principles, not before. Durão Barroso also requested that American and Soviet experts be present during cease-fire negotiations, recognizing that a superpower presence might help to energize the talks.

In November, the MPLA started hinting about amending the constitution to establish a multiparty system but refused categorically to recognize UNITA until after a cease-fire. For its part, UNITA changed its demand from "recognition" to "legalization" to help the MPLA take the big political leap.

Trying to understand the MPLA's problem on the issue of recognition or legalization, we took advantage of the ninth tripartite Joint Commission meeting in Windhoek, Namibia, on 13 September 1990 to seek Cuban wisdom.[34] In a private meeting, Cuba's General Jesus Bermudez said it was the Angolan military that objected to UNITA's legalization. They saw UNITA not as a political party but as an army. To keep up the morale of their troops, who had been badly bloodied at Mavinga, the FAPLA generals were insisting on a cease-fire first, with legalization later. Bermudez said the FAPLA hierarchy were actually in favor of a long war of attrition. Although FAPLA had failed to crush UNITA at Mavinga, UNITA was not in a position to win the war, and FAPLA had first call on Angola's oil revenue to purchase arms. The Angolans also knew that political opposition to US support for UNITA was growing, which meant that UNITA was bound to become weaker.[35]

Bermudez had a point. Throughout 1990, a battle was waged in Washington between lobbyists for and against aid to UNITA. The withdrawal of Cuban troops from Angola, the release of Nelson Mandela from prison in South Africa, and the overall cooperative relationship between the two superpowers were making it harder to justify Cold War activities in Africa. UNITA supporters found themselves constantly on the defensive, but the commitment to Savimbi, "the anticommunist freedom fighter," remained strong. UNITA's registered lobbying office in Washington, the Free Angola Information Service, reported an annual expenditure of $800 000. In addition, UNITA's hired guns, the lobbying firm of Black, Manafort and Stone, reported annual expenditures of $350 000. Across the street, the Angolan government hired the law firm of Washington, Perito and Dubuc for an annual fee of $800 000 to promote both an end to UNITA support and formal US diplomatic recognition. In the Congress, Michigan Democrat Howard Wolpe, chairman of the House Subcommittee on Africa, led the campaign against UNITA.[36]

Testifying at closed hearings before the two congressional intelligence committees in September 1990, I determined from member feedback that continued support for UNITA was not in immediate danger. Nevertheless, everyone was so anxious to see an end to the Angolan problem that UNITA risked losing its support if it failed to negotiate seriously.

During consideration of the 1991 Intelligence Authorization Bill, Representatives Ronald Dellums, Lee Hamilton, and Mervyn Dymally, all Democrats, introduced an amendment prohibiting covert assistance for military operations in Angola. The amendment was defeated in the House on 17 October 1990 by a wide margin. Subsequently, however, the House narrowly passed the Solarz amendment, which called for a suspension of lethal aid to UNITA if the MPLA set a reasonable date for free and fair multiparty elections, stopped receiving military assistance from the Soviet Union or any other source, and refrained from launching offensives against UNITA. While his goals were laudable, I told Representative Solarz that we opposed his bill because it allowed the MPLA to determine when we would stop aid to UNITA. Nevertheless, passage of the Solarz bill showed growing congressional impatience with Angola.[37]

December 1990: superpowers to the rescue

The fifth round of negotiations in Portugal in late November failed to achieve a breakthrough on either UNITA's legalization or the MPLA's demand for a cease-fire. As usual, Angola was on the agenda for the next Baker–Shevardnadze meeting scheduled for Houston, Texas, 9–10 December. A week earlier, we received word from the secretary's office that he and Shevardnadze had agreed to meet with Angolan foreign minister Loy and Dr Savimbi respectively. We were instructed to request their presence in Washington on 12 December. Savimbi was delighted that he would be photographed with the Soviet foreign minister, a major milestone on his road to full legitimacy.

At the Houston meeting, my Soviet counterpart Yuri Yukalev, Foreign Ministry director for African nations, and I briefed the ministers on Angola for thirty minutes. Our message was that, conceptually, the two sides were not far apart on what was needed: cease-fire, legalization of political parties including UNITA, establishment of a multiparty system, merging of the two armies, encampment of troops during a transition, and elections. Unfortunately, the talks were stalled by the MPLA's refusal to accept mutual recognition without a cease-fire, and by UNITA's refusal to sign a cease-fire agreement in the absence of progress on other issues. These basic disagreements delayed the detailed exchanges needed for the complex problems of implementation. Nevertheless, we praised mediator Durão Barroso for focusing talks on essentials.

Shevardnadze graciously commented that the progress achieved to date was due to the good work of the African bureaus of the US and Soviet foreign ministries. He believed the Portuguese needed help from the superpowers to break the logjam. He proposed that Yukalev and I get together right there in Houston and construct a framework agreement. We should then summon the two parties and say, "This is the solution we have worked out for you. Now return to the table and negotiate the details." Baker agreed to this somewhat unorthodox approach.[38]

Yukalev and I saluted, retired to a separate room, and wrote a new concept paper. We then drafted an Angolan paragraph for the Houston communiqué, expressing continued confidence in the Portuguese mediator and announcing that Baker would meet with Foreign Minister Loy and Shevardnadze with Savimbi in Washington on 12 December.

It also said the ministers would propose a package involving a cease-fire, free participation of UNITA in a multiparty political process, free elections under international observation, and the end of all arms deliveries to both sides. That package would be discussed at a high-level meeting involving the MPLA, UNITA, Portugal, the United States, and the Soviet Union in Washington on 13 December. In effect, the superpowers had taken charge.[39]

Savimbi and Loy were already on their way to the United States, because they had been invited to meet with Shevardnadze and Baker. After the Houston discussions, we rapidly invited the Portuguese to attend the 13 December conclave. Richard Roth and I met with Savimbi and his top advisors on 11 December to go over the draft concepts paper. Savimbi suggested minor changes in substance, which I accepted. I gave Savimbi the time of his appointment with Shevardnadze for the following day, and he asked where the meeting would take place. He almost fainted when I said the Soviet Embassy, fearing the Soviets would find a way to kill him, most likely by poisoning. I said the Soviets would not want the embarrassment of his dropping dead as he walked out the embassy door. Savimbi responded, "They have poison that kills three weeks later."

On 12 December, Baker's meeting with Loy was valuable for its atmospherics. Loy was not in the negotiating loop and thus could not discuss details knowledgeably. But he appreciated the fact that the photo with Baker boosted the MPLA's legitimacy. The press also gave big play to Savimbi's call on Shevardnadze.[40] Afterwards, I asked Savimbi how it had gone. He said he was pleased and convinced the Soviets really wanted to end their Angola commitment. He also assured me he had not eaten anything.

If the Portuguese were unhappy about the Shevardnadze–Baker initiative, they did not show it. They sent Ambassador Antonio Monteiro, Durão Barroso's deputy mediator, who could not have been more enthusiastic. The Angolan government representative was Lopo do Nascimento, member of the MPLA central committee and newly designated chief negotiator. UNITA was represented by Jeremias Chitunda.

We met the morning of 13 December in the Africa Bureau conference room, with Yuri Yukalev cochairing with me. I went over the US–Soviet draft point by point, with Yukalev jumping in from time to time to emphasize certain points. He kept returning to the need for what he called "a negotiated political settlement," since a military victory by either side was impossible. Our paper had seven central provisions:

- Legalization of UNITA.
- Holding of free elections, with the determination of a date a precondition for a cease-fire.
- Creation of a unified national army before elections.
- Constitutional legalization of a multiparty democracy.
- Cessation of lethal military supplies from all sources, known as the "triple zero" option.[41]
- UN involvement in cease-fire monitoring.
- Presence of international election observers.

Ambassador Monteiro praised the superpower initiative, describing our document as an important supplement to the work already done in five negotiating rounds. He added that continued superpower involvement would serve both to build trust and to "guarantee" the outcome. Yukalev emphasized the importance of a neutral army and the presence of UN observers. Chitunda placed particular stress on international guarantees for both the negotiating process and implementation.

Lopo do Nascimento was more than a new face. He was a breath of fresh air. In contrast to his predecessors, who tended to be arrogant in defense of Angolan sovereignty, Lopo (as everyone called him) was polite and reasonable. His attitude toward the UNITA delegation was especially warm and brotherly. He and Chitunda exchanged compliments and expressions of respect.

After we had gone through the paper once and had a coffee break, Yukalev asked the Angolans if they were ready to initial the document. Chitunda said yes, but Lopo said he did not have a mandate to sign. He attempted to end the discussion, claiming an urgent need to return to Luanda.[42] I countered that our document was not sacrosanct, and he was welcome to make suggestions. Lopo then stuck his toe in the water by commenting on the first point. When he found the water comfortable, he relaxed and commented point by point. After another four hours, we came up with a document that all could initial *ad referendum*. Lopo had achieved his two main objectives: A cease-fire had to precede everything else, and the Angolan government's sovereignty would be preserved throughout. UNITA was willing to concede these because it had obtained everything else it wanted.[43]

At the end, I insisted that the agreed "Washington Concepts Paper" was not a substitute for documents already negotiated, nor was our meeting a substitute for Portuguese mediation. Nevertheless, a break-through had taken place because obstacles to an agreement on princi-ples had been overcome. What remained were those devilish details concerning the election date, the composition of a new national army, and the role of the UN. Major disagreements remained, but the Angolans were finally in a position to tackle them.[44] As I reported to Under Secretary Bob Kimmitt, "The concept paper clears up a number of problems: UNITA's political legalization, acceptance of U.N. monitors, and linkage of a cease-fire to a change in the constitution. We are approaching the goal."

January–May 1991: the tough details

As "official observers," we and the Soviets henceforth had to prepare to be useful. Overall coordination was centered in the Office of Southern African Affairs, with Deputy Director Richard Roth as point man. The entire operation was supervised by Senior Deputy Assistant Secretary Jeff Davidow, a veteran Southern Africanist, formerly ambas-sador to Zambia. I was kept informed but had to divide my time among Ethiopia, Liberia, and the Sudan in addition to Angola. During the detailed negotiations from January to May 1991, I was one of the team members deployed when necessary to help move the talks along.

The interagency process was employed intensively to help the negotiations. Since the toughest problems were military, we made sure the talks did not fail for want of technical expertise. Colonel Charles Snyder, our army exchange officer, was in charge of our military repre-sentation. He was assisted by Colonel Kim Henningsen from Jim Woods's staff in the Pentagon and by our Office of Defense Cooperation in Lisbon. In the Pentagon, Woods established an Angola working group to support the US negotiating team. It included representatives from the Joint Chiefs of Staff, the Defense Intelligence Agency, and the armed services as needed. In anticipation of both negotiating and implementa-tion requirements, for example, the group developed a putative force structure for the new Angolan unified army, as well as a document on the likely tasks required to implement a cease-fire.

Richard Roth led our delegation in the political and constitutional talks, with assistance from Jeff Millington, political counselor in Lisbon, John Byerly, the State Department's assistant legal advisor for Africa, and Karl Troy, officer in charge of Angolan affairs. In Washington, we stayed close to the experts in the Bureau of Intelligence and Research, who daily sifted through the raw intelligence, providing both timely and insightful analysis.

During January 1991, the Portuguese prepared three documents for signature or initialing during the sixth negotiating session scheduled for 5–8 February – the Washington concepts paper, fundamental principles for the establishment of peace in Angola, and a framework cease-fire agreement. The cease-fire agreement could only be initialed and not signed, because its coming into force required both an agreement on elections and a constitutional amendment authorizing multiparty democracy.

UNITA took advantage of negotiating intervals to send people to Washington for instruction on implementing a cease-fire, how to merge two armies, and how to run a free election. While this was going on, Jeff Davidow went to Luanda to help ease the MPLA's fears. He also negotiated agreements giving international relief workers access to war zones. In effect, we networked nonstop to give the process a cachet of American involvement and support.

The bulk of the serious negotiations took place during March and April in the town of Bicesse, twenty miles from Lisbon near Estoril. The Portuguese sequestered the two delegations in a hotel training school where they negotiated, took their meals, and slept. They were served by the hotel trainees. Durão Barroso and Monteiro set up offices there along with appropriate support staff and equipment.

I personally made two visits to Bicesse to help overcome deadlocks. Each time, I met with the Portuguese press, which could not get enough news about the Angola talks. Each time, I made a point of praising the tireless work of Durão Barroso and his team. In March, I found the delegations far apart on the issue of an election date. UNITA was in a hurry. The MPLA was thinking of three to five years after the cease-fire. With compromise difficult, if not impossible, I proposed that Portugal and the two observers make their own recommendation. I suggested the formula "no less than 15 and no more than 18 months after the signature of a cease-fire." Since the proposal came from outsiders, both sides found it easier to agree.

I will never forget the very last plenary session the night of 25 April. Durão Barroso was in the chair. A last-minute problem arose over the police, which would remain exclusively under government control. UNITA told me they felt uneasy with this, suspecting the police would be used to intimidate UNITA supporters. They wanted to reopen the issue. I approached Pitra, the MPLA delegation head, who told me it was out of the question. After much debate, I suggested that the UN be requested to supply one police monitor for each province who would be teamed with one UNITA and one MPLA representative. The teams would investigate reports of police misbehavior. The MPLA and UNITA agreed. With that issue settled, we suddenly realized there was nothing left to discuss. From a corner came a howl of delight from Richard Roth, who proceeded to dance a jig. Needless to say, the party went on for some time.

The documents were initialed in Bicesse on the first of May. An unofficial cease-fire went into effect 15 May, and the formal gala signing by dos Santos and Savimbi took place in Lisbon on 31 May. Secretary Baker witnessed the signing along with the new Soviet foreign minister Alexander Bessmyrtnykh, UN Secretary-General Javier Pérez de Cuéllar, and the entire Portuguese hierarchy. I flew in from London, where we had played a role in ending the Ethiopian conflict a week earlier. It was quite a heady week for me, with the Bush–Baker foreign policy in Africa looking good. Baker's formal statement paid tribute to the courage of the Angolan protagonists, to the good work of the United Nations, and to the Portuguese mediators. He pledged that the United States would support the peace process in its role as official observer in the Joint Political Military Commission, and would refrain from sending lethal military items to Angola pursuant to the accords, thereby ending five years of military aid to UNITA.[45]

Baker met with Savimbi to assure him that although arms supplies would be terminated, shipments of nonlethal goods would continue. Savimbi was pleased, because UNITA needed to open political offices in at least eighteen urban centers. He also asked Baker for a source of advice on running a political campaign. Baker said he would try to establish a liaison with American experts outside of government channels. Finally, Baker obtained a promise from Savimbi that all remaining stocks of Stinger ground-to-air missiles would be returned to US inventories quickly in order to maintain congressional support. Flying home in Baker's plane, I decided that the coordinating apparatus we had built to help mediate Bicesse would have to be maintained for another eighteen months to support implementation.

The making of an election

Flaws in the Bicesse agreements surfaced as soon as implementation began. We saw at least five:

- The Joint Political Military Commission, the key implementation mechanism, had only the two protagonists as its members, guaranteeing significant slowdowns and blockages caused by disagreements and mistrust. Certainly, Portugal, the United States, and the Soviet Union had official observers present at all meetings to intervene and break impasses. But the absence of an official tiebreaker exerted a significant drag on implementation.

- The MPLA insisted, over UNITA's objections, on limiting the UN Angola Verification Mission (UNAVEM II) to a few hundred monitors. In a country as vast as Angola, with abundant opportunities for cheating, the monitoring task was daunting. UNAVEM II was headed by a skillful senior UN civil servant, Margaret Anstee, and staffed by experienced civilian and military personnel. But they could not adequately cover the whole territory.
- UNITA insisted, over the MPLA's objections, on linking the cease-fire to a firm, relatively early date for elections, thus making the implementation process hostage to anyone who wished to sabotage the elections. In the rush to complete processes prerequisite to the election such as unification of the two armies, cutting corners produced potentially disastrous consequences. Linked sequencing – process B does not begin until process A is completed, no matter how long it takes – would have been preferable.
- The agreement to allow the Angolan government complete control over the police was a mistake, and my compromise at Bicesse providing for UN police monitors was inadequate. The government took advantage of the loophole to develop what I called the "fourth army," a paramilitary "antiriot" police that raised the level of UNITA's paranoia considerably.[46]
- The other side of the paramilitary police coin was UNITA's right under the agreement to provide armed security for its own political leaders, enabling UNITA to send fighters to areas they had been unable to penetrate while the war was still on.

Despite problems systemic to the Bicesse agreement, implementation proceeded, with many favorable developments. As official observers in the JPMC, we were able to continue an activist role and wasted no time gearing up for it.

Jeffrey Millington, our man in Lisbon, went to Luanda to open the US mission, designated "The United States Liaison Office to the Joint Political Military Commission" (USLO). Besides Millington, who knew all the players on both sides from the Bicesse marathons, we sent two other State Department officers, communications and secretarial personnel, and Portuguese-speaking military officers, who were our eyes and ears on the crucial issues of military encampment and unification.

Back in Washington, considerable interagency discussion focused on how we might help overcome obstacles to implementation. We identified three major areas where we had comparative advantage: food deliveries, transportation of people and cargo, and election assistance. We decided to exploit all three and to participate actively as official observers in the JPMC. As of September 1991, for example, the Angolan government had still not selected a firm date for the election. The three observer governments sent a high-level joint delegation that included me to Luanda. We made it clear in advance that we did not want to arrive without an announced election date. A few days before our mid-September arrival, dos Santos declared the election would be held 29–30 September 1992.

September and October 1991 were busy, with visits to Washington by both dos Santos and Savimbi.[47] President dos Santos's unofficial visit on 1 September fulfilled Baker's promise of March 1990 in Namibia. Dos Santos had the brilliant idea of bringing his 21-year-old daughter, a student in England. She was vivacious, attractive, and spoke perfect English. Bush, who was strong on families, just melted when she walked into the Oval Office. From that point, it was not easy for him to talk tough to dos Santos, but he did forcefully urge more expeditious assembly and cantonment of troops and an early decision on an electoral calendar.[48]

I personally made six visits to Angola during the twelve-month period from 1 November 1991 to 30 October 1992. Jeff Davidow and others also traveled there to keep the transition moving ahead. Although we tried to project a neutral posture as official observers, we maintained a special relationship to UNITA. Whenever I visited Luanda, I met with both sides on an equal basis, but the conversations were on different levels. With dos Santos and the MPLA, conversations focused on implementation. With Savimbi, we talked strategy and tactics aimed at coping with problems and winning the elections.

As Baker had promised Savimbi in Lisbon, we continued to supply nonlethal equipment to UNITA. The termination of arms supplies made it easier to continue congressional financial support.[49] Instead of clandestine flights from Zaire landing at Jamba in the middle of the night, we had commercial trucks coming from Namibia in broad daylight. By late 1991, Savimbi was ebullient about UNITA's prospects. His arrival in Luanda in September had been triumphant, drawing large crowds wherever he went. Shortly after the Lisbon ceremonies on 31 May 1991, experts were giving the MPLA the advantage in the elections.[50] By the end of 1991, however, reports from travelers and

UNAVEM monitors indicated that UNITA was ahead, because the people were tired of the MPLA's economic mismanagement. Sensing this, some senior MPLA officials sent their families to Europe in anticipation of losing the election.

In general, our relations with UNITA remained positive until March 1992. At that time, two developments made us uneasy. First, the UNITA campaign became ethnic and racist. Its nasty rhetoric about "foreigners" was code language for the mestizo, or mixed-ancestry, Angolans, many of whom were leaders in the MPLA. Secondly, reports surfaced of human rights abuses at UNITA's headquarters in Jamba. In April, two top UNITA officials, Foreign Minister Tony Fernandez and Interior Minister Nzau Puna, suddenly turned up in Lisbon announcing they had defected. They accused Savimbi of killing opposition members and claimed they had escaped just in time.

Our big problem with UNITA arose from the death of Tito Chingunji, UNITA's representative in Washington until mid-1989 when he was recalled to Jamba. Tito, as everyone called him, had been a popular representative, especially among the friends of UNITA. An admirable man, he was highly articulate and got along well with friends and adversaries alike. After his return to Jamba, we received reports that he was in political trouble. We asked all visitors to Jamba to check on Tito's health. Aware of our concern, UNITA made sure that Tito was shown to be healthy and working hard. In March 1992, however, we learned that UNITA had executed Tito. Fernandez and Puna witnessed the killing. Even more horrible, Tito's wife and children had also been put to death.[51]

When I informed Baker about the executions at a morning staff meeting, he was furious. He instructed me to send Savimbi a tough message seeking an explanation. He demanded an immediate investigation.[52] When I visited UNITA in Luanda shortly thereafter, 10–14 April, Chitunda handed me a document summarizing the findings of their investigation: While Savimbi was responsible for everything that happened within UNITA, the killings were perpetrated in Jamba after Savimbi had moved to Luanda to campaign. The killers were none other than the two defectors, Nzau Puna and Tony Fernandez. Chitunda asked that I read the document carefully and consider issuing an official State Department expression of confidence in the report's integrity and conclusions. Omitting diplomatic niceties, I told Chitunda it was out of the question. That exchange cooled our relations.[53]

The Angolan and Portuguese press criticized me personally for not denouncing UNITA over the killing of Tito Chingungi. I told the press

I had read the investigative report but would have no comment on an internal UNITA matter. That was the first time, to my knowledge, that the United States had not backed UNITA on such a problem. In May, Savimbi responded to Baker by accusing Chingungi of having worked with the CIA to overthrow him. There was no follow-up, and the matter was closed, but it could only hurt UNITA in the elections.

One year into the transition, observers could argue whether the glass was half full or half empty. Everything was behind schedule, but some preparations fared better than others. At least the cease-fire was holding up well. Election preparations were not too bad. The United States had waived restrictions on aid to the Marxist regime, allocating $14 million for election support. The government spent considerable amounts from its own budget to set up voter registration facilities, including machines to produce laminated voter cards. Impressively, UNITA organizers were able to fan out across Angola, setting up offices and support groups with minimal harassment. Savimbi's public meetings were also peaceful. Also impressive was the successful registration of four million voters, with election workers transported by US aircraft and fed with surplus military rations.

Encampment of troops, sequestration of their arms, and integration of troops from both sides into the new national army were painfully slow. UNITA was doing its part well. UN military commanders were in awe at the organization and discipline of UNITA's fighters. The encampment sites, in the bush, had no facilities of any kind. Used to this type of primitive environment, UNITA soldiers quickly built native huts and started cultivating vegetable gardens. They stayed together. By contrast, FAPLA troops were used to barracks life in urban centers and did not stay long. Their rapid disappearance from the sites came to be known as "spontaneous demobilization." The ability of UNITA fighting groups to remain intact, in contrast to the disintegration of FAPLA units, facilitated UNITA's postelection decision to revert to war. For the new national army, a headquarters was established with both MPLA and UNITA senior officers ensconced but not much else. We were resigned to having the election take place with three armies in existence, FAPLA, UNITA, and the still embryonic new national army.

Then there was the "fourth army," the new antiriot police the government established pursuant to its rights under the Bicesse accords. They were trained by Spanish advisors and heavily armed. With their distinctive black uniforms, the people called them "Ninjas." UNITA complained bitterly about this force, because five thousand "demobilized"

FAPLA troops had been recruited for it. At our request, dos Santos ordered the Ninjas confined to barracks during the election season, so they did not have an impact on the voting. Nevertheless, they served as a convenient excuse for UNITA to keep arms hidden just in case these riot police might be used against their supporters.[54]

In addition to the $14 million provided for election support, the United States also supplied surplus food to keep encamped troops fed and air transport to help move troops to demobilization points. At the end of July, the White House announced that it had instructed the Defense Department to deploy three C-130 transport aircraft to Angola for six weeks. The White House was careful to state that it had acted at the joint request of dos Santos, Savimbi, and UN Secretary-General Boutros-Ghali.[55]

During the last three months of the transition, our sources within UNAVEM and the humanitarian relief community indicated that UNITA's support had peaked and was declining steadily. UNITA was beginning to frighten people with a campaign emphasizing militarism, racism, and revenge. UNITA rallies had substantial armed protection, and the rhetoric reminding voters about blown-up bridges, destroyed electric power plants, and sabotaged water lines did not necessarily cause the listeners to swell with pride. In addition, the speeches alluded to "evil foreigners" and spoke ill of certain ethnic groups controlling the MPLA. UNITA also promised to deal harshly with "black marketeers." This was especially maladroit because in the Marxist system, buying and selling in the black market was necessary to make ends meet. Listeners to UNITA's message ended up more frightened than reassured.

By contrast, the MPLA campaign emphasized peace themes and free markets. Dos Santos hired a Brazilian public relations firm, which plastered posters all over Angola depicting him as a man of peaceful reconciliation. Normally reserved and quiet, dos Santos was persuaded to leave his isolated seaside redoubt south of Luanda at Fitunga and mingle with ordinary people. Angolan television showed him visiting schools, playing soccer with the kids, and mingling with the crowds at native markets. Savimbi was shown in military fatigues surrounded by armed guards with automatic weapons.

We talked to Savimbi about revising his rapidly souring campaign approach, but his agents throughout Angola were reporting good news about strong voter support for UNITA. They saw no reason to change the format. We also questioned UNITA closely about their defenses against electoral fraud. They assured us that a UNITA representative would be at every polling place, would witness the count, and would instantly radio the result to UNITA central.

The official observer delegation, with Portuguese State Secretary Durão Barroso as leader and myself and Russian deputy Africa director Anatoly Smirnoff, paid its last two preelection visits in August and September 1992. The atmosphere was tense. Diplomats were describing the election as too close to call. MPLA dignitaries continued to send their families abroad. UNITA remained optimistic and almost cocksure. The "troika" decided that nothing should be allowed to postpone the election, including the absence of a fully established new national army.

Durão Barroso and I decided to lean hard on both dos Santos and Savimbi to pledge to form governments of national unity regardless of who won the election. There could be no other way to dissipate the fears that would certainly grip the losing side. Without enthusiasm, dos Santos reacted positively but would not make a public statement to that effect. He had no objection to the "troika" telling the press of his pledge, however. Savimbi was enthusiastic and told us he would treat the MPLA with magnanimity and invite them into his government. After all, the MPLA had most of the trained people needed to run the country. After our call on Savimbi in September, he told the press of his determination to establish a national unity government if he won.[56]

On 9 September, at a rare private meeting at Savimbi's headquarters in the posh Miramar neighborhood, he said something that gave me a frisson of anxiety. He confided that his military commanders were telling him an election was not necessary to win power. The Bicesse accords had given UNITA fighters the freedom of all of Angola, and they were everywhere. With FAPLA essentially demobilized, UNITA had the capability of taking power by military means. Savimbi assured me he had told his commanders that they must fulfill UNITA's commitment to the democratic process. I left that meeting hoping more than ever for a UNITA victory.

The operation was a success, but the patient died

Observers, both official and unofficial, considered the actual voting on 29–30 September successful. The Angolans took very seriously their first opportunity since independence in 1975 to vote in a multiparty election. Voters walked miles to the polling stations and waited hours to vote. Volunteers did guard duty the night of 29 September to prevent ballot box tampering.

The trouble started when the first results were released the 2nd and 3rd of October with only 10 per cent of the vote counted, showing a majority for the MPLA in both the presidential and parliamentary elections. UNITA panicked immediately, finding no other way to explain the MPLA lead than to claim fraud. To make matters worse, UNITA threatened to abandon the peace process if it did not win.[57]

While this crisis was unfolding, I was in Rome helping to midwife the peace agreement in Mozambique, signed on Sunday, 4 October. Jeff Davidow called from Washington on 3 October recommending that I call Savimbi and ask him to refrain from threatening language. If UNITA had evidence of fraud, they should give it to the independent electoral commission and to the UN. My calls reached Savimbi's villa easily, but neither he nor his top lieutenants were available.

Unable to reach Savimbi by phone, I had no choice but to go public. I called Jeff back and asked him to arrange for the Voice of America Portuguese Service to interview me so that I could broadcast a personal message to Savimbi. The VOA agreed, and I read the following message:

> Dr. Savimbi, now is the time to think about the people of Angola. I have heard your statement about the election. I believe you should think again, and have confidence in the United Nations which is supervising the elections. You are a great political leader in Angola. Because of your struggle, it was possible to have free and fair elections. I do not know the results of these elections. The counting is still going on. But if it happens that you are not elected president, the United States believes that you still have a great role in the reconstruction of Angola. Eduardo dos Santos has assured us that you will play an important role in the process of reconciliation. So you will be a great statesman if you accept the results of this election, and together UNITA and the MPLA should bring about a wealthy new Angola.[58]

My answer came the next day. A journalist found UNITA General Ben Ben and asked him if he had a response to my appeal. Ben Ben said, "Assistant Secretary Cohen can drop dead." Worse than the insult was Ben Ben's decision on 5 October suspending UNITA's participation in the new national army. All former UNITA officers and men who had been incorporated into the national army disappeared from their units and rejoined UNITA, an action we considered unacceptable. On 6 October the State Department declared, "This is an unfortunate step which is not in accordance with the spirit or letter of the Angolan peace accords."[59] Acting Secretary Eagleburger sent a personal message to Savimbi saying "I must also tell you as a friend that threats from UNITA to return to armed struggle find no support here."[60]

The first three weeks of October witnessed contradictory statements by UNITA and some turbulence. On 3 October, Savimbi claimed massive fraud and criticized the observers. On 8 October, Savimbi retreated from his war threat provided the UN would investigate. The UN quickly set up a special committee of experts to investigate the allegation.[61] On 12 October, street fighting erupted in downtown Luanda, with UNITA supporters the main targets.

On 17 October, the final election results were announced. The MPLA won the parliamentary elections with 54 per cent to UNITA's 31 per cent. Dos Santos led the presidential vote with 49.6 per cent to Savimbi's 40.1 per cent. A runoff between them would be necessary. The same day, UN Special Representative Margaret Anstee declared, "While there were certainly some irregularities in the electoral process, these appear to have been mainly due to human error and inexperience."[62] We supported Anstee's statement, urging the parties to sit down and arrange the runoff election as soon as possible.[63]

The observer "troika" tried to save the peace process on a post-election visit 18–20 October. I brought letters from President Bush to both dos Santos and Savimbi urging dialogue and a return to the Bicesse process. When UNITA military personnel pulled out of the new national army, Jonas Savimbi was whisked to the central highlands city of Huambo, one of his strongholds. His nephew and economic planning secretary, Elias Salupeto Pena, was left in charge in Luanda. The Portuguese military assistance contingent flew us to Savimbi in Huambo, where he was ensconced in the governor's house. We pleaded for reason and dialogue, but Savimbi reverted to his earlier line that the election was stolen. We were very depressed.

At the same time, South African Foreign Minister Pik Botha was in Luanda. The South Africans were active behind the scenes as Savimbi's advisors and Angola's growing trading partners. Botha, too, was doing shuttle diplomacy trying to promote dialogue. In his view, Savimbi needed a dignified solution that would save UNITA's honor. That meant meaningful power-sharing. Dos Santos had just offered UNITA the Ministry of Culture and the deputy minister of defense and interior slots. It was not enough. Botha then asked to see me and Durão Barroso separately. He gave each of us the same message. Salupeto Pena had told him, he alleged, that UNITA was planning to assassinate Durão Barroso and myself.

In his invective-filled daily press conferences, Salupeto Pena threatened dire punishment for Luanda if the government implemented the election results. I therefore found the assassination threat plausible, reinforced by our own meeting with Salupeto Pena, during which he was drunk and quite incoherent. In addition, UNITA sabotage units were setting explosions all around Luanda. Tensions ran high.

On the weekend of 31 October–1 November, combat broke out in Luanda between government security forces and UNITA fighters. The government had distributed weapons wholesale to MPLA militants, who proceeded on signal to liquidate all the UNITA supporters they could find. The special antiriot police fired their weapons against UNITA's headquarters in the Miramar section of town a few doors from the American liaison office.[64] This action created a nightmare for both our staff in USLO and those of us at the other end of the telephone in Washington.

Our ambassador-designate to Angola, Edmund de Jarnette, had arrived in Luanda a few days before to replace Mike Millington. When the fighting broke out on 31 October, all the other embassies in Miramar evacuated their personnel in time, but the Americans were trapped in the crossfire. Ed de Jarnette and his colleagues took shelter in a depression on the compound grounds, safe from bullets passing overhead. When there was a lull, they would go into the office to report by phone. That situation was frightening enough, but what really worried us was that UNITA had learned the Americans were still in the neighborhood. For about twenty-four hours we feared we might be facing a hostage situation.

Manning the UNITA office were Vice President Chitunda, Salupeto Pena, and a number of other senior officials. We spent a lot of time on the phone with them from Washington and could tell they were weighing their options. We also talked directly to President dos Santos, who promised to be helpful but was unable to change the situation at the embassy compound. On 4 November, while we were studying our options, de Jarnette came up on the phone to report that the UNITA people next door were gone. They had driven away, trying to break out of their encirclement and disappear into the surrounding shantytowns.

Chitunda and Salupeto Pena were killed when their car crashed, as we later learned from Abel Chivukuvuku, UNITA's foreign minister. He was in a Luanda hospital with a shattered leg from the same accident. Unsurprisingly, the government's action to liquidate UNITA's presence in Luanda, as well as the deaths of Chitunda and Pena, did not bode well for peace. I was particularly sad about Chitunda, who had become a valued interlocutor and sympathetic colleague.

The period between November 1992 and March 1993 was one of heavy diplomacy designed to find a way to restore the peace process. The Portuguese had effectively bowed out as mediators in favor of the United Nations. Diplomats, including ourselves, were constantly shuttling between the two parties in search of formulas. Face-to-face negotiations between UNITA and government representatives were arranged in Addis and Abidjan to discuss UNITA's role in the government and how the national army might still be revived. I even had a strange telephone call from Dr Savimbi on 27 November in which he insisted that UNITA still liked me. He said, "I speak for UNITA, and I consider you our friend." In that conversation he also assured me that UNITA would send its people to sit in Parliament and would accept government ministerial portfolios if offered. All he wanted was increased supervision by UNAVEM.[65]

Despite the promising diplomacy, UNITA fighters were busy establishing new facts on the ground by spreading throughout Angola to areas previously denied to them. By the end of February 1993, it was estimated that UNITA either controlled or denied access to government forces in 70 per cent of Angola. While no analysts believed UNITA could win a military victory, UNITA's generals might have thought differently. In any event, they were interested neither in negotiations nor in observing the Bicesse cease-fire. In a speech from Huambo on 9 March 1993, Savimbi was very much the conqueror, with many non-negotiable demands. As with the government side in September 1990, a new cease-fire could not be envisaged until another test of force had been exhausted. I departed the Bureau of African Affairs with the war heating up, thoroughly disgusted with the waste of it all.

The incoming Clinton administration reviewed our Angolan policy in February 1993 and decided to remain fully engaged in peace efforts, with the United Nations in charge. In March, the UN Security Council formally condemned UNITA, officially designating them as spoilers of the peace process but offering continued good offices.[66] On 19 May, President Clinton announced formal diplomatic recognition of Angola.

The war continued with much destruction until November 1994, when a new peace agreement was signed in Lusaka, Zambia. The long negotiations had been mediated by UN special representative Blondin Beye, with strong assistance from retired US ambassador Paul Hare. Although UNITA no longer enjoyed support from either the United States or South Africa, it captured valuable diamond fields in Angola's northeast. Diamond sales enabled UNITA to maintain an arms and fuel supply line via Zaire. But the government's substantial oil revenues financed crushing arms purchases and private sector technical assistance, thereby overcoming UNITA's initial advantages and eventually forcing it to sue for peace. On the government side South African mercenaries from a company called Executive Outcomes proved decisive. Ironically, many of the same South African fighters who had supported UNITA prior to August 1988 helped the government retake much of the territory that had fallen to UNITA after September 1992.[67]

The Lusaka agreement of November 1994 built on the 1991 Bicesse accord, with two major modifications. UNITA was guaranteed a share of power through ministerial portfolios and the position of second vice president, which was offered to Savimbi. On the military side, UNITA fighters were required to enter cantonment areas to be disarmed and to be demobilized or integrated into the national army, a requirement not imposed on government forces. Angola suffered far more damage between Bicesse and Lusaka than between 1975 and 1991.

Implementation of the Lusaka agreements between 1994 and 1998 was no more successful than implementation of the Bicesse accords between 1991 and 1993. In both cases during the cessation of hostilities, UNITA rebuilt its military capabilities and prepared for a return to fighting. For UNITA, peace negotiations were in effect another form of warfare, not an attempt to achieve compromise, consensus, and reconciliation. The fact that two parties to a conflict engage in a peace process does not necessarily mean that one or both are serious about peace. We learned that the hard way in Angola. Savimbi was the master of delay and deceit.

Could we have done it better?

The international community invested a great deal of effort and money in support of both the 1991 Bicesse agreement and the 1994 Lusaka agreement. Neither agreement brought peace to Angola. As of December 1998, the government and UNITA had returned to full-scale war. Could the United States, as a third party intervenor, have done more in the Bicesse stage of the process to avoid the sad outcomes of 1992 and beyond?

Encouraging negotiations

Right from the start our intervening in Angola had a solid policy foundation. President Bush had pledged to help UNITA achieve national reconciliation even before taking office. We also sought a cooperative relationship with the Soviets, and Angola presented an obvious opportunity in view of our respective clients there. Our aid to UNITA, a Cold War vestige, was increasingly unsustainable in the Congress. Both we and the Soviets needed an honorable exit from our commitments. Encouraging negotiations was thus both desirable and necessary.

Our efforts to bring about negotiations were tactically effective. As UNITA supporters, we could not pretend to be neutral, but we could and did apply appropriate pressures and call on old friends for favors. Our conservative allies in the Congress let UNITA know that our assistance was enough to prevent military defeat but insufficient to ensure victory. Our liberal friends in the Congress let the MPLA know that it was unrealistic to base their policy on the termination of US assistance to UNITA. Our friends among Angola's neighbors put pressure on the MPLA to accept dialogue with UNITA – their Angolan brothers, not men from Mars.

The high-level State Department decision to undermine the Gbadolite process in 1989, against the Africa Bureau's better judgment, proved unfortunate. A comparison of the Gbadolite power-sharing formula with the 1994 Lusaka agreement shows more similarities than differences. If we had leaned heavily on Savimbi to accept the Gbadolite process as the basis for further negotiations, as Mobutu requested, it might have been possible to avoid the 1989–90 fighting, as well as the 1992–94 generalized conflict. But Baker's decision that we support Savimbi's demand for elections was understandable, given Savimbi's strong support among conservatives.

Our acquiescence in Savimbi's repudiation of Gbadolite made it inevitable that we would have to greatly accelerate our assistance to UNITA against the government's final offensive at Mavinga in late 1989, setting the stage for military stalemate and real negotiations. Both Baker and Shevardnadze deserve credit for their subsequent coordinated efforts to push the protagonists to accept face-to-face negotiations with Portuguese assistance.

Facilitating negotiations

Our approach to the actual negotiations was not to crowd the Portuguese, who appeared to have the situation under control. We kept in close touch through Jeff Millington and the defense attachés in Lisbon, but we did not attempt to supervise. Shevardnadze's brilliant idea that the United States and Soviet Union collaborate to devise a framework document and then "sell" it to both parties provided the breakthrough that moved the negotiations to a serious level.

I learned two things from this experience. First, leverage is significant only when used, but the timing has to be right, as Shevardnadze clearly understood. Second, there is an indefinable psychological element in African negotiations. In essence, when strong powers are involved, the confidence level is higher because the protagonists perceive them as guarantors. On its own, Portugal was not able to fulfill that role.

Regarding the Bicesse agreement, should we feel guilty for having blessed a flawed document? Were we driven by a "signature obsession," ready to accept any agreement as long as both sides were willing to sign it? I believe emphatically that if UNITA had accepted the results of the election in good faith, as it had promised, Bicesse would have survived. I made this point in a number of press interviews in October and November 1992. Certainly, the Bicesse Accords were imperfect. But the main reason Angola went back to war was UNITA's refusal to live up to its commitments.

The big question on the Bicesse accords, therefore, is why did we accept such an agreement, which failed to prevent UNITA from denouncing the election and returning to war? In this respect, Bicesse contained two key flaws: failure to provide an adequate number of UNAVEM monitors, and failure to link encampment and disarmament of fighters to the timing of the election.

At the December 1990 Washington conference, UNITA vice president Chitunda had talked about the need for "thousands" of UN monitors and continued to argue for this at Bicesse. To prevent "internationalization" of the conflict, in contrast, the Angolan government insisted on a small number of monitors. In retrospect, UNITA's strong advocacy of a large UN monitoring effort indicates to me that they were not planning to go back to war until they actually did it.

Regarding the election date, the government wanted a long transition of three to five years, whereas UNITA wanted early elections. At Bicesse, the government representatives continually argued that it would be impossible to have a fair election until the military transition was complete. They were right. Yet, the government side was mainly responsible for delaying the military transition.

Our view of both these issues was tainted. We knew that the number of UN monitors would be too small. But both we and the Soviets were not unhappy at the thought of a small price tag for the Security

Council operation. It turned out to be penny-wise and pound-foolish. We should have known better. Because we sympathized with UNITA's analysis that an early election would be favorable to their chances, we were not troubled when the early election date was traded for a small UN contingent. If both sides were happy, who were we to object? In the end, the "signature obsession" carried the day.

I believe the atmosphere was too tense, and the level of hatred and mistrust too high, for the choosen scenario: cease-fire, military transition, and elections within fifteen months. If we could do it all over again, a more plausible scenario would have been a coalition government of national unity, cohabitation in governance for three to five years, military transition to one national army over two to three years, liberalization of political life, and elections after five years. In effect, this is what Mobutu wanted to achieve at Gbadolite in his own African way, but he botched the job.

Supporting the implementation phase

The US performance during the implementation phase was something to be proud of. All agencies were looking for ways to be helpful. The entire US national security apparatus had a "can do" attitude. The White House even authorized the dispatch of military transport aircraft to assist the elections and the demobilization of fighters. Defense supplied surplus field rations, our "Meals Ready to Eat" (MRE), as well as three C-130 aircraft from National Guard assets. The Office of Foreign Disaster Assistance (OFDA) also supplied surplus food, and USAID financed election experts to help organize the elections and train election personnel. The high-level policy commitment from the White House guaranteed such positive responses.

Efforts to salvage the peace process

When UNITA declared the elections fraudulent, withdrew their fighters from the new national army, and moved rapidly to deploy their still-intact units throughout northern Angola and the central highlands, the United States did not give up on the peace process. We deployed much diplomatic time and effort to bring about new negotiations and proposed several creative new formulas, most of which found their way into the agreements signed in Lusaka in November 1994. When negotiations actually began under UN auspices, Ambassador Paul Hare attended every session as the US observer and played an important role. In the Lusaka agreement, we rectified our error at Bicesse and accepted a costly major deployment of 7000 UNAVEM monitors. After Lusaka, the United States pledged $175 million for reconstruction, reflecting a strong Clinton administration commitment to peace.

Over three administrations – those of Reagan, Bush, and Clinton – the United States remained committed to peace in Angola. Though ultimately frustrated, its contribution was never less than professional and fully dedicated to conflict resolution.

5
Liberia: A Bold Plan Hijacked

In a technical sense, Liberia's civil war began on 24 December 1989 when a hundred armed insurgents of the National Patriotic Front of Liberia (NPFL) crossed into Nimba County from neighboring Côte d'Ivoire. In a larger sense, the war began on 12 April 1980 when seventeen inebriated noncommissioned officers of the Armed Forces of Liberia (AFL) invaded the Presidential Palace and assassinated President William R. Tolbert, Jr. These same soldiers then took power by establishing a "People's Redemption Council" (PRC), with Master Sergeant Samuel Kanyon Doe as chairman and head of state.[1]

Background to a tragedy

Military coups were not unusual in Africa between 1965 and 1985. What made this particular coup significant was that the leaders were from the "tribal" or "country" people of Liberia, those of indigenous stock, who make up 95 percent of the population. President Tolbert's death effectively ended 133 years of minority rule by "Americo-Liberians," descendants of the freed American slaves who settled on the Liberian coast between 1816 and 1847. In the eyes of many Liberians, the rise of the "country" people marked the beginning of a new era of majority rule.[2] Thus, although Doe and his lieutenants were cruel, crude killers, their regime was popular with the masses. Naturally, the Americo-Liberian community did not welcome the coup. Many fled to exile in the United States, where they constituted a political lobby opposed to any US support for the regime.

Among the political elite murdered by Doe's regime was A. P. Tolbert, the late president's son. Because his wife Daisy was the adopted daughter of President Félix Houphouet-Boigny, Tolbert had obtained protection in the Côte d'Ivoire Embassy, whose ambassador placed him in the French Embassy for safekeeping. Houphouet sent a delegation to Doe, who granted Houphouet's request to guarantee Tolbert's safety. During Doe's absence abroad, however, his henchmen discovered Tolbert's hiding place. In violation of international law, they invaded the French Embassy, captured Tolbert, and executed him shortly thereafter. The action deeply angered Houphouet, who would not easily forget or forgive. He would get his revenge.[3]

After a year in power, Doe had eliminated most of his serious rivals and opted for a traditional Liberian pro-American posture. He had closed the Libyan People's Bureau and established diplomatic ties with Israel, leading the outgoing Carter administration and the incoming Reagan administration to reconfirm the traditional US–Liberian special relationship. In 1982, Reagan offered Doe an official visit to Washington, where he urged Doe to end all political executions. Doe readily agreed, since most Liberians who might be a threat were now dead or living in exile.

During 1980–85, US economic and military assistance increased substantially. During that 1982 official visit, Doe granted special military deployment rights to the US military, enabling it henceforth to use Robertsfield International Airport and the port of Monrovia with only twenty-four hours' advance notice. Having once received commando training from a visiting team of US Green Berets, Doe felt comfortable with the American military, the only external influences he had ever known.[4]

Doe's major problems were domestic, not foreign. The overthrow of minority Americo-Liberian rule alienated the country's most influential group. In addition, during his first few years in office, Doe's tribal favoritism alienated the rest of the population. His Krahn tribe, about 7 percent of the population, monopolized power and resources with the help of some corrupt Americo-Liberians. The Krahns also gained control of the army, especially the Israeli-trained Presidential Guard, giving them unchecked power. Within five years, the Doe regime went from the embodiment of indigenous majority rule to an oppressive government dominated by Liberia's most backward ethnic group. The other tribal people now regretted the ouster of the Americo-Liberians in 1980.

In a presidential election held in October 1985, the deeply unpopular Doe was defeated in the general voting in the view of most observers. Since he controlled the election machinery, however, Doe declared himself the winner with a convenient 50.9 percent of the vote. The US government accepted the result with a lukewarm endorsement, causing dismay in the Congress and marking the start of a steady decline in US–Liberian relations. With the Cold War still dominant in 1985, however, the Reagan administration was determined to keep Liberia as a close ally. In 1986, for example, the United States began sending military equipment to the anticommunist UNITA rebels in Angola, using Robertsfield in Liberia and Kinshasa Airport in Zaire to refuel our aircraft. That project alone justified good relations with both the Doe and Mobutu regimes, neither of which enjoyed much support within the Congress.[5]

US–Liberian relations unravel

In January 1987, within a few days of my arrival at the National Security Council staff as senior director for African affairs, I accompanied Secretary of State George Shultz on his first trip to Africa. His truly interagency entourage included Assistant Secretary of State Chester Crocker, US Agency for International Development (USAID) Administrator Peter McPherson, and Deputy Assistant Secretary of Defense James L. Woods.

Shultz liked briefing sessions on the plane en route to each country. During the Liberia briefing, I learned how difficult our relations had become. Doe's management was so bad that Liberia's arrears on loan payments to the United States were mounting to the point where legislation mandated that aid be suspended. In addition, human rights abuses gave ample ammunition to the anti-Doe lobby in the United States pressing for reductions in military assistance. Asked by Shultz if he had any new ideas, McPherson proposed assigning a team of retired financial experts to work with the Liberians for two years to get their books and procedures in order. If Doe agreed to cooperate, USAID could release $10 million in economic support assistance (ESA) waiting in the Liberia pipeline.

My memory of Shultz's meeting with Doe is dominated by a picture of Doe, a short man in full military regalia, screaming in a high-pitched whine. He complained bitterly about American abandonment. He had incurred risks defending US foreign policy, especially at nonaligned summit conferences. What was his reward? Aid budget cuts and carping in the Congress about the human rights situation. Shultz couldn't get a word in edgewise, so he delivered his message about the need for improved economic management during the exchange of toasts at the formal luncheon that followed.[6]

Publicly, the secretary's visit constituted a US–Liberian love feast. But privately, we all went away as frustrated as when we arrived.

We and Doe just did not speak the same language, and he did not have a clue about Washington realities. Although he relaxed tensions a bit by reluctantly agreeing to McPherson's financial management team, none of us had any illusions that Doe even understood he had a problem.

At Ambassador James Bishop's request, I visited Monrovia again in September 1987 as the "White House guy," to impress upon Doe the importance of cooperating with the financial management team. I found him completely unchanged from the previous January, understanding nothing. From his point of view it was a simple matter of reciprocal loyalty. He gave unstinting support to US foreign policy. In return, he expected our enthusiastic support for him as the legitimate ruler of Liberia. US recognition of his legitimacy seemed more important than material support. Congressional problems and management issues were irrelevant to Doe's concept of US–Liberian relations.

In January 1989, when the Bush administration came into office and a full eleven months before the start of the civil war, Liberia was already a cause of concern. It was the subject of my first interagency Africa Policy Coordinating Committee (PCC) meeting as assistant secretary, on 19 May 1989. Growing congressional disenchantment with Doe threatened to undermine our rights to three US national security facilities near Monrovia.

A large diplomatic and intelligence communications relay station comprising two 500-acre antenna fields and several buildings serviced fifteen American embassies in Africa. The Voice of America had a 1600-acre relay station transmitting seventy-five daily broadcasts to Africa. The US Coast Guard operated an "Omega" maritime navigational tracking station, one of only six worldwide essential for airplane and ship navigation. In addition, the US military had unlimited access to Robertsfield Airport, which we used for twelve flights per month in support of activities throughout Africa. In return for these facilities, we paid a ridiculously small rent of $100 000 per year. Meanwhile, the Congress was eliminating bilateral aid.

The PCC meeting considered contingencies, particularly possible exorbitant Liberian demands for increased rent to make up for lost bilateral aid. The meeting confirmed that all the facilities were important and virtually irreplaceable. Replicating them elsewhere would cost hundreds of millions of dollars.[7]

These 1989 concerns did not lead to new policies. While the agencies debated a response to expected Liberian demands for more rent, we in State expected to tough it out with Doe on the basis of our historic special relationship. In October 1989 on my first visit to Liberia as assistant secretary, the only tangible result was my promise to deliver the commencement address at Doe's graduation from the University of Liberia in December 1990. In the absence of any viable alternatives, we persisted in a business-as-usual posture, despite growing animosity towards Doe in Washington. The McPherson financial reform project ended in November 1989 after it became evident that Doe would not subject more than a trickle of revenue to budgetary controls. Government-owned enterprises were his personal cash cow.

Against this grim backdrop, we greeted the unexpected arrival of anti-Doe insurgents in Nimba County on 24 December 1989 almost as a relief. With a problem we could finally sink our teeth into, our first instinct was to take charge of it. The close historical relationship made US diplomatic intervention logical.

The NPFL makes its entry

Our embassy in Monrovia believed the Liberian military could easily deal with the Christmas Eve 1989 incursion in Nimba County by the National Patriotic Front of Liberia.[8] The Liberian army had, after all, defeated an attempted coup following the1985 election by its former commander, Brigadier-General Thomas Quinwonkpa, and had already rounded up and killed several groups of infiltrators associated with the NPFL incursion.[9]

Buoyed by past successes against coups and infiltrators, the Armed Forces of Liberia set out to suppress the incursion, with little concern for tactics or for the nature of the threat. When they suffered their first deadly ambush, they discovered they were facing dangerous guerrillas. Instead of regrouping to devise an appropriate response, however, they punished the civilian population for harboring the guerrillas.[10] The result was predictable. Tens of thousands of Liberians abandoned their homes and moved to Liberia's large cities as internally displaced persons or crossed into Guinea or Côte d'Ivoire as refugees. Further, the AFL's scorched-earth policy in Nimba County's fertile agricultural areas caused severe food shortages across Liberia.

By the fall of 1989 we had lost patience with Doe for refusing to cooperate with the financial advisory group, which Ambassador Bishop sent home prematurely. In January 1990, nonetheless, we leaned towards helping him with the Nimba County crisis. Although we knew little of the rebels' composition, leadership, and aims, we saw credible reports of Libyan sponsorship. The rapid buildup of refugees and displaced persons particularly troubled us.

Reports of AFL human rights violations against civilians provoked our first public reaction. The NPFL rebels were killing members of Doe's Krahn tribe, but behaved well toward other ethnic groups. Doe in turn sent in his Krahn troops, who specialized in pillaging, killing, and extortion – like every other AFL activity, the war in Nimba County had become a business. The Gio majority ethnic group in Nimba County suffered greatly, thereby furnishing many new recruits for the NPFL. Gaining momentum between January and April 1990, the NPFL retaliated for the killing of Gios by Krahn soldiers with indiscriminate massacres of Krahns. An ethnic war was in full force.

The State Department granted Ambassador Bishop's request to address Nimba's human rights situation by sending two US Army officers from the embassy's military assistance group (LIBMISH) to Nimba on 2 January 1990. Since these officers worked closely with the AFL, we hoped the AFL would heed their counsel on civilian protection. We further hoped their presence might have a calming effect. We also arranged for President Bush to write to Doe expressing concern about AFL abuses.

In addition to its scorched-earth policy, Doe's cadre embarked on a major expansion of the army. Rapid recruitment sucked in thousands of unscreened youths, prison graduates, drug dealers, and previously expelled military delinquents. Expanding expenditures for equipment, arms, uniforms, and the like created new opportunities for corruption, thereby not only wasting money but also increasing repression and extortion against innocent Liberians.

Our small initial act of sending two LIBMISH officers to Nimba County ran into a firestorm at home. The Americo-Liberian lobby accused us of providing counterinsurgency advice to the AFL. They and other anti-Doe Liberians apparently viewed the NPFL as "freedom fighters" with a legitimate objective. In their eyes, our attempt to work with Doe's AFL, regardless of our stated motives, constituted an effort to preserve an illegitimate regime.

President Bush's letter failed to change Doe's practices. To exert additional direct pressure we sent a high-level emissary, Warren Clark, my principal deputy assistant secretary, with a personal letter from me to Doe. I hoped I might have some residual credibility as the designated commencement speaker for Doe's college graduation. In my letter I urged Doe to promote reconciliation, protect civilians, assure the safe return of refugees, halt the killing of civilians, and stop expanding the army. True to his genius for alienating US officials, Doe could not find time to receive Clark. At that point, therefore, we stopped delivery of the remaining $4 million in military assistance.

At the end of March 1990, we faced a full-fledged civil war in Liberia. For Doe and his cronies, the fighting was a game of cops and robbers that opened opportunities for additional extortion and theft. They were totally unaware of the likely grave consequences of their action. As Jim Bishop stated in a telegram dated 26 March: "The rebellion in Nimba is a low-intensity conflict, but it is one the Government is currently losing. Doe's repressive approach is only swelling the ranks of the rebels."[11]

By this time, the rebels controlled several major towns. As I wrote in a memorandum to Under Secretary Robert Kimmitt: "The Doe regime is now threatened. Doe has refused to receive special envoy Warren Clark, and also refused to grant a farewell visit to [outgoing] Ambassador Bishop. We are reviewing evacuation procedures for 5000 US citizens."

Who is Charles Taylor and what is the NPFL?

An invasion that in January looked containable became in April a major insurgency threatening the regime's existence. Learning more about the National Patriotic Front of Liberia and its leader Charles Taylor thus became an imperative.

Doe's entourage gleefully informed us that Taylor was a fugitive from both Liberian and American justice. In Doe's first government in 1980, Taylor had headed the general services agency.[12] In August 1983 he allegedly stole $900 000 and escaped to the United States one step ahead of the Liberian police. He was arrested and jailed in Massachusetts on a Liberian extradition warrant.[13] Awaiting extradition papers, he languished in prison for two years before escaping to Burkina Faso, where he received asylum. By escaping from prison, Taylor had committed a felony under state law.[14]

Our intelligence reported between January and March 1990 that Taylor and some of his fighters trained in Libya and had links with Liberian exiles in Côte d'Ivoire. The army of Burkina Faso supplied staging areas, weapons depots, and training facilities in the town of Po. The American embassy in Abidjan, Côte d'Ivoire, heard from residents near the Liberian frontier that Taylor's rebels regularly crossed and recrossed the border, unhindered.[15] The American Embassy in Ouagadougou, Burkina Faso, reported Libyan cargo planes unloading there at night and Liberians retrieving military supplies in vehicles that had transited Côte d'Ivoire.[16] Expatriates in contact with Taylor reported a force of 1000 well-armed commandos operating from a base just inside Côte d'Ivoire.[17]

Taylor used a satellite telephone to contact any place in the world. Our first high-level NPFL contact came from Tom Woweiyu, his "minister of defense," who called the Bureau of African Affairs in January 1990 from his roofing company in Newark, New Jersey. Woweiyu assured us the NPFL insurgency aimed only to depose Doe, after which they would install democracy. Taylor himself called to say the same thing, assuring us he meant no harm to US citizens or installations. In his first conversation with me, Taylor claimed no political ambition except evicting Doe.

What Taylor told us, however, was not what he told others, especially media interviewers. In April 1990, for example, he told the *Financial Times* he would capture Monrovia, depose Doe, and rule by decree for five years to prepare for democratic elections.[18] Worried by his Libyan connection, we were not yet ready to embrace Taylor during the first few months of 1990. In March 1990, NPFL representatives approached our embassy in Abidjan in search of a formal dialogue. The State Department, however, in reply to the embassy's request for guidance, asserted: "The USG has no interest in dignifying Taylor's Libyan-supported group by engaging in contacts that could later be flaunted, thereby causing further complications in our already troubled relations with the Doe regime."[19]

By the end of March 1990, security had deteriorated so much that the need to protect our expensive and irreplaceable facilities led us toward a dialogue with Taylor, the Libyan connection notwithstanding. Meanwhile, in the presidential palace, "Chairman" Doe slowly began fading into his own alcohol- and drug-induced fantasyland.

Washington hand-wringing: to take charge or not?

The Liberian conflict was not comparable to the two others that we had begun addressing in 1989. In Angola and Ethiopia, civil wars had been going on for fifteen and thirty years respectively. In both cases, the international community was adequately addressing the humanitarian dimension. In neither case were we faced with an emergency. We had the luxury of spending time to analyze core issues and develop strategy.

In Liberia we faced a fast-breaking situation. Although we did not contemplate evacuating American embassy personnel *in extremis* in March 1990,[20] the Doe regime was crumbling and the NPFL seemed about to move into a most threatening position. We no longer believed the AFL could handle the threat, and we lacked the luxury of time.

We had only a brief window of opportunity to develop both strategy and tactics and determine the desired degree and substance of US involvement. To that end, the Policy Coordinating Committee for Africa met on 6 April.

A dearth of viable options

The session opened with a military briefing by William Thom, the highly professional director of African analysis for the Defense Intelligence Agency, describing the phases of the rebellion. A planned major uprising in December failed with the capture of NPFL infiltrators. In January and February, NPFL rebels engaged in small-scale ambushes. AFL atrocities in retaliation led Gio ethnics to flock to the rebels' side. In March, the rebels began "large-scale attacks" designed to inflict maximum casualties on the AFL. Thom confirmed previous reports that rebel forces consisted of 200 original insurgents trained in Libya, 500 new recruits trained inside Liberia, and 1000 Gio "followers" carrying shotguns.

After that grim briefing, I asked the three agencies owning facilities in Liberia to update us on their outlook and needs. All three reconfirmed their statements of May 1989 that the facilities were "vital" or "critical." The Voice of America told us of major plans to refurbish their relay station in Fiscal Year 1992. The CIA, which operated the ATO (African telecommunications office) diplomatic relay station, said their two sites could not be replaced in kind before 1994, when satellites would take over. The Coast Guard emphasized the need to keep its Omega navigational station in operation until at least 1994 as a vital component of Atlantic Ocean ship and aircraft transit.

Two opposing views emerged in the PCC discussion. The minority believed Doe was faltering but far from defeated, and he still controlled the areas surrounding our facilities. If Doe's forces perceived us in their growing paranoia as favoring the rebels, we faced possible grave damage. In addition, there were 5000 US citizens needing protection, which in turn required the regime's cooperation. In short, it was too early to take out a protective insurance policy with the rebels.

But the majority emphasized distancing ourselves from Doe's human rights abuses. We were unable to shore up Doe because the human rights situation in Nimba County was so horrible, and the Americo-Liberian lobby made sure everyone knew it. We had no choice but to keep him at arm's length, making it hard for us to be mediators.

As chairman, I summed up the PCC meeting as follows:

- The United States cannot and should not be passive in Liberia. The historical ties, the close relationships, the need to help the refugees, and congressional pressures made it important that we be active.
- We must disassociate ourselves from the worsening military repression.
- We must continue to safeguard our three important installations.
- We should develop contingency plans to evacuate up to 5000 American citizens.[21]

Without a clear consensus in the PCC, we limited our immediate action to an announcement suspending military assistance to keep the anti-Doe lobby at bay for a while and reiterated our support for the Liberian people and their need for humanitarian assistance.[22]

Military developments

The period 15 April–15 June 1990 was busy with initiatives on several fronts. Doe's military situation deteriorated rapidly, although he refused to acknowledge it. From mid-April to July the rebels broke out of Nimba County, captured Buchanan, Liberia's major minerals and timber port, took Robertsfield International Airport, and placed Monrovia itself under siege. Rebel advances were attributable more to AFL desertions and refusal to fight than to rebel military prowess.

Throughout this period, Doe spent most of his time seeking arms from neighbors and friends. On 13 April, ignoring our suspension of military aid, Doe asked our chargé d'affaires Dennis Jett for rifles and ammunition to equip 3000 new recruits. He told Jett that we should view the crisis as a Libyan plan to undermine America's friends worldwide.[23] Running out of both credit and friends, Doe received his last arms delivery from Romania in May.

Especially ominous was the outbreak of ethnic killings in Monrovia. Krahn military massacred hundreds of Gio prisoners in camps near the capital. Anyone from Nimba County was fair game for retaliation.

The military situation stimulated considerable activity among politicians, who understood the importance of finding a political solution. Opposition politicians proposed a coalition government that could assure an honest presidential election in October 1991. Such an arrangement aimed at attracting NPFL participation and ending the fighting. It was soon evident, however, that the NPFL would accept no solution that kept Doe in office until 1991, while Doe sought only military victory. Having committed so many atrocities against the people of Nimba County, Doe and his cronies reasoned, correctly, that the war had become a tribal fight to the death.

Failing to make any headway with Doe, Liberian politicians looked to us forcefully to convince both Doe and Taylor that a solution lay in a free election monitored and guaranteed by the United States. To make sure the politicians understood his intentions, Doe told the press on 25 April that he would never negotiate with Taylor. Only a military solution was acceptable to him. Nevertheless, in a gesture to the opposition, he proposed sending an all-parties delegation to Washington to encourage the United States to play an active role.

In May, with time running out, we had to take some key decisions. The safety of American citizens was our foremost concern. By the end of May, the embassy staff was reduced 75 percent to about 100 people. A nightmare scenario was the potential need to evacuate thousands of Americans from the Monrovia peninsula with both the international airport and overland escape routes blocked and inaccessible.

To deal with evacuation planning and operations, we established a Liberia working group under the direction of Jim Bishop. A "working group" is an ad hoc assemblage of interested State Department bureaus and other agency representatives who assemble in a designated work space in the department's Operations Center to manage a specific emergency twenty-four hours a day.

Fearing a possible worst-case scenario, the working group requested a US naval task force deployment to the Liberian coast to assure emergency evacuations if required. We encouraged Americans to leave while the airport was still open, but most were dual nationals with closer ties to Liberia than to the United States. We could not persuade them to leave early by threatening to be unavailable later. We had to be ready to help them at any time. Sailing time from the United States or Europe was five to ten days. Clearly, waiting for an emergency to call in the ships would be too late. Our only option was to have ships hovering near the coast until the crisis was over, though they might have to wait there for weeks.

A decision to deploy US naval forces could not be made unilaterally by the State Department, nor even by Defense, but only by a presidential decision. Unfortunately, we thus had to elevate control of our Liberia policy to a higher interagency level. I wrote to Under Secretary Kimmitt on 30 April recommending we start the process of requesting deployment of the USS *Saipan*, a helicopter carrier on station in the

Mediterranean Sea as part of the Marine Amphibious Readiness Group (MARG).

Political developments

In anticipation of the "high-level" all-parties delegation Doe was sending to Washington in early May, the Liberia Working Group did some brainstorming on what a political solution might look like. We began with the following basic givens:

- According to military analysts, Doe could be defeated militarily.
- Doe was out of touch with reality in his determination to pursue a military victory. His troops refused to fight and continued to fall back toward Monrovia. Doe assumed we would come to his rescue because of the special US–Liberian relationship and Taylor's Libyan connection.
- Doe had no friends left in West Africa. His visits to Togo, Guinea, and Nigeria had yielded no support.[24] The Nigerians told us they were upset by his unwelcome visit. Togolese President Gnassingbe Eyadema told us that all heads of state in West Africa either hated Doe or considered him an embarrassment.
- Doe lacked money for arms, having drained the government-owned companies of their cash.
- Doe retained the loyalty of 1000 special forces troops guarding the palace. As the war progressed, it appeared increasingly that he was preparing to make a stand within Monrovia itself.
- Until late May, Taylor seemed well disposed towards the US presence and US assets. American businesses continued to operate in NPFL-occupied areas.
- The NPFL could not accept any political scenario in which Doe remained in power, even for a short period.
- Charles Taylor professed a commitment to democracy.

On the basis of the foregoing, we concluded that a solution would have to begin with Doe's departure to a comfortable exile. His wife and children had already gone to London on an extended holiday. With Doe gone, the Liberian political factions could negotiate a democratic transition with Charles Taylor in a roundtable setting. In consultation with other interested agencies, we decided to seek a solution like the one in the Philippines, when President Ronald Reagan sent Senator Paul Laxalt to Manila to escort President Ferdinand Marcos to exile in Hawaii.

For Doe's exile we selected Togo by process of elimination. I called President Eyadema and followed with a letter on 28 April 1990 requesting political asylum for Doe. Eyadema responded on 30 April that he would be willing to grant asylum but only if it were requested by the United States, not by Doe. Eyadema wanted to be able to inform the other West African heads of state, who might become annoyed, that he was doing it only as a favor to Washington.[25] With Eyadema on board and my immediate superiors in the State Department not objecting, we felt exhilarated at the prospect of organizing Doe's departure as the starting point for a democratic transition. Sadly, however, Doe lacked the capacity to understand what was required.

At the beginning of May 1990, our tactical position was to:

- Encourage all American citizens to leave Liberia.
- Seek presidential approval for the deployment of a naval force to Liberian waters to help evacuate our citizens.
- Begin a negotiating process via the all-parties high-level mission coming to Washington the first week of May.
- Begin preparing Doe psychologically for a high-level suggestion that he go into permanent exile.
- Step up contacts with Taylor to assure protection for US facilities, and encourage a negotiated democratic transition via an all-parties interim government in which Taylor's power would be diluted.

It was a worthy menu of objectives. We were confident about assuring the safety of our citizens but not sanguine about being able to influence a political settlement that would spare Liberia additional suffering and initiate a democratic process. But at that point, we were the only game in town and anxious to give it our best shot. The situation inside Liberia was so fluid and confused that we could not say we had taken charge of conflict resolution. Nevertheless, we had what looked like a viable tactical plan.

Hijacked at the NSC: Liberia is not our problem

May 1990 was a threshold month for our involvement in Liberia. The first glimmer of negotiations between the Doe regime and the NPFL began under our auspices; we began trying to get Doe used to the idea of going into exile; and overall US policy on Liberia was addressed for the first time at a level higher than the PCC on Africa, namely, the Deputies Committee of the National Security Council.

Liberians come to Washington

On 2 May the all-parties delegation from Liberia arrived in Washington, headed by Winston Tubman. A practicing lawyer, former foreign minister, and nephew of the late president William V. S. Tubman, who ruled from 1944 to 1971, Winston Tubman was a neutral, representing neither the government nor any political party. Included in the delegation were politicians Carlos Smith (United Party), Baccus Matthews (United Peoples Party), and Representative William Glay, a close associate of Doe. Also present was Council of Churches Chairman Levi Moulton.

In an initial meeting with Liberian Task Force Director Jim Bishop, Tubman said the delegation was authorized to speak to Liberians of all political persuasions except for "armed rebels," meaning he could not talk to the NPFL. But Bishop persuaded him that technically a political representative should not be considered an "armed rebel." On that basis, we sent a message to the NPFL via a special channel through our embassy in Abidjan. We informed them that the Liberian delegation was available for talks in Washington and that we would pay the airfare and expenses for one person. We received a rapid response indicating that "Minister of Defense" Tom Woweiyu would be coming.[26]

In a formal meeting on 8 May, Tubman summarized Doe's position. A solution had to be constitutional. The government had the right to defend itself against armed opposition. The 1985 election was flawed, and the lack of popular confidence was therefore understood. To restore confidence, the government was willing to form a government of national unity that would guarantee that the next election, scheduled for October 1991, would be free. International observers would guarantee a transparent and honest election. The United States should acknowledge this good faith proposal and urge the rebels to accept a cease-fire, disarm, and participate in the process. Negotiations with the rebels on political and economic reforms could begin on that basis. The United States should also persuade neighboring countries to stop the arms flow to Liberia and should resume its military assistance to the government.

In response, I emphasized the lateness of the hour, with the rebels only fifty miles from Monrovia, and the need for dramatic action. I reminded them that the AFL's atrocities made it impossible for us to provide military aid. I also stressed the importance of opening a dialogue with the armed opposition. I told them of my experience with the Angola negotiations, where it was not feasible to ask the opposition to disarm before beginning negotiations. To their obvious discomfort, I emphasized that talking to the people with guns was unavoidable.

I told them that the "dramatic action" I had in mind consisted of unilateral government steps to challenge the insurgents to participate in a process of peaceful, democratic transition. I suggested moving up the presidential election one full year to October 1990, with international monitoring by non-Americans. If such an offer were made in a free dialogue with the rebels, and if the rebels turned it down, then the international community would shift the blame for the crisis from the government to the NPFL. Another "dramatic" option would be to offer to withdraw all AFL troops from Nimba County in return for a cease-fire, followed by negotiations. I concluded by insisting that negotiations had to be with the rebels and not with the US government.

The reaction was one of chagrin and disappointment. The delegation gave a litany of reasons why they could not take up my suggestions: They did not have a mandate; the constitution would not allow an early election; amending the constitution followed by a national referendum would take time and money; a military solution was still possible if the United States would exercise its leverage to shut off arms flows from neighboring countries. Later, we heard that my remarks were considered "tough" and "sobering," especially by Doe's cronies like Representative Glay. They were apparently afraid to report my remarks back to Doe.[27]

En route to Washington to meet with Tubman, Tom Woweiyu was quite open with officers at our Embassy in Abidjan about the NPLF's war aims. Woweiyu was not in the mood for a real negotiation. As far as he was concerned, Doe was "dead meat." The best thing we could do was convince Doe to depart and allow Taylor to take over while the economy and infrastructure were still intact. Woweiyu reassured us that Taylor would safeguard US lives and property and would install a democracy. At one point he said, "I know you won't believe me, but this is what Charles Taylor wants. If once all this is over he could be assured that a stable democratic system could be installed in Liberia and that future leadership changes could take place without bloodshed, he would be only too happy to step down."

Woweiyu made two additional comments of interest. Liberians, he said, the NPFL included, considered the United States to be the father of Liberia. As father, the United States had the power to end the conflict by disciplining its children. Second, the NPFL became convinced it could defeat Doe as soon as we announced the suspension of military assistance. This was a reminder of the occasional unintended side effects of US decisions.[28]

Talks between Doe's delegation and Woweiyu did not take place. Woweiyu received last-minute orders from Taylor not to sit with Doe's representatives.We suggested proximity talks, which the government side rejected.

Doe's possible exile became a hot issue during May. We instructed Dennis Jett in Monrovia to introduce the idea and to continue hinting about the pleasures of early retirement. We also asked former USAID administrator Peter McPherson, whom Doe liked, to call from California, where he was a senior official with the Bank of America. Doe's reaction to the idea blew hot and cold. On a formal level, his response was essentially, "They will have to kill me to get me out of here." But in several talks with Dennis Jett he gave the impression he was considering the idea seriously. In one conversation he asked if the US government could arrange a scholarship to either Harvard or Cambridge university. In another he asked if we could fly him and his family and friends to his home in Grand Geddeh County. He was particularly anxious to know if our transportation offer included twenty-five cases of assorted soft drinks.

Finally, it seemed possible to usher Doe to the exit door with one high-level push from a special envoy with a dedicated aircraft. Our proposal to station the Marines off the Liberian coast was therefore amended to include the positioning of a military C-130 aircraft in nearby Freetown, Sierra Leone, for delivery of Doe, his family, and his soft drinks to Togo.

Also during May, we were treated to a number of direct telephone calls from both Doe and Taylor. When Doe called, I pushed him hard on advancing the elections to 1990 to challenge the NPFL's commitment to democracy. Doe retreated behind the constitution, claiming it did not permit an election prior to the prescribed October 1991 date. On the other hand, moving it up three to six months might be possible (*sic*).

Charles Taylor called to reiterate his pledge to protect US assets. I called his attention to the three communications sites that were full of displaced Liberians trying to escape the war. He assured me his people would do no damage and would leave all property intact. He also reiterated that he had no personal ambition. "My only objective is to get rid of Doe."

Our timid awakening to activist diplomacy opened a dialogue with the Liberian exile community. Our announcement suspending military assistance was apparently the signal everyone had been waiting for. After having denounced our sending military officers to Nimba County in January, the exiles were now ready to discuss their agenda with us. Their main spokesman was Dr Amos Sawyer, former professor of political science at the University of Liberia and chairman of the commission that drafted the Doe Constitution. He lived in exile in Chicago, where he headed the Association for Constitutional Democracy in Liberia (ACDL). His agenda was (a) an immediate cease-fire, (b) Doe's immediate resignation, (c) a roundtable all-parties conference, and (d) a free election. Sawyer and all the other exile groups not involved in combat operations expected the United States to guarantee them a seat at the table.[29]

The NSC is seized with Liberia

One layer above the Policy Coordinating Committee (PCC) that I chaired is the Deputies Committee, part of the national security decision-making system. The "deputy" designation refers to the second-ranking official in each agency represented. In 1990, the committee was chaired by Deputy National Security Advisor Robert Gates, a career CIA official brought into the NSC by President Bush under National Security Advisor General Brent Scowcroft. Actual attendees for meetings on African issues were usually the third- or fourth-ranking agency officials.

The difference between the PCC and the Deputies Committee was that those who attended my PCC meetings were Africa specialists. In the Deputies Committee, the participants were generally poorly informed about Africa because they had other, higher-priority issues to worry about. Those of us on the Africa PCC filled the back rows at the deputies meetings in the White House Situation Room. The State Department representative I accompanied was almost always Robert Kimmitt, under secretary for political affairs.

The deputies meeting to consider the PCC proposal for the deployment of the Marine Amphibious Readiness Group to Liberia met on 24 May 1990. It was the first policy meeting on Liberia above the PCC level since the crisis began. Bob Kimmitt gave a review of the situation in Liberia as of that date. Doe was in the process of losing both the war and his political base. Our efforts to stimulate a dialogue between Doe and the NPFL had failed so far, but we would try again to broker discussions in the days and weeks ahead.

The official US government community in Liberia was down to 100 persons. The private American citizen community had declined from 5000 to about 1100 persons who had declined departure assistance. Including noncitizen dependents, an emergency evacuation would involve about 3000 individuals. A seaborne departure might be necessary if the war came to Monrovia and the regular air and land escape routes were cut off. Thus, the PCC recommended the forward deployment of naval assets that could undertake a noncombatant evacuation operation, or NEO, before the fighting reached Monrovia. If the operation were delayed, US fighters might have to suppress potential opposition using force. For this reason, the MARG was desirable because of its complement of 2500 US Marines with assault and transport helicopters.

Kimmitt described our initial efforts to push Doe into exile, including an informal statement to his friends in the official delegation that earlier visited Washington informing them that a place of exile had been arranged. Doe appeared to be resisting, so the time was not yet ripe to send a special envoy to demand that he leave, as we had done in the Philippines. Kimmitt also described our contacts with the NPFL and our efforts to persuade them to establish a broadly based successor regime. The NPFL was treating American citizens and property correctly and was solicitous of our concerns. Our scenario for a Liberia that did not include a continuation of Doe in power naturally struck a friendly chord with Taylor. Kimmitt also informed the committee of our diplomatic efforts to persuade other countries to stop arms flows to both sides.[30]

The 24 May deputies meeting achieved consensus on deploying a Marine group from Europe to Liberia to facilitate the departure of American citizens, if necessary using the prescribed noncombatant evacuation operation. We were instructed to work harder to persuade people to leave while it was still possible to fly them out by charter aircraft, so that an emergency evacuation would be unnecessary.

Two aspects of the deputies meeting, however, were discouraging. First, Chairman Robert Gates refused to recognize any special US responsibility for Liberia's crisis on the basis of our historical ties. We needed to weigh our interests carefully and act accordingly, especially in protecting American citizens, but we were not responsible for solving the Liberian problem, no matter what the Africans or anyone else expected. Secondly, the "vital" and "critical" importance of US facilities in Liberia, so vigorously expressed in the Policy Coordinating Committee, was not repeated in the Deputies Committee. The CIA, USIA, and DOD (representing the Coast Guard) failed to stand up and be counted against Gates's browbeating. In the end, none of the agencies recommended the use of force to protect those facilities. That "vital" and "critical" they were not. In my mind, as I sat behind Kimmitt at the meeting, was to use not force but some vigorous diplomacy. So far, that element of our plan had not been shot down, but Gates's disclaimer was not promising.

The Marine Amphibious Readiness Group arrived off Monrovia during 3–4 June. Since US forces were now close to a fighting zone and might have to be deployed into a dangerous environment, the Deputies Committee had to meet frequently to keep abreast of the facts on the ground. In a meeting on 4 June, we heard that the MARG's arrival had stimulated several hundred additional American citizens to depart. This led us to arrange weekly charter flights as further inducement, with the arrival of fighting in Monrovia seemingly imminent.

At the 4 June meeting, we described our ongoing efforts to find a political solution, including enhanced pressure on Doe to leave. In his telephone conversation with Peter McPherson, Doe had revealed he was contemplating two alternate scenarios. One was to defend the presidential palace, which would be difficult for the rebels to capture because they were unaccustomed to set-piece combat. The other was to hold out in Krahn country in Grand Geddah County, where Doe had 2000 troops. We believed Doe had not excluded departure, and Kimmitt told the committee that I would be going to Monrovia with an aircraft and an invitation for asylum in Togo, to give him the final push.

Our thinking about Liberia's political future was also taking shape. We had already proposed a constitutionally viable scheme to both sides. In effect, Doe would resign in favor of Vice President Harry Moniba, who would appoint Charles Taylor as the new vice president and then himself resign. Taylor would become president of Liberia but would have to organize an election in October 1991 pursuant to the Constitution. Government and civil society groups, such as the Liberian Council of Churches, expressed interest in the scheme as a constitutional way out. The NPFL was less enthusiastic about the October 1991 election deadline, but we were slowly persuading Taylor of the importance of constitutional respectability. Doe's departure and Taylor's coming to power were the heart of our policy. The biggest impediment to this scenario was Doe's refusal to leave. Hence, it was increasingly urgent to send a high-level envoy.[31]

On 5 June 1990, we were jolted by an ice-cold bureaucratic shower. Deputy Secretary Larry Eagleburger received word from the National Security Council that the president had decided the United States would not take charge of the Liberian problem, and I should not, therefore, travel to Monrovia to escort Doe into exile. We would confine our efforts to the protection of Americans. Needless to say, at the PCC level we were dismayed because our diplomatic effort had just begun to gain momentum. Liberians with guns were listening and taking us seriously.

My not going to Monrovia to pressure Doe was less of a disappointment than the admonition not to take charge of the problem. What I wanted was to use the considerable influence of the United States to push frightened Liberians into a "win-win" solution that might spare the country further agony. If the United States refused to take risks to do that, who else would? I was personally outraged, particularly by the absence of any real dialogue between those with the knowledge and those with the ultimate power of decision.[32]

Drawing in the West Africans

That the Marines were sitting in the Atlantic Ocean 15 miles from Monrovia the first week in June not engaged in any activity in Liberia graphically illustrated our decision not to address the conflict. By this point, the rebels had entered the Firestone rubber plantation near Robertsfield, indicating that Monrovia itself was threatened.

Fortunately, other entities were willing to fill the vacuum. The Liberian Council of Churches (LCC), whose chairman had been in the official Liberian delegation visiting Washington in May, proposed a roundtable negotiation in neutral territory in Freetown, Sierra Leone. Taylor called us on 7 June to ask that we inform the Liberian government of his willingness to participate, but without a prior cease-fire. We considered this a possible breakthrough, because the NPFL had previously refused to meet government representatives while Doe remained in office. Our decision to play only a passive role had signaled Taylor that Doe could not hope for any US support to remain in power.

The talks began in Freetown on 12 June. We offered the American Embassy as the venue but did not take part. We did, however, send Ambassador-designate to Liberia Peter Jon de Vos to monitor the talks in Freetown. I informed a PCC meeting on 12 June that our posture was one of "facilitation and not mediation." Our interagency discussions thus concentrated on evacuating citizens, protecting the American Embassy, and finding refuge for Liberians trying to escape the fighting. Augmenting the Marine security guard to 200 would assure Embassy protection. We decided to allow Liberians seeking safety to take shelter in our Greystone compound, across the street from the Embassy.[33] Subsequent meetings of the Deputies Committee, which occurred frequently, also concentrated on security issues, but the option of a negotiation under our umbrella was no longer on the table.

The negotiations in Freetown were not the breakthrough we had hoped for. While Taylor showed some flexibility, he insisted there could be no deal as long as Doe remained in office. Doe, on the other hand, felt he should remain in power until an election could be held. As he saw his military situation deteriorating, however, Doe told us he would be willing to accept our proposal to move the election up one year to October 1990. He himself would not run. That solution could have been face-saving for him, but it came too late.[34]

As June gave way to July, the plight of the Monrovia population steadily worsened. Food, fuel, and water were in short supply, and displaced people kept arriving. We also received disturbing information about the NPFL. In April, after the AFL had won a rare combat victory over the NPFL, Taylor insisted on summary justice against his commanders who had lost the battle and executed them. This produced a split, with a breakaway group under the leadership of Lieutenant Prince Yeduo Johnson forming the Independent National Patriotic Front of Liberia (INPFL).[35] The emergence of the INPFL turned the war into a three-way fight, with each side battling the other two. In addition, we received horrible news from Buchanan, where NPFL forces were killing any Krahn or Mandingo ethnic they captured, including women and children.

As he tightened the noose on Monrovia, Taylor made additional errors of judgment beyond these. Thousands of citizens from neighboring West African countries trapped behind Taylor's lines depended for their safety on Taylor's protection. Most were English speakers from Nigeria, Ghana, and Sierra Leone. Taylor's main backers in the West African subregion were francophone Burkina Faso and Côte d'Ivoire, which facilitated the transit of arms to NPFL fighters. Taylor perceived that Doe enjoyed sympathy in Nigeria and Ghana, where younger military officers had also taken power through coups. He was particularly suspicious of General Ibrahim Babangida, president of Nigeria, who had been close to Doe during the 1980s. Taylor's decision to keep the West Africans hostage to dissuade Nigeria and others from intervening on Doe's behalf proved a serious lapse in judgement.

Needless to say, as soon as it became clear that at least 3000 Nigerians and thousands of other West Africans were being detained in Liberia, the neighboring governments became alarmed. Concern for their nationals grew into concern for the stability of the entire subregion, which faced arms proliferation and floods of refugees. Liberia's neighbors, under the umbrella of the Economic Community of West

African States (ECOWAS), decided to take on the Liberian question in May–June 1990. That decision was the exact opposite of what Taylor had hoped for.

Enter ECOWAS and ECOMOG

By the first week of July 1990, the NPFL had cut off Monrovia, except by sea and the road northwest to Sierra Leone. Several Krahn generals had already abandoned Doe and left the country. Monrovia was in danger of a sanitary and nutritional crisis because thousands of displaced people flocked into the city as the flow of humanitarian assistance dwindled. We feared a catastrophe if there were a pitched battle for the city. Although they normally tended to avoid combat, the Krahns in Monrovia had no choice but to fight to the death. Krahn troops knew that if captured they would be killed. The impact on the city could be devastating.

In one of many telephone chats, I acknowledged to Charles Taylor that victory was in his grasp and suggested that it would be better for everyone if a battle for Monrovia could be avoided. I said the way to achieve that was to give the Krahns an overland escape route. If he agreed, then the road to Sierra Leone should be left open. Taylor inferred from our conversation that we expected an NPFL victory. He was thus conciliatory and promised to keep the road to Sierra Leone open. The NPFL nevertheless attacked Monrovia on 2 July for the first time, and on 5 July Taylor predicted Monrovia's fall within a few weeks. The escape route for the Krahns was never opened. As predicted, they defended Monrovia ferociously, as if their lives depended on it, which was the case.[36]

Both our desire to keep open the road to Sierra Leone and Taylor's hope to conquer Monrovia quickly were dashed in mid-July when Prince Johnson's INPFL fighters suddenly appeared on Bushrod Island, west of Monrovia, effectively sealing the road to Sierra Leone. Suddenly, Taylor had to worry about two armed adversaries instead of one, the Krahn-dominated AFL and Johnson's INPFL.

Liberia was high on the agenda when the ECOWAS heads of state gathered in Banjul, the Gambia, in May 1990 for their annual summit. Normally, Africans were unaccustomed to discussing such strictly internal problems. In the Liberia case, however, they determined that the state had effectively collapsed. In addition, the war was creating refugee flows, arms trafficking, and growing banditry and lawlessness.

They reacted by calling for an immediate cease-fire and establishing an ad hoc mediation committee mandated to contact both sides to work out a compromise.[37]

The mediation committee, which included both Nigeria and Côte d'Ivoire, contacted various factions in mid-June, picking up the mediation burden where the United States had left off. After the failure of the Sierra Leone talks in June, the committee tried to schedule a second session under ECOWAS auspices. In their informal phone discussions with Doe and Taylor, they had reached the point where Doe was willing to resign but only if Taylor would not take over immediately. On 2 July, Doe actually did offer to resign if the NPFL and ECOWAS would guarantee his personal safety and prevent retribution against his fellow Krahns. But by this time, sensing military victory, Taylor hardened his terms. He insisted on taking power, guaranteeing only that Doe could leave Liberia safely.

The second negotiating session in Freetown was scheduled for 12 July. My statement to a PCC meeting the same day showed how distanced we had become from the crisis:

> Our role in these talks is one of interested observer. We are not providing facilities as we did last time, and we are not providing a solution to the conflict. The Sierra Leone Government is providing the site and ECOWAS is providing the mediators.[38]

That statement reflected the thinking of a loyal civil servant who wanted to make sure the bureaucracy followed policy guidance from on high that "we will not take charge of the Liberian problem." It was a lot easier to assume this posture at that moment because only 500 American citizens remained in Liberia, a hard core who refused all embassy advice to depart. Because of them, however, our naval force also remained.

The mediating team for the Freetown talks was led by ECOWAS secretary-general Dr. Abass Bundu, a Sierra Leonean. His approach appeared eminently fair and reasonable. Doe should resign in favor of a coalition interim government that would take Liberia through a transition to an election. No Liberian should have a claim to power unless he had popular support as expressed in an election. Doe liked the proposal because it would protect both himself and the Krahn ethnic group from reprisals. Taylor, however, thought it robbed him, unreasonably, of the fruits of victory. His NPFL movement controlled most of Liberia, and he refused to be deprived of power. His only concession was to accept an interim government, with a deadline for an election, provided he was named interim president. Under the ECOWAS proposal, the interim president would have been a neutral person, ineligible to run for reelection. Taylor was saying, in effect, "I have won the war. I want power. Democracy will come, but under my control."

To Taylor, the ECOWAS refusal to name him interim president proved that Nigeria hated him and secretly supported Doe, a conclusion bolstered by the ECOWAS secretariat's location in Nigeria. The view of Côte d'Ivoire president Houphouet-Boigny, a major NPFL supporter, that ECOWAS was a vehicle for Nigerian domination of the subregion encouraged Taylor's jaundiced view of Nigeria. After one week, the talks broke up in deadlock on 19 July. Accordingly, Taylor kept the Nigerian citizens trapped behind his lines as hostages to deter a Nigerian intervention.

During July, fighting inside Monrovia became particularly intense. Bullets passed close to the Embassy, requiring an increase in the number of Marines. Much of the combat was between Prince Johnson's INPLF and the AFL, with the NPFL waiting outside Monrovia for the two enemy groups to tear each other apart. Increased tension incited the AFL to attack a Lutheran church sheltering hundreds of the displaced from Nimba County. About 200 were massacred. If Taylor captured the city, we knew that retribution would be horrific.

The church massacre, increased urban fighting, and growing food shortages finally persuaded the remaining Americans to depart. MARG helicopters with armed Marines flew to an assembly point inside Monrovia to lift the evacuees to the ships and then on to Freetown. To assure a peaceful evacuation, the deputy chairman of the Joint Chiefs of Staff, Admiral David Jeremiah, called Taylor requesting there be no shooting. US embassy personnel did the same with the AFL and Prince Johnson, who had become a regular visitor to the chancery. The evacuation of 2500 people, including US citizens and their noncitizen dependents, was completed in peaceful conditions during the first week of August 1990.[39]

America's successful military evacuation did not relieve the tension for the West African governments whose nationals remained trapped, especially the Nigerians, whose citizens were deliberately detained. The flow of refugees into Guinea, Côte d'Ivoire, and beyond to Ghana and Sierra Leone continued. The ECOWAS mediation committee went back to the drawing board, meeting at the head-of-state level in Banjul on 6 and 7 August. Agreeing that an external military force was needed to rescue West African citizens, restore stability, and assure a democratic transition, they decided to send a force of 2500 troops taken from the armies of Nigeria, Ghana, Guinea, Sierra Leone, and the Gambia. The commander was a Ghanaian general, but the majority of the troops were Nigerian. The force was baptized ECOWAS Monitoring Group, or ECOMOG for short.

To establish an interim regime, a national conference of Liberian political parties and civil society would select the government and its interim leader, who would be ineligible to run for president.[40] His exclusion as head of the interim government and ECOMOG's domination by Nigerians convinced Taylor he would be the loser. He therefore objected strongly and noisily, warning the Nigerians not to come in. Taylor's detention of their citizens and protests against their alleged support for Doe convinced the Nigerians they had no option but to intervene.

Ambassador de Vos and others were skeptical about the prospects for ECOMOG's success, because the NPFL was so heavily armed. In the State Department, however, we saw the ECOMOG operation as the only hope for ending Liberia's downward slide into anarchy and expressed our support. The plan was well conceived and had the extra merit of involving Africans working to solve an African problem. Within the ECOWAS mediation committee, however, one major, ominous problem arose. Côte d'Ivoire registered a vigorous dissent to the intervention, arguing that the committee lacked jurisdiction to send troops to a member country. Only a full plenary of ECOWAS heads of state had that power. Nigeria, Ghana, and Guinea, a majority in the committee, disregarded the Ivoirian objection and proceeded with the deployment. That left the Ivoirians alienated, furious, and determined to continue transferring arms to the NPFL. If Taylor wanted to fight ECOMOG, he would get help.

ECOWAS established a $50 million emergency fund to finance ECO-MOG and requested assistance from donor countries, including the United States. We debated this request in the PCC, where military representatives expressed concern that a US contribution would lead to follow-on requests for direct military support. The PCC decided it was a risk worth taking and recommended that the United States contribute. Endorsement by the Organization of African Unity gave the operation added legitimacy. Acceptance of the PCC recommendation produced only an initial contribution of a symbolic $3.3 million, but it showed solidarity with an important African initiative.

As agreed by the participating heads of government, two ships of the ECOWAS peacekeeping force landed troops at the port of Monrovia on

24 August and secured the port and central city. The landing had the important immediate effect of opening the besieged city to humanitarian relief, thereby rescuing thousands of hungry people from literally starving. It also prevented further AFL atrocities like the Lutheran Church massacre. The ECOMOG operation's one negative impact was that it preserved the AFL as a military establishment, a factor that was later to complicate efforts for a lasting solution.

ECOWAS sponsored an "All-Liberia" Conference in Banjul during the period 27 August–1 September. The conference chose an "interim government" and appointed Dr Amos Sawyer president. The NPFL boycotted the conference, warning that the interim government would be unable to fulfill its mission. In any event, security conditions inside Monrovia were not yet conducive to the arrival of the interim government and the problem of its legitimacy remained moot.

By 31 August, ECOMOG had expanded its perimeter and captured the in-town Spriggs Payne Airport, with only token resistance from the NPFL. It also freed the hostages. But ECOMOG had been required to use lethal force and had taken casualties. The emergency humanitarian situation in Monrovia had been alleviated, for which we were thankful, yet the outlook for a peaceful transition was not bright. Worse, the continued arms flow to Taylor from Burkina Faso and Côte d'Ivoire further widened the ECOWAS split.

The United States takes a back seat

The State Department working level happily greeted the ECOWAS initiative. ECOMOG's arrival effectively saved Monrovia from mass starvation. That alone would have justified the effort. In addition, however, the West Africans' taking charge of the problem assuaged our guilt feelings over abandoning our Liberian offspring. Finally, having Africans themselves accepting responsibility for security in their own neighborhood had set a good precedent. The OAU's rapid approval reflected Africa's new activist approach to internal conflict.

As of the end of August 1990, the United States was essentially relegated to a secondary role. The small financial contribution we proposed to make to ECOWAS was insufficient to give us a major voice in West African policy.[41] Monrovia was still dangerous enough to require an augmented Marine detachment at the Embassy, and a reduced MARG contingent remained stationed offshore, just in case. All three of our "vital, irreplaceable" facilities were out of commission and thoroughly looted. Doe was still in the executive mansion claiming to be president. The "interim government" had not yet taken office. Prince Johnson, head of the renegade INPFL, was inside Monrovia cooperating de facto with ECOMOG in opposing the NPFL.

On 9 September, Doe made a fatal mistake. He accepted Prince Johnson's invitation to meet on "neutral" territory in ECOMOG headquarters, ostensibly to forge an alliance against Taylor. But it was a trap. With the ECOMOG people looking the other way, Prince Johnson seized and tortured Doe, then let him bleed to death from his wounds.[42]

Doe's death did not end the crisis. Far from it. Taylor had also received a significant amount of new military supplies, guaranteeing that the fighting would not end soon. As noted in a document I prepared for the PCC meeting of 4 September 1990: "The arrival of military supplies for Taylor's force seems to have improved its fighting ability. Burkina Faso shows no sign of withholding support for Taylor, quite the contrary."[43]

Having saved their nationals, the ECOMOG governments could reasonably start thinking about pulling out to avoid additional expense. Taylor knew this and probably thought he could "wait ECO-MOG out." He also knew from the "national conference" held in Banjul on 27 August and the "all-parties" negotiations in Freetown on 12 June that he would be in a minority position in any normal political process. All the unarmed political factions were terrified of Taylor. In short, his incentive for cooperating in a transitional process under an ECOMOG umbrella was minimal. He had conquered most of Liberia by military force and was not about to yield at the negotiating table what he had won in battle.

For their part, the ECOMOG governments and their military commanders in Liberia could not have been nicer to Taylor. Disregarding his insults, they constantly referred to him as a key leader with a major role in the transition. They could not, however, meet his nonnegotiable demand that he be installed as president, whether interim or permanent.

Where did this leave the United States? Could we be helpful in any way? My own inclination in allocating my time was to drop Liberia to a lower priority. I already had a lot on my plate working on conflicts in Ethiopia, Angola, the Sudan, Zaire, and South Africa, places where we could pursue an activist role. High-level reticence on Liberia led us in early September 1990 to decide:

- To maintain our embassy staff at a reduced level, protected by a strong Marine detachment.

- To communicate regularly with the ECOMOG commanders but not identify too closely with them, because they were in a combat rather than a peacekeeping mode.
- To withhold recognition of any interim government without Taylor; and
- To continue trying to persuade Taylor (a) that he should negotiate with ECOMOG; (b) that we were not hostile; but (c) neither did we recognize his claimed right to rule without a democratic process.

The Unites States jumps back in – temporarily

In view of our "no zeal" policy in Liberia, and with the death of Samuel Doe not really changing anything, I turned my attention elsewhere at the beginning of September. But I was soon wrenched back to Liberia, which had become alive again in the media. Taylor was advancing toward central Monrovia, bullets were flying around our Embassy, and civilian suffering was increasing. ECOMOG appeared unable to cope with the NPFL. As criticism of our inaction mounted, the NSC decided to increase the US profile by sending me on a "fact-finding" mission to West Africa, just to show we cared. With my executive assistant Karl Hoffmann, I left Rome on September 15 in an Air Force jet bound for Sierra Leone, Liberia, Côte d'Ivoire, Nigeria, Ghana, and Burkina Faso. Deputy Assistant Secretary Jim Woods from Defense joined us in Abidjan.

Arriving in Freetown, Sierra Leone, on September 17, we were immediately transferred to a Navy helicopter and flown to Monrovia, landing in the Embassy compound on Mamba Point. The helicopter was surrounded by heavily armed Marines, who escorted us to the chancery. Other Marines were in fortified elevated guard posts that gave them the capability of shooting at potential attackers at fairly long range. Gunfire sounded frequently. Briefings by various agency representatives indicated that ECOMOG would have to become much stronger if it intended to neutralize Taylor and start a political transition. Embassy morale was high, as it usually is when there is danger.

After Monrovia, we made lightning visits to the presidents of Côte d'Ivoire, Nigeria, and Ghana. President Félix Houphouet-Boigny in Abidjan said his country was the main victim of the Liberian war, having received well over 100 000 refugees. As for alleged Ivoirien help to the NPLF, Houphouet brushed aside the accusation, saying, "I have never even met Charles Taylor." His defense minister, however, acknowledged that supplies for the NPLF transited Côte d'Ivoire because the Ivoiriens did not have the capability of stopping the flow, not because of complicity.

Presidents Ibrahim Babangida and Jerry Rawlings, of Nigeria and Ghana respectively, told us they had increased ECOMOG's troop strength and believed the NPLF would soon be under control. Taylor would have no choice but to negotiate. They both asked us to put pressure on Côte d'Ivoire and Burkina Faso to stop arming the NPLF. The bottom line for these two major troop contributors to ECOMOG was their determination to stay as long as necessary to bring about a negotiated political solution. At an overnight stop in Ouagadougou, Burkina Faso, we actually saw Libyan cargo aircraft on the airport runway. The embassy confirmed that arms for the NPFL had arrived in those planes.

On 20 September, in the most interesting experience of the mission, we flew to the northern Côte d'Ivoire airport at Man. There, joined by our ambassador in Abidjan, Kenneth Brown, we boarded four-wheel-drive vehicles and crossed ten miles into Liberia to meet with Charles Taylor. The most striking, and frightening, aspect of Taylor's forest hideaway was the overwhelming presence of heavily armed 14-to-16-year-old boys.

The discussion went over familiar ground. Even though Doe was no longer alive, Taylor could not trust the Nigerians. They had supported Doe and they hated him. They were determined to prevent him from ruling Liberia. I told Taylor that on the basis of my talks with Babangida and Rawlings, I was persuaded that ECOMOG was there to stay, and he should find a way to negotiate.

Taylor responded that any such negotiation would require both the assistance and the guarantees of the United States. Otherwise, he could not participate. If the United States would send troops to Liberia, he would surrender the NPFL to them. Picking up on his pro-American statement, I asked Taylor if he would be willing to accept a cease-fire if we could persuade ECOMOG to go along. He immediately said yes.

Upon returning to Abidjan we quickly got word to Monrovia. ECOMOG agreed, and an informal cease-fire went into effect. When it was announced, an NPFL spokesman said, "With the United States involved, we can have peace."[44] The implication of the American-brokered cease-fire was that we would continue the process as mediators. Taylor, at least, saw it that way. The ECOMOG governments did not seem to mind an American brokering role either, although they considered themselves neutral parties, too.

Unfortunately, US policy promptly defaulted to the position prior to my "fact-finding" mission. My US-brokered cease-fire was disowned at the NSC level, which correctly saw it as a slippery slope to full involvement, or "taking charge of Liberia." Needless to say, while my superiors in the State Department were quietly smirking, the folks over in the NSC, especially Deputy National Security Advisor Bob Gates, were furious at me for "going beyond my mandate." Thus was the second favorable window of opportunity slammed shut by the NSC.

With the United States once again abdicating a leadership role, the situation continued to degrade. Trying to take advantage of the informal cease-fire, ECOWAS called for political negotiations in Freetown on 27 September, but Taylor refused to attend, apparently because of the US absence. With no peace talks, ECOMOG had to undertake a limited military offensive, because NPFL lines were too close to the port. Their guns could hit any part of the ECOMOG contingent. Consequently, ECOMOG, with the help of Prince Johnson's INPFL, spent most of October pushing the NPFL away from Monrovia to a "security arc," placing the city beyond artillery range.

In the summer of 1990 our very able Liberia task force director Jim Bishop left to take up his post as ambassador in Somalia. Replacing him was another African veteran, Ambassador Donald Petterson. In early October I sent Petterson to West Africa on a tour depicted as a follow-on to my September trip. I gave him a letter imploring President Houphouet-Boigny to do something about Liberia. By this time, Houphouet surely understood that his protégé Charles Taylor could not gain power without ECOMOG cooperation.

Petterson told Taylor himself that it was unrealistic to expect ECOMOG to fade away and he should therefore accept negotiations. Taylor was adamant. He would speak to anyone about peace, but not to ECOMOG. Houphouet's response to my letter was to call an ECOWAS summit conference for 15 October 1990 in Yamoussoukro, Côte d'Ivoire. The anglophone countries and Guinea saw Houphouet's move as a ploy to discredit ECOMOG and therefore boycotted the conference, thereby aborting it.

Houphouet later said that he had called the meeting only at the request of the United States. Increasingly, the war was becoming a surrogate fight between Côte d'Ivoire/Burkina and Nigeria/Ghana. In any event, Houphouet, now partially pregnant, as it were, was beginning to take responsibility for the problems he himself had helped create. At that particular time, however, we had a good reason for taking a soft line with Houphouet. Côte d'Ivoire was one of three African nations then on the UN Security Council. The United States was counting on them to support a war against Iraq, making it impossible for us to get tough with them over Liberia. They were under Secretary Baker's protection.

At the beginning of November, we reviewed both trips to the region, my own and Don Petterson's. In a meeting on November 8 the PCC made three important decisions:

- We would disengage the MARG from Liberian waters and draw down the augmented Marine security detachment.
- We would release $3 million that we had been holding for ECOWAS, but to the ECOWAS humanitarian fund, not ECOMOG. Our avoidance of support for ECOMOG was a gesture to Taylor, who saw it as his principal enemy. At the same time, our support for ECOWAS sent a signal to Taylor that we were edging toward a dialogue with the interim government he considered an ECOMOG puppet.
- We would establish a working relationship with the interim government without granting it formal recognition.

After the 8 November PCC, I reported our assessment of ECOMOG to Under Secretary Kimmitt:

> The PCC feels that the ECOWAS's experience to date has on balance been positive. ECOMOG has performed its mission in a restrained and responsible fashion. The expansion of its perimeter beyond Monrovia has been a blessing for the malnourished citizens of the capital. ECOMOG has played a pivotal role in the distribution of relief.[45]

For most of 1991, what seemed like an endless series of peace conferences took place in several African capitals under the ECOWAS umbrella. There were so many conferences that we started numbering them (Yamoussoukro I, II, III, Banjul I and II, and so on). The results were all the same. There was always to be a cease-fire agreement, followed by the formation of an all-parties interim government and an election under international supervision. Beforehand, the armies were to encamp their troops and disarm to ECOMOG.

Charles Taylor came to most of the meetings and signed the final documents. The trouble always came later when he found excuses for reneging. His bottom-line demand was always the same. He must be the interim president. He also insisted that ECOMOG depart so that the Liberians could negotiate without "outside interference." Unsurprisingly, a few ECOWAS heads of state became fed up with Taylor and his antics by the time of Yamoussoukro III in September 1991.

Bankrolling the Senegalese

Between October 1990 and September 1991, the United States remained relatively passive in Liberia. Though we took no responsibility for anything beyond relief, we presumed we had a right to look over everyone else's shoulder and criticize. If our historic relationship with Liberia meant anything, we thought, it gave us the right to tell everyone else what to do. At one point we even considered bringing the Liberia issue to the UN Security Council. We asked the Soviets to be our stalking horse for informal consultations. They came back to say that Côte d'Ivoire, one of three African members on the Council, was adamantly opposed and had enough support among the nonaligned members to keep Liberia off the agenda. So much for superpower hegemony.[46]

In June 1991, I encountered Burkina Faso president Blaise Compaore in Abidjan. We talked about Liberia, and I asked him about Burkina's arms supply to Taylor. Compaore said he had decided to support Taylor in 1989 because he found the Doe regime in Liberia hopelessly repressive and corrupt. At the time, getting rid of Doe seemed a good deed, but the operation had turned hideously wrong. Regrettably, instead of entering a new era, Liberia had become a disaster. Left unsaid was Compaore's commitment to continue aiding Taylor until final victory. Despite my urging, he had invested too much to stop in midstream.

During this same twelve-month period, the situation on the ground was not static. The Interim Government of National Unity (IGNU) started to develop a personality of its own but had neither troops nor guns. Taylor and his NPFL developed economic interests in territories they controlled. International firms made deals with him for the illicit export of timber and minerals. As more time went by without a government, and with many young boys becoming brutalized by living with guns, negotiating a settlement became all the more difficult. In addition, new armed factions appeared, the most important of which was the United Liberation Movement for Democracy in Liberia (ULIMO), an amalgamation of bands connected to the Armed Forces of Liberia and the Krahn and Mandingo ethnic groups, all bitter enemies of Taylor.[47]

In September 1991, the third Yamoussoukro peace conference whetted our appetite for renewed involvement. For a change, Taylor was cooperating, negotiating diligently with interim president Amos Sawyer on the composition of an electoral commission and Supreme Court. Moreover, everyone took seriously Taylor's apprehensions about disarming to the Nigerians, whom he considered biased. Thus, there was serious talk about reconfiguring ECOMOG to include troops from countries not previously implicated in Liberia, such as Senegal and Guinea-Bissau. Taylor himself said, "Send me Senegalese troops and I will be happy to disarm to them, because they are trustworthy."[48]

President Bush's strong personal relationship with President Abdou Diouf of Senegal was pivotal to our possible contribution to a new Liberian peace process. Secretary Baker told me in early 1989 that Bush considered Diouf one of Africa's most reasonable and intelligent statesmen. The two had seen a lot of each other during Bush's many visits to Africa as vice president. Diouf was therefore one of the few Africans Bush invited for a state visit.[49] I was also friendly with Diouf, having been American ambassador to Senegal during 1977–1980.

For Diouf's state visit in September 1991, we put Liberia on the agenda. With a view toward involving Senegalese troops as peace-keepers, Bush expressed the view that Taylor might be getting serious about a peaceful transition. Senegalese troops would give Taylor confidence that he was dealing with a neutral party. Diouf, whom I had briefed beforehand, said that Senegal could not refuse to play such a role if peace in Liberia depended on it. But Senegal could not afford to equip, transport, and maintain 1500 troops in Liberia on its own. Could the United States assist Senegal in this regard? Bush replied we would try to be helpful and suggested Diouf discuss it further with Baker.

The Bush–Diouf meeting in the Cabinet Room was followed by Secretary Baker's luncheon in his eighth-floor dining room. Baker asked Diouf what was required. Diouf responded that the Senegalese army needed everything that would equip a 1500-man battalion to operate in Liberia for a year. He pledged to send the troops if the United States could equip them. Baker said we would study it and get back to him. The implication of both the Bush and Baker statements was that we wanted to provide support.

In the bureaucracy, we took the statements as a provisional commit-ment and started working to meet the need. Deputy Assistant Secretary Leonard Robinson, who worked exhaustively for peace in Liberia, took charge.[50] Robinson persuaded the Defense Department to invite the Senegalese chief of staff to go over their requirements. After much interagency discussion and horse-trading, we found various legislative authorities to provide Senegal with the necessary support. Equipment for the troops was to come out of Defense Department stocks, with cash outlays coming from Economic Support Funds controlled by State.[51] In addition, we found a transportation windfall in the form of 50 mili-tary trucks the Doe regime had ordered from South Korea that were sitting idle in a Senegalese warehouse. Senegalese coastal ferries would transport the troops to Liberia, with US air transport moving the initial contingents. The exercise illustrated how well the different agencies can work together if properly motivated, especially, as in this case, when the president and secretary of state both wanted it to happen.

The Senegalese deployment took place in November 1991 over the objections of the French military, jealous of US–Senegalese collaboration. The French also knew that the operation would place Senegal in direct opposition to the pro-Taylor policy of Côte d'Ivoire, France's other important regional client. Although hopeful, we had our own doubts, reflected in a State Department message to Embassy Monrovia:

> If Taylor balks once Senegalese forces have been deployed at his request, we will consider appropriate US responses, which could include public censure, formal recognition of IGNU, presentation of Ambassador [Peter] de Vos's credentials, jawboning of US companies against doing business in Taylorland, and consideration of appropriate sanctions against such firms.[52]

Senegalese troops moved into NPFL-controlled territory slowly, although some roads were opened and some progress registered. A Liberia policy review meeting on 22 January 1992, chaired by Len Robinson, expressed disappointment with the slow progress. Some participants wanted to declare that Taylor was stalling, but Peter de Vos counseled patience. Nevertheless, talk of ways to pressure Taylor was quite lively as disillusion returned.[53]

The breaking point for ECOWAS, the Senegalese, and the United States came in May 1992 when six Senegalese soldiers on patrol in NPFL-controlled territory were deliberately killed in a village called Vanum. Captured after discovering an NPFL arms cache illegal under the Yamoussoukro III agreement, they were brutally executed. This act confirmed what we had already deduced. Taylor had gone back to his old ways, toughing it out in the bush in the expectation that everyone else would get tired and leave. After promising to cooperate if the Senegalese would provide "neutral" peacekeeping service, Taylor's deliberate killing of Senegalese soldiers was the last straw.

By the end of 1992, the overall environment in Liberia had changed drastically. ECOWAS began discussing sanctions against Taylor. Facing protracted war, ECOMOG distributed arms to the IGNU, ULIMO, and AFL. The AFL received back all of the arms ECOMOG had confiscated in 1990. For its part, the NPFL was resupplied massively by air through Robertsfield Airport. The Qaddafi spigot remained wide open, and the transit points through Burkina Faso and Côte d'Ivoire continued to be available. Taylor received sufficient arms to launch a major, quite damaging offensive on 15 October 1992. He came dangerously close to Monrovia but was pushed back. The net effect was to persuade Nigeria and Ghana to escalate their military effort and prolong the stalemate.

In November 1992, ECOWAS took the Liberia issue to the UN Security Council, where it obtained endorsement for its mission and an arms embargo on Taylor. In addition, the Council agreed to sponsor deployment of non-ECOWAS peacekeepers, namely from Uganda, Tanzania, and Zimbabwe, to entice Taylor into cooperating. The three African Security Council members took the lead in this flurry of activity.[54]

On 24 February 1993, soon after taking office, President Clinton signed a directive calling for a Liberia policy review by the now renamed Interagency Working Group (IWG). This last interagency policy review meeting over which I presided, the first IWG on Liberia, noted that the United States had spent $203 million for Liberian relief over three years, and $28.65 million for peacekeeping. The ECOMOG operation had cost over $500 million, most of which was provided by Nigeria. The IWG concluded that the forces of ECOMOG and the armed factions of AFL and ULIMO were together stronger than the NPFL, but not strong enough to defeat it. Continued stalemate could thus be expected. Taylor apparently expected a new, elected civilian regime in Nigeria in June 1993 to pull out of Liberia, thereby handing victory to the NPFL by default. In those circumstances, the United States had no alternative but to continue supporting ECOWAS.

That was my last involvement in Liberia policy before I was replaced by George Moose. A military coup in August 1993 aborted the expected transition to a civilian democratic regime in Nigeria, dashing Taylor's hopes for a Nigerian pullout. Negotiations and war continued until mid-1996, when fatigue finally overtook all the parties.

On 21 April 1996, a high-level US delegation, headed by principal deputy assistant secretary William Twaddell, arrived in Monrovia to lend its good offices to efforts to revive previous accords. Twaddell carried with him a conditional promise to provide $30 million in US assistance as an incentive to the parties to resume the transition. This was the first such official act of diplomatic intervention by the United States since the Senegalese project four years earlier.[55] The lure of America's historical tie to Liberia had proved irresistible to the Clintonites, unlike Bush's people. The impact was dramatic. The transition was resumed, leading to a presidential election in July 1997 considered cleanly run and basically free and fair. The winner was none other than Charles Taylor, the man we had wanted to install as president in 1990.

Postmortem: could Liberia have been spared?

The May–June 1990 decision that the United States would not play a leading role in peacemaking in Liberia was a big mistake. If we had been allowed to pursue the plan adopted in the interagency process to persuade Doe to go into exile, thus opening the door for Taylor to take power, years of devastating civil war might have been prevented. And without the collateral need for ECOWAS peacekeeping, a francophone–anglophone surrogate war could also have been prevented.

As the civil war continued year after year, Liberia became increasingly brutalized, hugely escalating human hardship. Had Taylor been allowed to take power in 1990, would he have been the same spoiler he became in his role of warlord? That is difficult to say. But the destruction of Liberia would have been avoided, and Taylor might have been more open to constructive external influence.

In 1993 Bush's national security advisor, Brent Scowcroft, told journalist Reed Kramer that he had feared a permanent US burden in Liberia if we had taken responsibility in 1990 for a change of regime.[56] In other words, he thought US troops would have been needed indefinitely as peacekeepers. That was not evident at the time, nor did it ever become evident in later years. I regret that Robert Gates, as chairman of the National Security Council's Deputies Committee, did not engage in dialogue on this subject within the committee. If he had, I believe we could have reached consensus on a limited, low-cost diplomatic operation. Had the change in regime not succeeded in stabilizing Liberia, a UN peacekeeping option would probably have been feasible. Although ECOWAS committed the troops, which remained bogged down in Liberia until the 1997 elections, the United States did not get off cheaply. As so often happens, failure to practice less costly conflict prevention resulted in US humanitarian relief expenditures of several hundred millions of dollars. But, as some congressional staffers kept telling us, "Humanitarian relief is a different budgetary line item."

Another key element in the US policy process on Liberia was the failure of those agencies having expensive and supposedly indispensable facilities in Liberia – the CIA, USIA, and the Defense Department for the Coast Guard – to speak up in favor of an aggressive policy. If they had protested the White House's decision, the diplomatic intervention option might have carried greater weight. Their refusal to defend their own agency interests constituted a death blow to any but a passive US role.

Once we decided not to take the lead and the ECOMOG forces had intervened, our policy of support for the West Africans' own effort was correct. Our contributions to ECOWAS peacekeeping were modest, but we carried the major burden of significant humanitarian assistance. Our financial support for the Senegalese troop deployment in 1991–92 was a major contribution to the peace effort, but served only to prove that Taylor was unwilling to cooperate with any process that did not guarantee him power in advance.

When it became clear that Taylor considered ECOMOG an adversary rather than a peacemaker, we might have played the role of honest broker and mediator. But even that possibility was aborted by the NSC after my brief effort to broker a cease-fire in September 1990. We could have done a better job in the use of pressure and publicity designed to embarrass Burkina Faso and Côte d'Ivoire into cutting off the arms flow to Taylor. The need for Côte d'Ivoire's vote in the UN Security Council against Iraq was a deterrent until the end of 1990,[57] but we had no need for reticence toward Burkina Faso.

The chilling effect of a White House stop order penetrates deeply. In Liberia, we thus remained on the sidelines, making gratuitous comments to the main players, refusing responsibility, and speculating on what might have been.

6
Rwanda: Could We Have Prevented Genocide?

On 6 April 1994, a well-planned, well-executed program of genocide was launched in the tiny central African republic of Rwanda. The perpetrators were elements of the political and military leadership who had taken power in a coup that same day after assassinating their own leader, President Juvénal Habyarimana. The main victims were men, women, and children from the minority Tutsi ethnic group. Also murdered were many members of the majority Hutu ethnic group who opposed the regime. The orgy of genocidal killing lasted until mid-June 1994. The exact number of people killed will probably never be known, but estimates vary from five hundred thousand to one million victims. Tens of thousands of ordinary apolitical citizens slaughtered their neighbors, acting obediently on the orders of their political masters.[1]

The Rwandan genocide occurred in 1994 during the Clinton administration, well over a year after I departed. Nevertheless, the crisis leading to the genocide began in 1990, only a year into my tenure. How we intervened during the buildup to the genocide may thus hold lessons regarding the disastrous outcome.

The October surprise: invasion from Uganda

On 2 October 1990, President Bush and Secretary of State Baker were in New York for the annual extravaganza known as the United Nations General Assembly "General Debate." The event is an occasion for the world's leaders to get together to make speeches, have bilateral meetings, and socialize. The secretary of state normally spends about a week in New York, the president one or two days, to make the "American speech." I accompanied Baker to New York each year to assist during meetings with African leaders.

The 1990 session was of particular interest because it began with the "Summit of the Child." That drew far more heads of state than usual, including 25 Africans, all of whom wanted to meet with Bush. Because Bush could not possibly meet each African counterpart individually, we decided to offer a presidential morning coffee for the Africans at the Waldorf Astoria Hotel, an event that turned out to be more exciting than anyone might have imagined.

A few hours before the coffee, we learned that 2000 armed men had invaded northern Rwanda from bases in southern Uganda the previous day, 1 October. It quickly became clear that the invaders were from the large, quasipermanent Rwandan exile community residing in Uganda since 1959. The invading army was made up largely of young men from the minority Tutsi ethnic group, whose parents had fled Rwanda as political refugees between 1959 and 1963, during Rwanda's transition to independence from Belgium. In addition to their Rwandan Tutsi heritage, most were career military professionals in the Army of Uganda, their country of permanent refuge. Thus, they were well equipped, well trained, and dangerous.

The heads of state of Rwanda and Uganda were both in New York for the summit, and both attended George Bush's coffee party. With the invasion only one day old, our hope was that the two presidents could at least set the stage for a peaceful solution to the crisis. But that was not to be. Afterward, an incredulous Rwandan President Juvénal Habyarimana told me that in a discussion lasting one hour, Ugandan President Yoweri Museveni kept insisting that he knew nothing about the invasion and was not in a position to do anything about it.

The next day in Washington, I went to the Ugandan ambassador's residence to meet with President Museveni, who had come to the capital for a series of appointments with business and political leaders. When I asked him to give me the background to the invasion, he looked at me with a poker face and said it was a big surprise to him. He considered the invading forces official deserters from the Ugandan Army subject to court martial, with a possible death penalty.

Later that day, the Belgian ambassador, Herman Dehennin, called to inform me that Museveni had called him with a message for the Belgian government: "Please do not send troops to Rwanda to help the Rwandan government cope with the invasion." Dehennin also told me that the French ambassador had received a similar call. In other words, Museveni was not such a disinterested bystander after all. We also learned that the invaders had a name, the Rwandan Patriotic Front (RPF).

Within a week, both the French and Belgian governments had dispatched small troop contingents to Rwanda. The French contingent's mission was to set up a blocking position to prevent the invaders from advancing on the capital city of Kigali and its airport. The Belgian troops were to help evacuate Belgians and other expatriates. Of equal importance, the general Rwandan population was not welcoming the RPF invaders as liberators fighting to oust a "corrupt and repressive regime." Far from it. Shortly after the RPF crossed the border, about 250 000 Rwandans left their homes in panic, becoming internally displaced persons. The human suffering that inevitably follows armed conflict became quickly apparent.

With Belgian and French troops in the country and the Rwandan army heavily outnumbering the rebels, the United States did not expect the conflict in Rwanda to get out of hand. We ourselves were busy trying to get negotiations going in both Angola and Ethiopia, with lesser initiatives in the Sudan, Mozambique, and Liberia. We saw no need to jump into Rwanda at that point. But Rwanda and its byzantine politics were not going away. As the crisis unfolded over the following two years, it became important for us to play a role. We did not shrink from playing our part. But did we, perhaps naively, make things worse rather than better?

Who started the Rwanda conflict?

The invasion of Rwanda by a band of young Tutsi exiles who had never actually seen their own country triggered some sharp memories as I contemplated the arrival in 1994 of yet another human tragedy in the Great Lakes region of central Africa. In 1972, when I was director for Central African affairs in the Africa Bureau, my responsibilities included the three former Belgian colonies, Zaire, Rwanda, and Burundi. I could never forget 1972, the year of genocide in Burundi.

Rwanda and Burundi are mirror images. Each has the same population density and ethnic makeup, about 85 per cent agrarian Hutus and 15 per cent cattle-herding Tutsis. Both groups speak the same language (called Kinyarwanda in Rwanda, Kirundi in Burundi), and live in close proximity on thousands of isolated hillsides with fertile volcanic soil. Through historical circumstance and German and Belgian colonial decisions, the Tutsis were the overlords and the Hutus the serfs in a feudal system. During colonial times, the Germans and Belgians ruled through the Tutsi royal families. The Tutsis thus dominated education and the professions. Although only 15 per cent of the populations of both countries, they held most of the school places, jobs, and businesses. When independence came to both countries in 1960, most people expected Tutsi domination to continue, and it did so in Burundi. But in Rwanda, with the help of certain Belgian political parties, the Hutus staged a revolution and grabbed power.

In the postindependence period, both minority rule in Burundi and majority rule in Rwanda brought violence to the ethnic groups out of power.

In the first years of Rwanda's independence, between 1959 and 1963, government-sponsored pogroms against Tutsi intellectuals, business elites, and just plain citizens caused many deaths and drove many into exile in neighboring Zaire, Uganda, Tanzania, and Burundi. In 1972, the Tutsi-dominated military regime in Burundi reacted to agitation for democracy by systematically murdering 75 000 Hutus. In effect, anyone who could read or write was targeted for murder. With literate citizens eliminated, voices for majority rule were effectively silenced. As in Rwanda, the ethnic killings in Burundi generated hundreds of thousands of refugees.

Unlike the 1994 Rwanda genocide, however, the 1972 mass killings of Hutu in Burundi received little public attention. Then, no CNN brought the tragedy into American living rooms. In the Office of Central African Affairs, we adopted a basic slogan for both Burundi and Rwanda to explain it all: "The Tutsis are condemned to rule."[2]

When the Bush administration took office, both Rwanda and Burundi were governed by the same authoritarian regimes that had been in power since the 1970s. A Hutu elite group was in charge in Rwanda, and a Tutsi military elite group, supported by Tutsi intellectuals, held power in Burundi. Hundreds of thousands of refugees from both countries were in neighboring territories. Rwandan Tutsi exiles were prohibited from returning, and Burundi's Hutu refugees were too frightened to return. By the mid-1980s, the international community, now accustomed to this arrangement, was not encouraging change in either country. Both countries were stable, hard-working, and faithfully implementing structural adjustment programs.

News of the invasion that hit Rwanda on 1 October 1990 triggered in me a flashback to mid-1987, when I was senior director for Africa on the National Security Council staff in the White House. During my visit to Rwanda that year, President Habyarimana had told me of his suspicions that Tutsi youth in the Ugandan army were plotting to invade their ancestral homeland. He asked me to check US sources, and I agreed to help. US relations with Rwanda were excellent, and the government was popular in the donor community because of its successful economic reforms. During this pre-democracy period in Africa, Rwanda was in the main stream of "benign dictatorships."

US intelligence sources then informed me that Rwandan Tutsi officers held positions of great influence in the Ugandan Army, but nothing indicated any invasion planning. Unfortunately, we stopped thinking about this possibility. Three years later it became a reality.

That both countries had been relatively without violence since 1972, when the last big outbreak had occurred in Burundi, lulled us into what proved wishful thinking that they might have reached equilibrium. A state of permanent civil war, in effect, prevailed in both Rwanda and Burundi between Hutu and Tutsi extremist elites. Even twenty years of calm could not fully mask the seething mass of subsurface fear awaiting the next eruption. As hundreds of thousands of Rwandan Tutsi refugees in surrounding countries rebuilt themselves to critical mass, they provided the popular heat and kindling to ignite the powder kegs. Thus, we should not have been surprised, as we were, by the RPF invasion of Rwanda on 1 October 1990. After the initial shock wore off, we knew instinctively that it probably would not go well. Initially, however, we acted as if the crisis would be short-lived.

Encouraging democracy and negotiations

Despite the surprise, the Rwandan Patriotic Front's invasion did not get very far. The arrival of the French blocking contingent effectively protected the capital city and its airport and gave the regime some breathing space. Between October 1990 and the beginning of serious negotiations in July 1992, the conflict settled into a classic, low-intensity guerrilla war. Nevertheless, even before the 1994 genocide, serious consequences confronted Rwanda:

- Military spending increased tremendously, with the army expanding from a normal complement of 5000 to well over 50 000.
- Because the Rwandan government paid cash for arms, much of which came by expensive air cargo, the economic stabilization program collapsed.[3]
- As the RPF incursions continued, the number of internal refugees among the majority Hutu escalated, reaching the level of 350 000. The mass flight to escape RPF incursions demonstrated how thoroughly indoctrinated the Hutus were with anti-Tutsi fear and hatred.

- The government took advantage of the invasion to increase persecution of resident Tutsi elites and to harass Hutu political opposition.[4]

Out of the insurgency and low-intensity civil war grew a quasisurrogate conflict between France, on the side of the Rwanda regime, and Uganda, on the side of the RPF guerrillas. France had a defense cooperation agreement with the Rwanda government, a commitment dating from the early 1970s that they were determined to uphold. For its part, Uganda continued to provide supplies, safe haven, medical facilities, and rear bases to the RPF, who were, after all, their army buddies.[5]

At the time of the RPF invasion, President Habyarimana was beginning to talk about Rwanda's "democratization." Earlier that year, Habyarimana's friend President Mobutu of Zaire had authorized multiparty politics; and, at the biennial France–Africa summit in La Baule, France, President Mitterrand had made an important statement encouraging democratic transition. A new political trend in Africa had begun. Rwanda was thus leaning toward democracy when the invasion occurred. Indeed, the event may have accelerated the process. The government announced a series of political reforms in November 1990 that included the issuance of new identity cards without ethnic identification and the convening of an all-inclusive national debate on Rwanda's future.

The Organization of African Unity waged the most aggressive external effort at conflict management in the Rwandan crisis. Ambassador Salim Salim, the newly appointed secretary-general, enthusiastically embraced an OAU role in conflict resolution and designated the Rwandan crisis the first test case.

Given these factors, we did not see a major role for the United States in the Rwandan conflict. The Africans themselves were in charge of negotiations. The major influences on the two sides were the Rwandan regime's French allies and the RPF's Ugandan advisors. We had enough on our plate in 1990–91 with Angola and Ethiopia. We therefore acted on the periphery, through humanitarian assistance to internally displaced Rwandans and efforts to persuade the Rwandan regime to maintain economic equilibrium and not overspend on arms. We also became acquainted with the RPF through discreet meetings in Kampala, Uganda.

Throughout 1991, no movement toward negotiations occurred. The Rwandan regime was preoccupied with moving from a one-party system to multiparty democracy. Habyarimana would not accept the argument that the RPF were Rwandans who wanted to come home and that negotiations were therefore necessary. In the regime's view,

Uganda controlled the RPF invaders. Despite the insurgency's devastating impact on Rwanda's economy, it remained, in effect, a Ugandan, not a Rwandan, problem. Habyarimana's message to the international community was: "Tell the Ugandan government to stop its invasion." The French apparently agreed that the conflict was above all a matter of Ugandan aggression. Since Uganda is an English-speaking country, some analysts saw an "Anglo-Saxon conspiracy" against French interests in Africa, a view scholar Gérard Prunier described as the "Fashoda syndrome."[6]

As 1991 went by with no progress toward a peaceful solution, and with Rwanda's economy and society deteriorating disastrously, US Ambassador Bruce Flaten in Kigali recommended that the United States assume a higher profile. Consequently, I undertook two missions to encourage negotiations.

On 8–9 May 1992, I went to Kampala for talks with President Museveni and the RPF leadership. I told both that the conflict was slowly destroying Rwanda's economy, that the RPF could not hope to conquer additional territory beyond its small enclave in northern Rwanda, and that negotiations were necessary. I pledged US support for talks and for the monitoring of a cease-fire.

Museveni said he was happy that the Americans did not agree with the French view that the war was strictly Uganda's problem. He said it was clearly Rwanda's problem, based on the regime's long-standing refusal to allow the refugees to return. He pledged to "use his influence" with the RPF to encourage good faith negotiations. For their part, the RPF said they were ready for negotiations, arguing that the regime refused to acknowledge their existence, except as a military threat.

On 10–11 May 1992, I visited Rwanda for talks with the government and with opposition party leaders. The opposition parties had recently been legalized by constitutional amendments abolishing the statutory one-party state. The US embassy had publicized my visit, which began on a Sunday. Consequently, I was not surprised that the opposition parties had organized demonstrations along the route from the airport to Ambassador Flaten's residence. They clearly wanted me to know they were neither docile nor unworthy of replacing the regime in power. Needless to say, the banners and placards were not kind to the regime.

President Habyarimana received me alone late Sunday afternoon. He was aware of the demonstrations in my honor and asked me what the demonstrators were saying about him. In my well-honed subtle approach, I said, "They are calling you a murderer and a thief." His response was, "They exaggerate a bit, don't you think?" After that preliminary bit of black humor, we talked about the war and politics.

Habyarimana was intransigent about the RPF. They were Ugandans, he insisted, and Museveni must be persuaded to order them to return home. He was willing to consider the right of return for refugees and had even established a commission to study it, but the RPF insurgents were Ugandan Army regulars who must go back. On democracy, Habyarimana assured me he would go forward with constitutional and regulatory changes needed to institute a multiparty state. Indeed, a government of national unity was already in place, with a prime minister and a foreign minister appointed from the opposition.

As Ambassador Flaten had recommended, I spent considerable time with the political opposition, some of whom held portfolios in the national unity government. Of particular interest were Prime Minister Dismas Nsengiyaremye and Foreign Minister Boniface Ngulinzira, both of whom were leaders of the Democratic Republican Movement (MDR). In contrast to Habyarimana and the traditional conservatives in the ruling National Revolutionary Movement for Development (MRND), they were both open to ideas and moderate in their discourse. I saw them as true democrats who believed in popular choice. Their hatred for the repressive regime that had controlled power since 1973 was unambiguous.

Despite their distrust of the Habyarimana regime, the prime minister, the foreign minister, and other opposition political leaders were not enamored of the RPF rebels either. The various opposition parties were refreshingly multiethnic, with Tutsi intellectuals holding important positions. Nevertheless, everyone saw the RPF as separate from other Tutsi oppositionists. Besides the RPF's Ugandan coloration, many among the Hutu opposition regarded the RPF as a throwback to the old days of Tutsi feudalism. For them, the RPF was less a force for democratization and more a threat of renewed traditional minority rule. I also sensed a fear of RPF "Tutsi Supermen" who would certainly put one over on them in negotiations. Thus the prime minister and foreign minister were almost as negative about negotiations with the RPF as was Habyarimana.

I spent considerable time with Foreign Minister Ngulinzira, arguing the case for negotiations. The RPF would not be going away, I said, and massive military expenditures were destroying the economy. A negotiated settlement, in the context of democratization, was imperative. He argued back that the RPF had posed unacceptable preconditions to negotiations, including the establishment of an interim regime without Habyarimana. He agreed with Habyarimana that the RPF should first go back to Uganda, with a promise that the refugee issue would be addressed as part of the political transition within Rwanda.

I recommended to Ngulinzira a negotiating framework that had worked well in other situations such as Angola, Mozambique, and Ethiopia. First, negotiations should be without any preconditions. We would reject any RPF efforts to impose them. Second, a negotiated settlement should be a complete package. No single element of agreement could be implemented unless all elements were implemented. With those ground rules, I argued, it would be impossible for the RPF to blackmail the government into paying a price for negotiations, or to employ salami tactics, pocketing one small concession after another until they won at the bargaining table what they could not win on the battlefield. The foreign minister told me he liked the proposal and would think about it seriously. I left Kigali without a promise of negotiations but felt confident that negotiations were inevitable.

On 24 May, Foreign Minister Ngulinzira went to Kampala to meet RPF representatives to explore possible negotiations. The French government then offered to host talks in Paris. The Rwandan government and the RPF held a preliminary meeting in Paris on 6 June and agreed to meet again in July to begin "comprehensive peace talks." That same day, the Rwandans devalued the currency 15 per cent to replenish state coffers drained by military spending.

Shortly after the first Paris negotiating session, my French counterpart, Henri Dijoud, director of African affairs at the Foreign Ministry, suggested that I join him in Paris for a discussion of Rwanda with the Ugandan Foreign Minister, Paul Ssemmogere, who was scheduled to be in France 19–20 June. Stating that the RPF had introduced unacceptable preconditions to negotiations, Dijoud suggested that joint French–American pressure on the Ugandans was needed to advance the negotiations. We agreed that continued military and logistical support to the RPF gave the Ugandans considerable leverage.

Dijoud, Ssemmogere, and I met at the Foreign Ministry Conference Center on the Avenue Kléber in Paris in the late afternoon of Saturday, 20 June. It was the last meeting after two days of French–Ugandan bilateral talks. Since Rwanda was the subject, Ssemmogere was accompanied by Ugandan military officers, most of whom looked typically Rwandan to me.

I opened with a frontal attack, telling Ssemmogere that the RPF's negotiating preconditions were unreasonable, especially their demand that Habyarimana step down in favor of an interim regime. Because Ugandan logistical support for the RPF was crucial, the Ugandans could do more to exercise leverage over the RPF to force the pace of negotiations. The continuing insurgency was not without cost. The United States and the donor community were devoting considerable resources to the care of hundreds of thousands of displaced Rwandans. Uganda was the recipient of major bilateral aid. If the Rwandan negotiations did not move forward soon, it might be necessary to finance continued assistance to the internally displaced by reducing assistance to Uganda.[7]

My statement to Ssemmogere both surprised and pleased Dijoud. He knew we did not agree with French views on the Ugandan nature of the Rwandan problem but saw it as a Rwandan problem first and foremost, with Uganda an important external player. Dijoud was therefore delighted that I had taken a tough line.

Under the close scrutiny of his military colleagues, Ssemmogere adhered to his script without flinching. His government, he said, continued to deny involvement with the RPF invasion and had no special leverage over the RPF. If the United States had evidence to the contrary, they would be glad to receive it. Nevertheless, he wanted to make clear that the Rwandan issue was handled not by the Foreign Ministry but by the Presidency. He would transmit my demarche faithfully. In other words, he knew that we knew, but it was out of his hands.

Official negotiations began in Arusha, Tanzania, on 12 July 1992 under the official auspices of the Organization of African Unity and Tanzanian President Ali Hassan Mwinyi. Later studies of the process leading to talks in 1991–92 generally gave credit to French and American diplomacy for "pushing" the conflicting parties to negotiations.[8]

The Arusha process: negotiating in Fantasyland

The Arusha peace talks began in July 1992 and ended with the signing of a comprehensive agreement on the future of Rwanda on 4 August 1993. The successive negotiating sessions were identified by number (Arusha I, Arusha II, and so on), and were chaired by Tanzanian diplomats. To police the cease-fire, the Organization of African Unity provided a monitoring force of 40 African military officers known as the Neutral Military Observer Group (NMOG). A Joint Political-Military Commission (JPMC) was formed to hold parallel discussions about military dispositions concurrently with the political negotiations. In the State Department, we were particularly pleased with the NMOG deployment because it marked the first involvement of the OAU in peace-keeping without UN support.

Between June and December 1992, it became clear that the talks were three-sided rather than two-sided. Foreign Minister Ngulinzira, a leader of the opposition MDR Party, led the Rwandan government delegation. He found himself negotiating on two fronts at the same time. On the one hand, he confronted a highly disciplined RPF, determined to achieve the right of return for all Rwandan refugees and to revamp the political system to guarantee that persecution of the Tutsi minority would never happen again. On the other hand, he had to negotiate with President Habyarimana and the MRND power structure, which controlled the army, as to the political-military bargains he would be allowed to strike with the enemy RPF. As a result of this somewhat unstable negotiating atmosphere, the RPF was able to exploit divisions on the government side to dominate the negotiations to a far greater extent than the military balance on the ground warranted, thereby setting the stage for eventual disaster.

Ngulinzira clearly wanted peace. But as a leader of opposition forces facing a transition from dictatorship to multiparty democracy, he wanted above all to forge a system that would allow the Rwandan people to remove a corrupt regime dominated by a minority of Hutu clans from Rwanda's northwestern corner. While claiming to embody Hutu majority rule, the regime was in reality a subregional family mafia. The RPF leaders understood the three-sided nature of the Arusha process – with the peace talks between the government and the RPF insurgents overlapping democratization negotiations between the regime and its opponents – and effectively undercut Habyarimana's position in the negotiations by making an alliance with his Hutu political opposition.

The US role in Arusha was secondary to that of the Tanzanian facilitators and other interested parties such as the OAU, the French, and the Ugandans. We encouraged the process and had a diplomatic observer there for every session, at first Ambassador Flaten. But as it became clear the negotiations would be lengthy, we preferred to keep Flaten in Kigali, where he could influence the regime, and assign someone else to observer duty.

Our official representative in Arusha, David Rawson, was a senior Foreign Service officer with extensive experience in Rwanda. He had been desk officer for Rwanda and Burundi during 1970–74 and subsequently served in Kigali as a political officer. He spoke fluent Kinyarwanda, learned as a child in a missionary family in Burundi. Rawson was effective with the protagonists in the corridors, steering them toward realistic negotiating positions. He also provided crucial reports to Ambassador Flaten in Kigali, who used the information in his dialogue with the regime. Rawson was also authorized to call in US military experts to assist in working out cease-fire problems and troop disposition issues. Thus, although our official participation in the negotiations was secondary, our influence was significant.

At the end of Arusha II (10–17 August), the prospects for success appeared fairly high. The session concluded with a protocol pledging to build a government of national unity based on respect for the rule of law, political pluralism, and human rights. From that point on, however, the divisions between the government's negotiating team and the regime's power structure began to appear, unsurprisingly because the negotiations had begun to address the future of political and military power in Rwanda. At Arusha III (7–18 September) and Arusha IV (6–31 October), Ngulinzira clearly was negotiating without authority or agreement from Kigali and the regime power structure. His dialogue with the military rulers had hardly begun.

Meanwhile, at Arusha the unofficial alliance between the RPF and the opposition forces representing the government were making mincemeat of future presidential powers. Ngulinzira and the RPF were outdoing each other in finding ways to reduce the powers of the presidency during a transition to multiparty elections. They agreed that the transitional coalition cabinet, which would include the RPF, would have full power to make major decisions and that all agreements reached at Arusha would take precedence over the Constitution and laws then in existence. On 31 October, they signed a protocol making the president a figurehead, with all executive powers vested in a Council of Ministers comprising all parties, including the RPF. One-third of the Council of Ministers could block all government actions, effectively giving the RPF a veto.

Needless to say, the protocols of Arusha did not arouse joy in the hearts of the ruling MRND. While talks were going on in Tanzania, ominous events were taking place in Rwanda. Anti-Tutsi violence in Kibuye Prefecture in August caused 300 deaths. A Hutu supremacist party called the Committee for the Defense of the Revolution (CDR) appeared and demanded a place at the table. Violent demonstrations became the CDR's hallmark. Like other ethnic-based extremist parties, the CDR created armed militias, the *Interahamwe* and *Impuzamuambi*. These groups received overt help from the Presidential Guard and were justified as "village defense," helping to defend the country against the RPF.[9]

On 15 November 1992, President Habyarimana made a public statement describing the Arusha protocols as "mere pieces of paper." He told Ambassador Flaten privately that the government negotiators had exceeded their authority. This marked the beginning of internal negotiations between Habyarimana and his negotiating team. The major sticking point was the composition of a transitional government and the distribution of cabinet posts among the various parties. Church mediators were called in. They proposed an equal division of cabinet posts among all the political parties, including the ruling MRND, which would have only three portfolios out of twenty. Although no agreement had been reached by the end of December, Ngulinzira insisted on returning to Arusha anyway.

If the agreements on the composition of a future transitional government made the Habyarimana power structure unhappy, RPF demands on the future of the military were guaranteed to push the regime into a state of total paranoia. While they understood the need to integrate RPF military units into a new army of national reconciliation, they were willing to offer them only 20 per cent of the new structure, pursuant to the Tutsi share of the population. The RPF, however, found such an arrangement to be incompatible with their security obsession. They demanded major concessions: a 40 per cent share of the army, a 50–50 share of the officer positions, the right to station a 600-man armed unit in Kigali to protect RPF political leaders during the transition, and the demobilization of 20 000 Rwandan army troops. Such an arrangement could give the Tutsis an equal role in the power structure: Their position of equality in the military would effectively neutralize Hutu majority political power.

All this was happening against a backdrop of increased hatred and violence perpetrated by government-sponsored extremists. In addition to the CDR party and its various armed militias, a so-called private radio station, *Radio Libre Mille Collines*, went on the air with the explicit mission to stir up ethnic hatred.

Extensive anti-Tutsi violence in the countryside at the end of 1992–beginning of 1993 led the RPF in February 1993 to break the cease-fire by retaliating against government military positions. That operation was so successful that it demonstrated how well the RPF had used the cease-fire time to build and train their forces. Their military success further emboldened the RPF to make political and military negotiating demands far beyond what the Tutsi community had a right to expect under majority rule.

The departure of the Bush administration in January 1993 led to a change of leadership in the Bureau of African Affairs. I was replaced as assistant secretary by Ambassador George Moose, a career Foreign Service officer with extensive African experience. Moose continued the policy toward Rwanda of encouraging the Arusha peace process, democratization in Rwanda, and a return to normal economic reform programs. The final Arusha agreement of 4 August 1993 effectively accorded the RPF all of its major demands.

Difficult as it was to negotiate the Arusha accords given the disarray within the government, implementing them was even more difficult. While the RPF and the oppositionists in the regime were trying to establish the interim government called for in the protocols, the true power structure in the MRND delayed as much as possible as they prepared to unleash the holocaust planned for 4 April 1994, in effect using the Arusha process as a cover for genocide.

During the tough negotiations in the second half of 1992, I was deeply involved in other crises, with little time to devote to Rwanda. On the surface, Rwanda seemed on the right track. In the pattern of conflict intervention we had developed since 1989, the most difficult step usually involved persuading parties to negotiate. Arusha was so well organized and making so much progress that we virtually took its eventual success for granted. Much tougher issues like the breakdown of the peace process in Angola and starvation in Somalia absorbed our attention.

Despite my minimal focus on Rwanda in late 1992, I took special notice of the Arusha decision allowing the RPF to control a 600-man armed unit in the city of Kigali during the transition. That RPF unit was not to be part of a new unified army but a discrete force that would protect RPF politicians participating in the interim regime. I remember thinking this a bad idea, although one could understand the RPF's need to protect its leaders. Considering how much the Hutu regime had demonized the Tutsis since 1963, the presence of 600 armed RPF in the middle of Kigali could not fail to strike fear in Hutu hearts, thus making them highly vulnerable to ethnic demagoguery.

As I left office in April 1993, my analysis of the Rwanda conundrum was less concerned about possible extremist action by the Hutu-dominated regime than by a slow and insidious return of minority Tutsi control, in a throwback to preindependence days. I was mesmerized by the skillful way the RPF was manipulating the Hutu opposition in Arusha. Thinking in terms of the Arusha agreement moving forward, I did not consider a nonimplementation scenario.

Did we try hard enough to prevent genocide?

In the confusion surrounding the genocide of April–June 1994, the RPF army conquered Rwanda. The Tutsis were indeed in control again – at a totally unacceptable cost in human lives, destruction, and gigantic refugee flows. For this critical study of US intervention during the Bush administration, we must ask: could the United States have done more to anticipate and prevent the genocide through better analysis and diplomatic advocacy during the period October 1990 to January 1993?

It is dangerous to play the retrospective analysis game to determine who was responsible for the genocide in Rwanda. Any attempt to establish how the ambiance for genocide was created could be interpreted as retrospective "justification" for that gigantic criminal action. It cannot be correct in any sense for an analyst to say the genocide was "caused" by the RPF invasion, or "triggered" by the overwhelming humiliation of the MRND power structure in the Arusha agreement. The Tutsis did not bring the genocide upon themselves.

A small group of politicians, military officers, and Hutu racists formulated and implemented the genocide. They decided to play the extreme version of the ethnic card to retain their power and wealth. The RPF invasion, as well as the humiliating terms of the Arusha accords, made it psychologically easier for the criminals to play the ethnic card; but the card might conceivably have been played anyway to stave off the inevitable pressures for democratization from within the Hutu majority. The following analysis of the US diplomatic intervention should therefore not be seen as establishing an "objective justification" for the genocide in any way, shape, or form.

Even superpowers must think before they leap

Looking back to the first day of the crisis, 1 October 1990, why did we automatically exclude the policy option of informing Ugandan President Museveni that the invasion of Rwanda by uniformed members of the Ugandan Army was totally unacceptable, and that the continuation of good relations between the United States and Uganda would depend on his getting the RPF back across the border? That the RPF were children of the Tutsi refugees of 1959–63 who were forbidden to return gave the event a certain romantic poignancy. Had we analyzed the potential for disaster, however, we probably would not have silently acquiesced in the invasion. The fact that tens of thousands of Rwandans immediately became internally displaced as the RPF advanced should have served as a warning. Rwandans, including Tutsis, clearly did not view the RPF as liberators.

At the time, the international donor community favored Uganda under Museveni's leadership because of its successful economic reforms, its substantial economic growth, and its revival of Ugandan society after the disastrous years of Idi Amin and Milton Obote. We had no desire to challenge Museveni over Rwanda and thus quietly looked for other avenues of conflict management.

Although we joined the French in 1992 in "pushing" the two sides in Rwanda to enter into formal negotiations, we should first have joined the French in 1990 in designating the invasion as an act of aggression by Uganda. France's ridiculous attempt to make it an anglophone–francophone dispute should not have deterred us. To balance the diplomatic pressure on Uganda to call the RPF back, we should have demanded that Habyarimana immediately remove the prohibition on the return of refugees, work with the UNHCR to organize repatriation for those who desired it, and speed up the process of political liberalization.

Instead of selecting these options, we engaged in "rote diplomacy," calling routinely for a cease-fire and negotiations. The Rwanda crisis taught us that this option can sometimes do more harm than good.

Pushing a flawed negotiation

On my visit to Rwanda on 10 May 1992, I saw graphic evidence that Rwanda's internal situation was, to say the least, extremly agitated. Was it wise for us to push them into a negotiation with the RPF at that point? The military situation was stabilized, with the French forces blocking an RPF breakout.

We could more constructively have offered initially to mediate between the regime and the opposition to help formulate a democratic political transition. Under RPF pressure, the internal negotiation might have moved quickly. If that had been accomplished first, the actual negotiation with the RPF could have been more realistic and more likely to succeed than the Arusha fantasy exercise. To "succeed" meant establishing a political and military transition less threatening to the power structure and thus less susceptible to ethnic hysteria.

In the end, the Arusha negotiation had an "empty chair," and the absent Habyarimana clique did not feel bound by the results. We were foolhardy to believe it could have been otherwise. But in our mindset, negotiations are inherently beneficial, so we liked Arusha.

Relations with the French: a missed opportunity

Much of the postmortem analysis of the Rwanda genocide treats the French unkindly. As principal arms and military training suppliers to the Rwandan Army (the FAR), France has been directly and indirectly linked to the mass killings. While I believe the French guilty of mistakes of judgment, I do not agree they were "accomplices" to the genocide.

France had the same military cooperation agreements with Rwanda as with most other French-speaking African countries. In 1990, moreover, many Western governments, including Germany, Switzerland, Belgium, and the United States, were assisting Rwanda. Like other African authoritarian regimes, the Rwandan government had a good track record for economic management with moderate foreign policies. In short, we were all helping the Habyarimana government. French military assistance was not out of the ordinary.[10]

Immediately after the RPF invasion, the French exhibited their "Fashoda syndrome" in foolish knee-jerk fashion, accusing that "Anglo-Saxon agent" Museveni of trying to expand anglophone influence at France's expense. Paris refused to be persuaded that the RPF were indeed the children of permanent Tutsi exiles who wanted above all to return to the land of their forefathers. French troops were dispatched to Kigali to signal the RPF that they would not be permitted to defeat the regime and that negotiations were the only avenue to peace. As allies of Habyarimana, the French wanted to demonstrate loyalty to a friend in need.

Where I fault the French is not that they honored their security commitment to Rwanda in the face of what they considered aggression from Uganda. It was their failure to use their leverage for conflict resolution, or to take notice of genocidal trends festering within the power structure to which they, better than anyone, related. By offering continued loyalty and material support without pressure for political liberalization, the French effectively signaled the Rwandan government they could count on French backing no matter what they did. Although French backing could not knowingly extend to gross human rights violations or genocide, the Rwandans would not have understood that, given the unambiguous support signals coming out of Paris. Instead, the French should have influenced the internal political struggle by pushing Habyarimana toward a moderate position against his own extremists.

Because we were annoyed with the French characterization of the RPF invasion as an Anglo-Saxon plot, we avoided a frank dialogue with them about Rwanda. That was a mistake. We should have worked closely with them to help resolve conflicts among opposing Rwandan political factions. Had we done that, we might have persuaded them to stop supplying arms to the military in the final stages of the crisis.

Obsessing over negotiations and signatures

Conflict intervenors, mediators, and facilitators *like* negotiations, especially those leading to signed agreements. Sometimes, negotiations and signatures become an end in themselves. This appeared to be the case in the Arusha process.

Because Arusha was an African show and the United States was on the periphery, we wanted to keep a low profile, intervening only when we had some value to add as a superpower. Accordingly, we contributed to the decision to negotiate and to the negotiation process itself. But seen with 20–20 hindsight, we were clearly negligent in not doing the same type of analytical preparations that proved so useful in such conflicts as Angola, Ethiopia, and Mozambique. If we had, we might have reached vastly different conclusions. Would those conclusions have helped the international community prevent the genocide? That question is unanswerable. As the Arusha process unfolded, however, it inadvertently guaranteed the genocide.[11]

Angola and Ethiopia as Soviet clients. They viewed US military assistance to anticommunist insurgencies in Afghanistan and Angola as models for other potential efforts elsewhere.

During 1987, DOD and CIA argued for similar US recognition and support for the RENAMO insurgency. They argued that RENAMO was the Mozambican equivalent of UNITA in Angola, anticommunists fighting for legitimacy against a repressive Marxist regime within the Soviet ideological orbit.[2]

In addition, some analysts, mainly in the Defense Intelligence Agency, argued that RENAMO was then on an upward trajectory in the war. The Mozambican Army (FAM) was unable to defeat RENAMO, which had nighttime control of much of central Mozambique. RENAMO could mount guerrilla attacks anywhere in the country with impunity, including the outskirts of Maputo, the capital. It commanded strong tribal support in central Mozambique, these analysts claimed, among the Ndau, the Macua, and the Shona ethnic groups, who had never had decent relations with any central authority. The FRELIMO regime, furthermore, had made the terrible mistake of persecuting traditional tribal authorities, judging them feudal entities incompatible with what they considered "scientific socialism." The government, it was thus argued, was demoralized and weak.[3]

On the basis of this analysis, both the CIA and DOD believed that RENAMO was "the wave of the future," and the United States should catch the train before it left the station. Conservative groups outside government supported this view, as did some politicized evangelical church groups particularly concerned about FRELIMO's persecution of organized religion in its early years. A "Mozambican Information Office" was housed in the same Washington building as the ultraconservative Heritage Foundation and served as RENAMO's US propaganda base.

The State Department disputed this favorable view of RENAMO. They argued that the intelligence services of the white minority regimes of Southern Rhodesia and South Africa had created RENAMO to keep Mozambique destabilized and skittish about supporting nationalist guerrillas engaged in cross-border warfare. South Africa also sought to substantiate its argument that it was surrounded by Marxist regimes that were part of the Soviet "total onslaught" strategy to conquer southern Africa.[4] Vigorously supporting State's anti-RENAMO view were liberal US political groups, which deemed illegitimate by definition any African movement receiving support from *apartheid* South Africa, including UNITA in Angola. Ironically, State's analysis of RENAMO later proved erroneous. Only when we rectified it were we able to contribute to the peace process.[5]

During 1987, Defense Secretary Caspar Weinberger joined the RENAMO issue, urging President Reagan to support the Mozambican rebels. As Reagan's principal advisor on Africa at the time, I tended to accept State's view that RENAMO's origins in Rhodesian and South African intelligence made it suspect, although I agreed with DOD that the movement had a real base of tribal support in some areas. More important, Assistant Secretary of State for Africa Chester Crocker already had enough political problems from strong liberal opposition to US support for UNITA in Angola. I did not think he needed additional obstacles to his efforts to negotiate Namibian independence and the withdrawal of South African and Cuban forces from Angola.

My bureaucratic tactic in 1987 was to avoid confronting DOD on the Mozambique issue, because it would have been unwise to take on Weinberger directly. He wielded considerable clout on national security issues, especially on causes espoused by conservatives. Instead, I stirred up anxiety among conservative supporters of UNITA in the White House and the Congress, declaring continued US support for UNITA our first priority. In its uphill battle to force the MPLA regime to negotiate a transition to democracy, UNITA faced 30000 Cuban troops and an Angolan army fully equipped and trained by Soviet advisors. We should not dilute this support within the Democratic-controlled Congress by opening up a dialogue with a group as controversial as RENAMO. We had to keep our priorities straight.

At the same time, the FRELIMO regime was clearly in the midst of significant change. The harsh Marxism and scientific socialism of 1975–85 were eroding in favor of political liberalization and market economics. Unlike Angola, Mozambique's regime did not depend on the Soviet bloc for its security, and its legitimacy was unambiguous from its origins in 1975. It had always enjoyed full international recognition, including that of the United States, which maintained a full embassy and USAID mission in Maputo. In view of Mozambique's favorable evolution, it would have been most unwise, in my view, to make FRELIMO a target of the Reagan Doctrine.

Political conservatives maintained pro-RENAMO pressure fairly steadily during the last two years of the Reagan administration, but not enough to force the issue to resolution at high levels. One of the rare briefings I was asked to give President Reagan on an African subject concerned RENAMO (apart from routine briefings, he received an hour-long briefing prior to visits by African heads of state).[6]

The president said he received many letters from his friends in Orange County, California, urging him to recognize RENAMO's anti-communist credentials. He asked my opinion as to why he should not listen to his friends. I explained that RENAMO was totally dependent on South African military support and had gotten its start with the indispensable assistance of the white-minority Rhodesian regime, defunct since 1980. We lacked substantial evidence of a popular RENAMO base within Mozambique, in contrast to Angola, where the popular UNITA was led by his good friend Jonas Savimbi.[7]

I reminded President Reagan of the good rapport he had developed with the late Mozambican president, Samora Machel, who had been in the process of liberalizing his country's political and economic systems when he died in an airplane accident in 1986. I explained that Machel's successor, Joaquim Chissano, was continuing the attempts to move Mozambique toward a market economy. In addition, no Cuban troops were stationed in Mozambique to defend "Marxism," as they were in Angola.

President Reagan said he had heard good things about Chissano from his daughter Maureen, who had visited Mozambique. He also expressed regret at the death of Samora Machel, with whom he'd had good personal chemistry. He was inclined, therefore, to tell his friends in California that the United States would not support RENAMO, provided that the Chissano government continued to move away from "Marxism" and showed willingness to start a peace process.

The president's reaction to my briefing was comforting in that he was unwilling to be rushed into applying his famous "doctrine" to a country just because of a "Marxist" label. He was also telling me, however, that he needed breathing space vis-à-vis his conservative supporters' enthusiasm for RENAMO. The most effective way to give him that breathing space, I believed, was to persuade President Chissano to accept negotiations aimed at transforming RENAMO from a guerrilla army into a political competitor.

That would not be easy. The more the State Department described RENAMO as a bunch of terrorists supported by South Africa with no Mozambican political base, the less Chissano was likely to give RENAMO legitimacy by negotiating with it. In Chissano's view, the RENAMO "bandits" would go away when *apartheid* was defeated in South Africa. Negotiations with the puppets of white South Africa were therefore not on.

Promoting negotiations: the hardest part of the process

Despite the Samora Machel–Ronald Reagan friendship, and despite Maureen Reagan's good feelings toward him, President Chissano had good reason to be leery of the conservative Republican administration in 1987. When Samora Machel paid a call on President Reagan in the fall of 1985, Chissano had accompanied him as Mozambique's foreign minister.

What Chissano had found during his private meetings in 1985 was not very comforting. NSC and DOD officials had bluntly informed him that they considered RENAMO the wave of the future and that it was only a matter of time before RENAMO received US recognition. Friendlier discourse from the State Department could only partially assuage his concerns.[8] Hence, US diplomacy had an uphill battle to persuade Chissano that the United States would be supportive if he accepted a negotiating strategy to end Mozambique's civil war.

To satisfy President Reagan's desire to see FRELIMO–RENAMO negotiations begin, we decided to jump-start the process by bringing Chissano to Washington for an official visit and exposing him to Reagan's charm. Assistant Secretary Crocker, his principal deputy Charles Freeman, my deputy at the NSC Alison Rosenberg, and I worked out the details. Together, we succeeded in getting Chissano invited for an official working visit on 7 October 1987.[9]

RENAMO topped the agenda for the Reagan–Chissano meeting. To make sure that Chissano understood our priorities, Chester Crocker briefed him beforehand on what Reagan would say. He urged Chissano to be forthcoming about the principle of opening a dialogue with RENAMO, who were, after all, Mozambicans and not men from Mars. Crocker argued forcefully that the international community could not be expected to make RENAMO disappear, nor should Chissano count on an early demise of *apartheid* in South Africa. Crocker also explained the need to help Reagan resist conservative pro-RENAMO pressure.

Chissano understood the scenario perfectly. He reacted positively to Reagan's forceful presentation, as he had promised Crocker he would, and agreed that a military solution was not possible. Dialogue was therefore the only way to go. He thought this should be possible, if RENAMO would accept constitutional government and recognize the legitimacy of the existing government. He promised to look for ways to open a dialogue. Listening to this conversation, I had the impression that Chissano was exploiting Reagan's strong arguments against the hard-liners in his own entourage who adamantly opposed talks with RENAMO. In any event, a seed for future negotiations had been planted.[10]

Unfortunately, on the ground in Mozambique very little happened to fulfill Chissano's promise for the rest of the Reagan administration.

The announcement of an unconditional amnesty for RENAMO fighters willing to lay down their arms was offset by Chissano's statement that "negotiating with murderers is out of the question."[11]

Throughout 1989, diplomatic activity mainly concerned negotiations about negotiations. How to initiate a dialogue was the key question. With positive changes discernible in South Africa under F. W. de Klerk's leadership, Chissano and FRELIMO found it difficult to reject the idea of dialogue. Everyone was doing it. People who talked to the Mozambicans all urged talks.[12] Slowly that year, trusted interlocutors began to appear. For the government, the Community of Sant'Egidio, an Italian Catholic lay order, became a nonthreatening link to RENAMO. For the insurgents, the Kenyan government, especially President Daniel arap Moi and his confidant, Permanent Secretary for Foreign Affairs Bethuel Kiplagat, provided advice and logistics.[13]

The United States played no substantive role in the 1989 prenegotiations. Consulted by Sant'Egidio early on, we encouraged their active role, and offered support when needed. However, the one missing ingredient for us was contact with RENAMO. We had quite correctly avoided any recognition of RENAMO as a legitimate political force in Mozambique during the Reagan administration to avoid jeopardizing the negotiations for Namibian independence. At the beginning of the Bush administration, however, as I was preparing to take over the Africa Bureau from Chester Crocker, I thought it made no sense for us to encourage Chissano to have a dialogue with RENAMO while refusing to talk to them ourselves. In any event, the tactical reason for refusing contacts with RENAMO had evaporated with the signing of the Namibian independence agreement.

During my Senate confirmation hearings in April 1989, conservative senator Jesse Helms was determined to extract a commitment to a dialogue with RENAMO. I was reluctant to make such a commitment without working the issue through the policy formulation process. However, I was mindful of Secretary Baker's prior instruction that I do as much as possible to keep Helms happy, or at least to avoid irritating him.[14]

During the question and answer phase of the hearing, Helms kept boring in on the RENAMO issue. "I'm not asking you to give military or financial assistance to RENAMO. All I am asking is that you talk to them. What's wrong with that?" After parrying the question two or three times, I decided to give Helms satisfaction. I replied, "Senator, if it will help the cause of peace in Mozambique, I will talk to anyone." Helms broke into a broad grin, gave me a thumbs-up sign, and walked out of the hearing in triumph. A few days later I was told that Baker was not amused that I had made policy during a confirmation hearing. But I am sure he was happy that Helms was happy.[15]

Although we played virtually no role in the prenegotiations during 1989, we followed them closely via our embassies in Maputo, Nairobi, Pretoria, and Rome, where contacts with Sant'Egidio were maintained by our embassy to the Holy See (the Vatican). We were pleased that Chissano had begun to talk about negotiations, but we were not happy with his preconditions. In effect, he was saying that the only issue for discussion was how RENAMO could be integrated into the existing one-party state under the existing constitution. Chissano was effectively telling RENAMO that after the end of fighting, nothing would change politically. The FRELIMO state remained the only legitimate entity, and RENAMO could take it or leave it. It was the earlier amnesty proposal warmed over, and there was no way RENAMO could accept a precondition that amounted to surrender. There was no justification for a RENAMO surrender since they had not been defeated.

Chissano was not just being stubborn. His negotiating policy had to be seen in the context of internal politics. In the liberalizing economic system, Marxist economics was giving way to the market. The ruling FRELIMO party was split on this issue, and Chissano had to maneuver carefully between liberalizers and hard-liners. Had he fully embraced realistic negotiations, he would certainly have faced internal opposition.

As negotiations on the basis of Chissano's preconditions were a non-starter, we invited him back to Washington to meet with President Bush on 12 March 1990. Bush spoke frankly, explaining that it was unrealistic to expect negotiations to take place under the announced preconditions. He urged Chissano to open talks without preconditions. Whatever Chissano thought of RENAMO, they were Mozambicans, and they had not been defeated. For our part, we would do everything possible to persuade South Africa's new president F. W. de Klerk to help make RENAMO more flexible by stopping assistance to the insurgents.

Chissano put up absolutely no resistance to Bush's recommendation, promising to enter into direct negotiations with no preconditions. That experience persuaded me that Chissano had known the proper course of action all along, but needed to have his close associates in FRELIMO feel pressure directly from the US president before accepting the inevitable. To make us even happier, Chissano allowed us to announce the "no preconditions" policy to the press.[16]

With both Reagan and Bush, Chissano in effect exploited the power of the US presidency to persuade his own hard-line colleagues in

FRELIMO that the international community would not solve the RENAMO problem for them. It was not just an issue of giving legitimacy to RENAMO by negotiating with them. That was bad enough. But negotiations with no preconditions meant that the one-party state under which FRELIMO held a constitutional monopoly of power had to be on the table, thus dooming it to replacement by a multiparty system. The FRELIMO elites must have found that perspective hard to swallow. Although another two years of tough bargaining remained after the Bush–Chissano meeting, the collaboration of two American presidents in helping Chissano break the political logjam in Mozambique probably constituted the principal US contribution to this particular peace process.[17]

Superpower support of the negotiations

The Mozambican protagonists began their serious negotiations in July 1990 in Rome, under the auspices of the lay Community of Sant'Egidio. The Italian government provided considerable assistance, including the hotel and living expenses of the negotiators, communications, and technical assistance. Mario Raffaelli, a Socialist member of parliament with significant African experience, was named chief mediator to the negotiation. Assisting the RENAMO delegates was Bethuel Kiplagat of Kenya, who kept in the background but was always available to provide advice and counsel. The negotiations lasted twenty-seven months, until President Chissano and RENAMO President Dhlakama signed a final cease-fire and settlement for a political transition on 4 October 1992 in Rome.[18]

The Mozambique negotiations began at approximately the same time as the Angolan talks but lasted seventeen months longer. The collapse of the Angolan peace process and return to war began on the very day the Mozambique agreement was signed (see Chapter 2). Implementation of the Mozambique agreement by the two parties, with the critical assistance of the United Nations, benefited from lessons learned during the Angolan implementation, thereby avoiding the tragedy suffered by Angola of a peace process gone wrong. In addition, because the Mozambique negotiations were considerably slower than Angola's, the negotiating process also benefited from some of the procedures, ideas, and solutions developed by the mediators in Angola. Lessons and examples from the Angolan peace process constituted a major contribution of the US government, the sole participant in both negotiations. Also significant was the role of the diplomatic corps in Maputo, which worked well together, followed the negotiations closely, and applied appropriate pressure as needed to the government and RENAMO.

While the United States did not play a high-profile leadership role in the Mozambique talks, we did provide important support. In the Bureau of African Affairs, this effort was coordinated by Jeffrey Davidow, my principal deputy assistant secretary, highly able alter ego, and supervisor of all southern African activities. During 1991–92, Davidow was extremely busy as our point man in Angola and Mozambique. He was particularly creative in finding support for the negotiating and implementation processes in both countries, making sure that the right technical people were deployed on a timely basis.

Cajoling and persuading

The mediators, the protagonists, and other interested parties constantly called upon the United States to intervene to break logjams by persuading one side or the other to be more reasonable or less fearful of bringing a particular subject to closure. We initiated contacts with RENAMO in Nairobi during the first half of 1990 and thereafter accorded them high-level treatment through our two deputy chiefs of mission at the US Embassy to the Holy See, James Creagan and his successor Cameron Hume, who arrived in January 1991. Jeff Davidow and I met with RENAMO's chief negotiator, Raul Domingos, whenever we stopped in Rome. I thus fulfilled my promise to Senator Helms.

With the Mozambican government, our major problem of persuasion concerned its sovereignty. With RENAMO the issue was legitimacy. Had it been possible, the government would have rejected all outside involvement in drawing up and implementing agreements. They were obsessed with sovereignty. We spent much time persuading them to accept outside involvement, to give RENAMO confidence. For their part, the RENAMO insurgents were obsessed with denying the government's legitimacy and kept insisting that Mozambican politics revert to square one, as if independence had just taken place. If the FRELIMO regime lacked any legitimate base, as RENAMO claimed, then political negotiations had to start from ground zero. Our burden was to persuade RENAMO's president Afonso Dhlakama and negotiator Raul Domingos that FRELIMO was a fact of life, had full recognition in the international community, and could not be asked to commit suicide, especially since RENAMO had not defeated it on the battlefield.

The issue of RENAMO's legitimacy as a Mozambican political force did not arise with President Chissano and his FRELIMO colleagues for a rather interesting reason. They could not believe that RENAMO had any political base and persuaded themselves that once South African support stopped, RENAMO would sink into oblivion. During my two visits with Chissano in Maputo, in 1988 and 1992, he spent a considerable amount of time telling me how incompetent Dhlakama and his top lieutenants were. "Dhlakama was just a low-ranking sergeant in the Mozambican Army," Chissano told me. How could a person like that aspire to high political office? Ironically, that sincerely held opinion of RENAMO kept Chissano confident about multiparty elections, making the political side of the negotiations that much easier. Needless to say, we did not try to dissuade him. He must have been shocked in 1994, therefore, when RENAMO won 35 percent of the parliamentary vote.

Between July 1990 and October 1992, Davidow made several trips to Angola in support of the 1991 Bicesse agreement. En route, he usually stopped in Rome to confer with Sant'Egidio, the negotiating protagonists, and the Italian Foreign Ministry. During every one of these stopovers, he was able to advance the negotiations by making cogent suggestions and by encouraging tough decisions. Davidow's intimate involvement in the implementation of the Angolan agreement enabled him to exploit its demonstration effect. Until the Angolan peace process broke down in October 1992, the various military and electoral dispositions in those accords afforded both positive and negative examples for Mozambique.

Although far less often than Davidow, I also visited Sant'Egidio in Rome several times. In April 1992, I met in Lilongwe, Malawi, with RENAMO President Dhlakama, primarily to persuade him to cooperate with humanitarian agencies for the distribution of famine relief.[19] Although I found him relaxed and self-confident, I could not persuade him to accord any degree of legitimacy to Chissano and his government. Dhlakama was negotiating with those "atheistic, corrupt dictators" only because of international pressure. He was highly suspicious about famine relief, fearing that as routes were opened, FRELIMO troops would be ready to pounce from behind every relief convoy. The only proposal he could accept was for talks with the International Committee of the Red Cross (ICRC) on a case-by-case basis.

Overall, the visits of senior US officials traveling from Washington and the day-to-day involvement of our embassy to the Holy See generated confidence in the process, based on the tacit moral guarantee that only a superpower like the United States could provide.

Stroking important interested parties

A number of important players in the search for peace in Mozambique, though not directly involved in the negotiations, nevertheless wielded a certain amount of influence, for better or for worse. Jeff Davidow and I, and our ambassadors in the field, spent a considerable amount of time trying to keep those players aware of developments and doing what they could to support the Rome talks.

Kenya – As mentor to Afonso Dhlakama, Kenya's president Daniel arap Moi took a keen interest in his welfare. Their friendship had roots in Protestant networks in which Bethuel Kiplagat was active. Thus, whenever possible I tried to enlist Moi as a source of positive influence over Dhlakama. During the Namibian independence celebrations in Windhoek in March 1990, for example, I called on Moi and we talked mainly about Mozambique. When I told him RENAMO had acquired a reputation as the Khmer Rouge of Africa, he said rather curiously, "How can people say Dhlakama is so evil when he goes around his territory giving out Bibles?" During the twenty-seven months of negotiations, Moi and Kiplagat did a credible job of guiding Dhlakama, thereby helping to avert the disaster that overtook Angola.

Zimbabwe – Mozambique's landlocked western neighbor had a clear stake in its civil war. To retain a minimum of economic autonomy from *apartheid* South Africa, Zimbabwe depended on the railway, hard-surface road, and pipeline to the central Mozambican coast at Beira. Because RENAMO was able to attack at will within Mozambique's Beira corridor, Zimbabwe had to maintain an expeditionary force of 7000 troops there to defend its vital transportation interests. This was an extremely expensive undertaking, in both budgetary and human terms. In addition, eastern Zimbabwe regularly suffered cross-border attacks by RENAMO terrorists, who killed civilians and stole food and livestock. The war also drove large numbers of Mozambican refugees into Zimbabwe.

Zimbabwe wanted the war to end as soon as possible, and it wanted the FRELIMO regime to prevail over RENAMO, which after all was the "puppet of *apartheid* South Africa." Furthermore, Zimbabwe owed a debt of gratitude to FRELIMO for its unstinting support for Zimbabwe's liberation struggle, which had ended in victory for majority rule in 1980.

Mozambique figured prominently in US diplomacy toward Zimbabwe. First, we kept in close contact to encourage their continued involvement militarily, despite the high cost, and despite our inability to assist them. Secondly, we did as much as we could to persuade the Zimbabweans to become involved in conflict resolution. The key to our approach was the Shona and Ndau tribal affiliations between

RENAMO's President Dhlakama and the Zimbabwe political leadership. Dhlakama and Zimbabwe's president Robert Mugabe were from the same extended ethnic family. In our regular dialogue with Mugabe and his key national security advisors, we emphasized the importance of his opening a dialogue with Dhlakama.

By the second half of 1991, the situation in South Africa had advanced sufficiently toward the demise of *apartheid* that President Mugabe could feel comfortable dealing with the war in Mozambique as a discrete subject. In late 1991 he was telling us that Dhlakama was a "real Mozambican" who had fought against Portuguese colonialism and deserved to have a role in deciding Mozambique's future. In January 1992, Mugabe decided to meet with Dhlakama to advance the peace process. Later, a cease-fire between RENAMO and Zimbabwe constituted the first confidence-building step in the overall peace process.

Despite his initial reluctance, Mugabe played a key role in inducing RENAMO to engage in serious negotiations, a role I believe we helped persuade him to take on. While the war and negotiations continued, in the background was the major southern African drought of 1991–92. America's rapid, massive, and effective humanitarian assistance gave us additional status and access. In the end, Mugabe's decision to revise his view of RENAMO from that of "armed bandit puppets of *apartheid*" to "Mozambican patriots" was vital to the negotiating process.[20]

Portugal – Mozambique understandably interested Portugal. The large Portuguese community in Mozambique departed in a state of panic and anger in 1975 during the independence handover. Unlike Angola, where the ruling MPLA regime was essentially installed by the short-lived Portuguese military junta of 1974, the FRELIMO regime took power as conquerors. Departing with bitterness, the Portuguese did everything to make governing difficult for FRELIMO, including deliberately destroying utilities, infrastructure, and enterprises. FRELIMO reciprocated by taking over abandoned Portuguese properties. Worse still, according to reliable reports, former Portuguese residents were financing RENAMO from their new bases of operation in Portugal, Brazil, and South Africa.

One thing I found striking in many visits to Lisbon was the intense interest of ordinary Portuguese citizens in Africa. The continent was high politics in Portugal, as demonstrated during Secretary Baker's one-hour bilateral meeting with Prime Minister Anibal Cavaco Silva in Lisbon on 31 May 1991 (on the occasion of the Angolan peace accords' signing). Baker expected the main subject to be the Azores base facility. But Cavaco Silva's priority was Mozambique. As Angola receded from the limelight, he did not want to miss the mainstream of activity in Portuguese-speaking Africa. Consequently, he spent over half the meeting persuading Baker to assume a higher profile in Mozambique and bring Portugal along as a participant.

Since Mozambique was neither a candidate for US–Soviet cooperation nor a major domestic issue, Baker was unenthusiastic about our becoming more deeply involved. Nevertheless, he found it expedient to offer US assistance because he had brought bad news on the Azores. The United States would henceforth stop paying Portugal, no longer poor, a subsidy for our use of Lajes Air Base. Thus, gaining acceptance of Portugal as an observer became one of our objectives in the Mozambique negotiations, accomplished when the talks opened to observers in 1992. We had had to persuade the reluctant Italians, though, who correctly saw the Portuguese as wanting to steal their show.

The Vatican – Because our official representative to the Rome negotiations was the deputy chief of mission at the US Embassy to the Holy See, our ambassador, Thomas Melady, wanted us to maintain close liaison on Mozambique with the Vatican Foreign Ministry. This was good, because the Vatican had much wisdom to share. Beyond its humanitarian concerns, the Vatican was troubled by the mass confiscation of Church property by FRELIMO during its manic "Marxist" phase between 1975 and 1980. As of 1991, virtually none of the property had been returned.

During my visits to Maputo, I usually met with the papal nuncio. Unable to recoup the seminaries and other confiscated properties, he had absolutely no sympathy for FRELIMO. When I raised this with the government, I was told that they had every intention of returning the properties. But first they must construct other facilities to house the official government boarding schools occupying the buildings. Our regular dialogue with the Vatican, I believe, helped contain the Church's leaning toward overt anti-FRELIMO hostility.

South Africa – The white South Africans had been the major trainers and suppliers of RENAMO. We therefore wanted them to persuade RENAMO to negotiate seriously and to stop supplying them. After de Klerk was elected president in 1989 and initiated negotiations with the ANC for majority rule, the white South Africans gladly agreed to stop arming RENAMO.[21]

The arms supply cutoff, however, meant the loss of South Africa's leverage. Each time we discussed the issue with Foreign Minister Pik Botha, he would say, "Dhlakama doesn't speak to us any more."

Meanwhile, we continued to receive reliable reports of clandestine deliveries to RENAMO through cooperating intelligence officials in Malawi. In addition, we knew that small planes were taking off for destinations within RENAMO-controlled territory from the many small airfields scattered throughout eastern South Africa. Reliable sources also reported continued RENAMO training in South African camps. Even though the small aircraft deliveries might have been completely private operations financed by Portuguese entrepreneurs, they helped prolong the war by making RENAMO less flexible about starting negotiations. Despite considerable effort, after all, we had little impact on white South African behavior in Mozambique. For them, it was a matter of honor not to abandon RENAMO.

Technical assistance

In contrast to the Angola negotiations, the Mozambique talks involved few face-to-face discussions between the protagonists. Mediators shuttling between the negotiating teams drafted most of the agreed texts. The FRELIMO side had the sophistication to determine whether or not the texts met their needs, RENAMO less so. RENAMO's main point of reference was the Angola agreement. Consequently, both RENAMO and the mediators felt more confident having American experts on the scene to help with the technical subjects, both juridical and military.

A great deal of credit for the success of the negotiations, therefore, belongs to such unsung heros as Lt-Col Charles Snyder, on loan to the Bureau of African Affairs from the Pentagon, John Byerly, the State Department's assistant legal advisor for African affairs, and William Jackson and Randall Lecocq, my desk officers for Mozambique. They made frequent trips to Sant'Egidio in Rome to help draft texts and advise the protagonists on what the language did or did not mean. Certainly, US government officials were not the only people able to provide competent technical assistance. Indeed, Italian military also became involved. But having the superpower involved tended to reassure all the players that much more.

Sometimes, not being in charge is an advantage

The final peace agreement was signed in Rome on 4 October 1992.[22] Implementation, which proved even more difficult than the negotiations, occurred mostly after the Bush administration left office. Success was achieved because the parties, both outside and inside, learned from the mistakes made in Angola. A key innovation was having the UN Special Representative act as the tie-breaking chairman of the Joint Political Military Commission established to oversee implementation. In Angola, the UN representative was a mere observer with no power. In Mozambique, the UN representative became the virtual czar of implementation.

In addition, the UN peacekeeping force in Mozambique numbered over 7000, compared with only 500 in Angola. Significantly, the Mozambique implementation was also subjected to strict sequencing. Elections were repeatedly postponed in order to make sure that the disarmament and encampment of fighters were completed first. In Angola, the election date was written in concrete as one of the elements of agreement required by UNITA and could not be postponed, even though disarmament was far from complete.

In the Mozambique negotiations, the American role was far less visible than in Angola. During the Angola negotiations, though officially observers, we were deeply involved on a day-to-day basis. In Mozambique, we were visiting supporters who showed up from time to time when we could be useful. Toward the end, we, Portugal, a number of other governments, and the UN became official observers. At no time was the United States in charge of the negotiations, an advantageous situation preventing the prestige of the United States from being eroded by day-to-day application. The combination of Sant'Egidio mediation and periodic superpower interventions – to put out fires or break a deadlock at strategic moments – worked out very well.

During the fall of 1991, our direct supervisor, Under Secretary Robert Kimmit, became ambassador to Germany and was replaced by Arnold Kantor from the National Security Council staff. During one of our weekly briefing sessions, Jeff Davidow and I told Kantor about our activities in support of the Mozambique negotiations, as well as our intensive work toward implementing the Angolan agreements. He listened carefully and responded with a question: "Apart from doing good, why are we involved in Mozambique anyway?" Stifling our urge to kick him, we explained that the United States was shelling out about $100 million per year in humanitarian relief to Mozambique, money that could be better used for development if the war could end.

Kantor was unconvinced. Seeing no "vital" US interest in Mozambique, he instinctively wanted us to drop out of that game. He so recommended in a memorandum to Deputy Secretary Lawrence Eagleburger. Eagleburger, who never forgot any detail, knew that Baker had made a

8
Somalia: Better Late than Never

Unlike other African countries suffering internal conflicts, Somalia was the only one with "strategic" implications for the United States. The US air and naval facility in the northwestern Somali port town of Berbera formed part of our military network defending the Persian/Arabian Gulf against Soviet aggression. Hence, our Somalia policy was important to the US Central Command (CENTCOM) based in Tampa, Florida. (CENTCOM is responsible for US military operations in the Middle East, the Gulf, and the Horn of Africa. It became well known to the public during the Gulf War against Iraq in 1990–91.) Because of Somalia's strategic position, US diplomacy felt obliged to cultivate close and cordial relations with one of the world's most vicious despots, Mohammed Siad Barre, president of the Somali Democratic Republic.

Siad Barre: our friend the military dictator

Mohammed Siad Barre seized power in a military coup on 21 October 1969. Somalia had previously been a "multiparty democracy," established at independence in 1960. Born of a union of Italian and British colonies, Somalia never developed a sense of nationhood, despite a common language and shared Muslim religion. Above all, these nomadic pastoralists are loyal to their clans and subclans. Somalis also have a warrior tradition linked to competition for scarce water and pasturage in a harsh, unforgiving desert-like climate. In Somalia's first elected government, clan loyalty meant winner-take-all, reducing government to the status of a family business. By 1969, the government had lost the last shred of citizen respect.[1]

Against the background of a corrupt and exclusionary "democratic" regime, Siad Barre's 1969 coup was initially popular.[2] That he overthrew a failed "democracy" also made it easy for him to establish a "one-party democracy," in line with prevailing African practice. He called it the Somali Socialist Democratic Party and adopted scientific socialism as its credo. Needless to say, an African military regime embracing Marxism, and sitting astride the strait of Bab el Mandeb at the back door to the Gulf, immediately attracted the Soviet Union. In addition, Somalia's long, unstable border with Ethiopia, a US ally hosting a US military facility, enhanced its value to the Soviets.

Siad Barre's regime had three main characteristics: an increasing tendency toward extreme harshness and murder to maintain itself in power; a total reliance on family and clan for governance; and an aggressive foreign policy of Somali irredentism. If anything could instill a sense of national solidarity among the Somali clans, it was the idea that all Somalis should live under one flag. Thus the Somali ethnic diaspora of about 350 000 persons living in Ethiopia's Ogaden region, in francophone Djibouti, and in northeastern Kenya were all seen as living in territories that rightfully belonged to Somalia.

The combination of strong irredentism, a warrior tradition, and a military regime enhanced the possibility of war between Somalia and its neighbors. Ethiopia, whose control of the Somali-speaking Ogaden region virtually separates northern from southern Somalia, was the most vulnerable. Conquered by Ethiopian emperors in the nineteenth century, the Ogaden was considered occupied territory. The Somali sense of loss was particularly bitter because the Ethiopian Ogaden had reverted to Somalia when the Italian colonialists briefly ruled Ethiopia from 1936 to 1941. When the British drove the Italians out of Ethiopia during the Second World War, they restored the Ogaden to Ethiopia. Unlike Kenya and Djibouti, Ethiopia did not enjoy the protection of former colonial powers. It was not surprising, therefore, that clashes along the Somali–Ethiopia border were frequent following Somalia's independence and threatened to escalate under Siad Barre.

Given the Cold War's intensity in the early 1970s, the Soviets could not resist the lure of Somalia. They inundated Siad Barre with arms, escalating the possibility of war with Ethiopia. The United States remained strongly supportive of the pro-West emperor of Ethiopia, who allowed us to maintain a communications station in Asmara that served our military and diplomatic needs in Africa and the Middle East. In return, we provided substantial economic and military assistance. The air force F-5 fighter jet program for Ethiopia was one of our most successful anywhere.

In 1974, in a watershed event, Ethiopian officers staged a successful coup against their emperor. Within a year, Marxists with a Stalinist bent were clearly in control, under strongman Colonel Mengistu Haile Mariam. Their dominant sentiments were strongly anti-American and pro-Soviet. Internally the regime duplicated the worst aspects of the Soviet system, including nationalizations, collectivization of agriculture, mass killings of "feudal reactionaries," and the incarceration of thousands of political enemies.

The Marxist coup made Ethiopia ripe for Soviet picking. With Soviet influence strongly entrenched in Somalia and the Americans ejected from their Asmara station, the Soviets quickly established themselves in Ethiopia in the traditional Soviet manner – with massive arms shipments and hundreds of military advisors. Moscow thought it was sitting pretty with two Marxist regimes strategically poised on the Persian Gulf's doorstep.

Unfortunately for the Soviets, they had misread the nature of the Somali regime and its foreign policy. Siad Barre's "Marxism" was just as superficial as his predecessors' "democracy." When the Americans were strong allies of his enemy Ethiopia, he adopted "scientific socialism" to attract Soviet aid. When the Soviets jumped into bed with Ethiopia's new Marxist ruler Mengistu, they fully expected brotherly solidarity between two socialist neighbors. They could not have been more mistaken. Siad Barre saw Soviet friendship with Ethiopia as an adulterous betrayal. His feelings shifted instantaneously from love to hate. In keeping with general African cynicism about the Cold War, Siad Barre decided to fall in love with the United States. Naturally, Washington did not resist, and allegiances were quickly reversed.

Between 1975 and 1979, US interest in Somalia was essentially as a window on the Indian Ocean and the Persian Gulf. It was not considered strategic. In Ethiopia, the Soviets had infiltrated the region's best military establishment, securing naval base rights in the Red Sea Dahlak Islands.

Soviet aggression in Afghanistan in 1979 elevated Somalia into the "strategic" category of US interests in the Middle East, an honor shared by only one other country in the Organization of African Unity, Egypt. As Somalia became strategic, our relations with Siad Barre became important. Here as elsewhere we became closely allied with an unsavory regime in support of our Middle Eastern and Cold War interests. Major economic and military assistance programs soon followed, with overall policy coming under Pentagon influence.

American objectives in Somalia, like those of the Soviets before them, differed from those of the Somali regime, a dissonance that produced constant strain. We wanted strategic base rights, made reliable by subregional stability. The regime wanted military assistance to enhance its internal power and its military capacity to liberate "occupied" Somali territory. From the moment Ethiopia fell into the Soviet orbit, Siad Barre assumed we would be delighted to support his efforts to liberate the Ethiopian Ogaden. Backing local wars, however, was incompatible with our concept of subregional stability.

To maintain our access to Somalia's ports and airfields, we had to keep Siad Barre reasonably happy, which required significant military assistance. But to discourage full-scale war with Ethiopia, we had to limit our military support. As displeased as we were with the nature of the regime in Ethiopia, our Cold War interests in Africa were not so strong as to motivate support for a regional war that would cause massive human suffering. Thus, for sixteen years we walked a tightrope between these mutually exclusive objectives. In addition, we found it increasingly difficult to avert our eyes from Siad's deepening internal repression and human rights violations, as one clan grouping after another slipped into armed opposition.

The Ethiopia–Somalia war and its tragic aftermath

Instability and power struggles among various military and civilian political factions marked the first three years of Ethiopia's revolution (1975–78). Purges and assassinations of military commanders degraded discipline and readiness. Siad Barre knew this and could not resist the temptation to try conquering the Ogaden.

In late 1977, the Somali army invaded and rapidly advanced toward the important Ogadeni Ethiopian towns of Harar and Dire Dawa. This offensive, not feasible using solely the defensive weapons and nonlethal equipment furnished by US military assistance, was powered mainly by large stocks of Soviet arms delivered between 1970 and 1974. So threatening was the Somali advance that the Mengistu regime requested Soviet help. As they had done in Angola in 1975, the Soviets brought in several brigades of Cuban troops, whose massive firepower drove the Somali invaders back across the border.

This defeat marked the end of Somali irredentism as the sole unifying factor in Somali politics. Nothing remained to inhibit the gradual alienation of those clans not included in Siad Barre's corrupt power structure. Severe discrimination against the former British Somaliland in the northwest led to the growth of an anti-Siad guerrilla group called the Somali National Movement (SNM). This group enjoyed safe-haven and logistical support inside Ethiopia for raids into Somalia. Knowing he could not hope to obtain US support for a second invasion of the Ogaden, Siad changed tactics and began to cry wolf. "Give me arms because the Ethiopians are planning to invade Somalia" became his leitmotif throughout the 1980s.[3]

The SNM's low-grade insurgency was followed by several clan uprisings that ended with brutal repression against civilians, which in turn sparked even greater resistance and widening insurgency. Through the mid-1980s, Siad Barre's territorial control gradually diminished as his repression increased. Antiregime insurgencies were also in progress in Ethiopia (see Chapter 2), led by the Eritrean People's Liberation Front (EPLF) and the Tigrean People's Liberation Front (TPLF). Both regimes were slowly being worn down. The Ethiopians had virtually unlimited access to Soviet arms, whereas Siad Barre was essentially limited to defensive weapons, except for what he could afford to purchase. To make matters worse, decreased prices for Somali exports diminished the national economic pie, increasingly reserved for Siad's own family.[4]

In April 1988, the Ethiopian and Somalian governments turned their full-time attention to their respective insurgencies. They saw mutual advantage in ending military tension along their border and signed a treaty of nonaggression and noninterference. The Ethiopians also pledged to close all SNM bases. The treaty, however, resulted in more rather than less warfare for the Siad regime. Rather than lay down their arms and become refugees inside Ethiopia, the SNM launched an all-or-nothing attack on their home area in northwest Somalia. By May 1989, the SNM guerrillas had captured Burao and entered the principal city of Hargeysa. In fierce fighting, the government gained the upper hand using artillery and aerial bombardment, at the cost of almost total destruction of the city.[5] Because most SNM fighters belonged to the Issaq clan, many clan members living in Mogadishu were massacred.

By the start of the Bush administration in early 1989, most of Somalia was under siege. Insurgent clan armies confronted the Siad Barre regime on many fronts.

The Somali state collapses; US strategic interests evaporate

The Somali government in January 1989 was essentially inoperative. Though it continued making ruthless war on its own people and collecting foreign exchange from livestock and banana exports, nothing else functioned.

Strategic interests in the Gulf continued to dominate US policy. Siad Barre's horrendous human rights performance had resulted in congressional suspension of military assistance in 1988. Economic aid, however, continued into 1989, maintaining a material tie to the regime. Despite Somalia's severe internal instability, CENTCOM continued to view the naval/air facility at Berbera as important to the defense of the Gulf. In Tampa, Florida, in late 1989, CENTCOM Commander in Chief General Norman Schwarzkopf pressed me on the need to maintain access to Berbera and, thus, constructive ties to the regime. I told Schwarzkopf that the Congress was losing patience and would probably end economic assistance. Nevertheless, we decided to continue working with Siad.

In 1989 and 1990, no analysts, to my knowledge, predicted the military demise of the Siad Barre regime. We therefore tried to promote internal Somali negotiations on the premise that the clan wars were unwinnable, developing contacts with insurgents wherever we could find them to encourage negotiations. We took the same line with Siad Barre. As of April 1990, the option of seeking the head of state's resignation and departure had been explicitly precluded by higher authority in the case of Liberia. This country-specific decision became Bush administration doctrine for all of Africa.[6]

The Somali National Movement, the best organized of the insurgent groups, maintained active offices in London and Washington. Knowing our interest in Somalia, the SNM assured us that the demise of the Siad Barre regime would not mean the end of our access to Berbera. On the contrary, they valued the facility because it provided employment and foreign exchange to northwest Somalia. In Nairobi, we talked to the United Somali Congress, which was carrying the war to southern and central Somalia.

As of mid-1989, the weakened Siad Barre regime was ready for serious negotiations. The opposition, however, insisted it was too late. Siad had committed too many crimes and had to go. Siad claimed he wanted reconciliation but continued targeting innocent civilians in enemy clans. We were disappointed at the insurgents' negative response but understood, sympathized with, and secretly applauded their sentiments. We also knew instinctively that Siad could not possibly be sincere. So, we decided not to press forward with conflict resolution efforts at that time, hoping for a better opportunity later.[7]

Two threshold events that occurred within months of each other effectively precluded the opportunity to promote peace and reconciliation and totally changed our outlook on Somalia: Iraq's invasion of

Kuwait in August 1990 and Siad Barre's military defeat and exile in January 1991. Within hours of the Iraqi military occupation of Kuwait, the United States asked for military base sites in Kuwait's immediate neighborhood, particularly in next-door Saudi Arabia. The requests were quickly granted, and US military forces were rapidly deployed to Saudi Arabia. Thus, eleven years of US military protection from "over the horizon" evaporated as the threatened countries welcomed US forces on their own territories. Military facilities in east Africa suddenly diminished in importance. African ports and airfields, previously seen as primary staging areas for US force projection, were downgraded to backup contingency facilities.

The Gulf War – "Desert Storm" – changed our strategic view of Somalia virtually overnight. It was too late, in any case, to embark on full-scale conflict resolution. Siad Barre's military situation had deteriorated considerably. His forces controlled only the capital city. We called him "the Mayor of Mogadishu." Despite Italian government entreaties right to the end, we stopped economic assistance in 1990 and reduced our embassy staff as the fighting advanced toward the capital.

On 27 January 1991, Siad fled south in a tank convoy, escaping across the Kenyan border. Preceding his departure, a wave of lawlessness erupted in the capital, overwhelming foreign entities. The large, new, state-of-the-art US Embassy compound, planned when Somalia was designated a strategic country, had to be evacuated *in extremis* the night of 5 January as hundreds of armed thugs stormed over the walls. Fortunately, US combat forces, nearby in the Gulf for Operation Desert Shield, were able to deploy large helicopters and carriers to make the rescue. In addition to the entire American embassy family led by Ambassador James Bishop, American helicopters also evacuated over a hundred diplomats from other embassies.[8]

While most of the expatriates escaped, hundreds of thousands of Somalis in Mogadishu were less fortunate. When the euphoria over Siad's departure wore off, those remaining behind faced a long period of precarious living as the city and southern third of Somalia sank rapidly into a state of violent anarchy.

In Washington, we were overjoyed by the rescue of the embassy staff, as well as the defeat and exile of Siad Barre. As for the rest, the assault on the Embassy by armed looters was the last straw for us with respect to the entire Somali nation. Assuming that the clan system would somehow find a way to bring order out of chaos, with US forces well accommodated directly in the Gulf, and with our embassy closed, we more or less dropped Somalia from our radar screens.

As Ambassador Frank T. Crigler, our chief of mission in Somalia until the summer of 1990, observed: "The United States turned out the lights, closed the door and forgot about the place."[9] Crigler was right, but Somalia had a way of coming back to haunt us.

Southern Somalia's descent into hell

The collapse of Siad Barre and the Somali state in January 1991 preceded the overthrow of the Ethiopian dictatorship by only four months. Subsequent events in the two countries could not have been more strikingly different. In Ethiopia, two well-honed insurgent armies rapidly filled the vacuum left by the ousted Mengistu regime, restoring law and order and government operations with little delay.[10] In Somalia, no obvious replacement for the Siad regime existed. The SNM decided to take power only in its Issaq clan territory in the northwest, the former British Somaliland. That left the remainder of Somalia to be fought over among the other insurgent movements, all linked to specific clans.

The clans' fight against Siad Barre became a fight against each other. There was no sense of nationhood or political tradition that could serve as the basis for a transition from civil war to civil peace. It was every clan for itself, with armed gangs taking advantage of the law-and-order vacuum to terrorize and pillage.[11]

Between January and July 1991, three events set the stage for tragedy in Mogadishu and the southern third of Somalia.

First, the United Somali Congress (USC), the political arm of the Hawiye clan, declared their leader Ali Mahdi, a Mogadishu entrepreneur, "Interim President" of Somalia. The USC military wing, led by General Mohammed Farah Aideed, rejected this self-appointment as "illegitimate." Aideed claimed he was the military commander who did the most to oust Siad Barre and the one who therefore deserved the presidency. Although Mahdi and Aideed were from the same Hawiye clan, their belonging to different subclans made it easier for them to hate each other.

Second, the end of the Ethiopian civil war, and the total collapse of the Ethiopian Army in April–May 1991, unleashed a flood of weapons into regional markets, much of which ended up in the hands of Somali clan militias and bandit gangs, aggravating tensions countrywide.

Third, the Somali National Movement abandoned all pretense of being a nationwide political party and declared an independent state in the former British colony, which they named Somaliland. We did not recognize the new entity, because we had no confidence in any declarations in Somalia.

Neighboring Djibouti generated some optimism by sponsoring two Somali reconciliation conferences, in June and July 1991. Because the conferences looked promising, I sent Deputy Assistant Secretary Irvin Hicks to Djibouti to demonstrate support and visited Djibouti myself shortly after the July conference to do the same. In a press conference, I endorsed the decisions, including Ali Mahdi's designation as interim president. I also pledged US support for the restoration of a Somali governmental structure and reiterated our refusal to recognize Somaliland, despite the Issaq clan's suffering under Siad Barre. Unfortunately, within a few months, our optimism dissipated as the various clan movements repudiated the agreements one after the other.[12]

Between August 1991 and January 1992, lawlessness, looting, and factional fighting spread in Somalia's southern districts. Within Mogadishu itself, an armed struggle for control of the capital city commenced between the two rivals in the United Somali Congress, General Aideed and Ali Mahdi. By mid-November 1991, our embassies in Nairobi and Djibouti, as well as the NGOs and UN personnel working in Somalia, were reporting the situation as out of control. There was no internal mechanism capable of restoring law and order, nor was there any mediating body that could bring the parties into some sort of dialogue.

The most troubling aspect of the growing anarchy was the looming threat of widespread starvation. To stay in business, the armed factions had to generate revenue to pay their fighters. In the general chaos, the main source of income was humanitarian food aid. Much of the armed action was designed to control food, which had effectively become the coin of the realm. Tens of thousands of hungry people were thus denied access to food, because the fighting had also disrupted normal crop production and food market operations. These tens of thousands, especially those living away from the coast, were in danger of mass starvation and severe malnutrition.

At the beginning of 1992, emergency action was needed to restore security in Mogadishu and open internal food supply routes. The international humanitarian relief community had stockpiled plenty of food in Mogadishu port, but moving that food to the needy was becoming virtually impossible. With the airport, seaport, and road network controlled by the clan militias, we concluded that it would require international intervention to feed the hungry, straighten out the chaos, and restore some semblance of normality. From our perspective, that intervention could take place only under UN auspices.

Disaster fatigue envelops the bureaucracy

In the Bureau of African Affairs, we had been so busy with the conflicts in Ethiopia, Angola, Mozambique, Sudan, and Liberia during 1991 that we failed to notice a qualitative change in the international attitude toward failed states like Somalia. We had witnessed the ease and enthusiasm with which the UN Security Council had authorized peacekeeping operations in Namibia and Angola in 1988 and 1991. The United States had been a leading advocate in the Security Council for multilateral solutions to such problems starting in late 1988.[13]

Following the Angolan and Namibian precedents, our strategy was to seize the UN Security Council with the Somali problem and recommend an appropriate peace operation to reopen relief routes and restore governmental authority. It was then, in January 1992, that we discovered the world had changed. The State Department's Bureau of International Organization Affairs (IO) showed little enthusiasm for any kind of UN initiative in Somalia beyond regular humanitarian food relief.

The bureaucracy dealing with multilateral affairs was suffering from "conflict fatigue." When the Somalia crisis exploded, the UN was already running a dozen peacekeeping operations on five continents. The system was saturated. In addition, the UN peacekeeping budget had ballooned, as had the 30 percent US share. Bad timing also afflicted Somalia. In October 1991, the Security Council authorized a $2 billion peace operation in Cambodia, the costliest ever. The United States was no longer willing to "throw the UN" at every Third World crisis. Somalia was out of luck.

When the Africa Bureau (AF) recommended a UN peace operation in Somalia, the IO Bureau bluntly disagreed. AF argued that Somalia was a security crisis. IO countered that Somalia was a food problem. If people were starving in Somalia, the UN's main job was to coordinate the shipment of food assistance, nothing more. AF had only one other ally in the interagency community, Andrew Natsios, the Massachusetts Republican serving as assistant administrator for food and humanitarian assistance in the US Agency for International Development. Speaking through his Office of Foreign Disaster Assistance (OFDA), Natsios was a lone voice supporting AF's contention that Somalia was a security problem.

We were not without friends, however. An important ally in the UN itself was the newly elected secretary-general, Boutros Boutros-Ghali of Egypt. As an African diplomat and expert on the Horn of Africa, he decided to champion the Somalia cause.[14] When he raised the issue in the Security Council in early 1992, the US delegation repeated the same refrain: "Somalia is a food problem, not a security problem." The United States continued to block action for several months despite alarming reports of starvation and mounting evidence that food was not getting through to the hungry.

Boutros-Ghali badgered the Security Council with alarming reports from his field mission in Mogadishu. He also appealed to the collective conscience of the Council and instilled a sense of guilt, reportedly accusing the Council of "fighting a rich man's war in Yugoslavia while not lifting a finger to save Somalia from disintegration."[15]

Additional support for a "security" intervention came from two other sources, the humanitarian relief community and the Cable News Network (CNN). Natsios realized early on that Somalia was a security problem, and he was not the type of person to keep quiet about it. His approach was double-barreled. He gave open testimony to interested congressional committees, and he issued periodic bulletins on the status of humanitarian aid in Somalia.[16] His bulletins pulled no punches. Statements like "50 percent of all Somali children under five have already died of starvation" were typical.

Sharing a common analysis, AF and OFDA cooperated in getting information to the public and encouraging NGOs to speak out. I also testified before congressional committees and met with NGOs.[17] Around March 1992 CNN discovered Somalia and filled the tube almost daily with pictures of starving mothers with dying children.

While Boutros-Ghali assailed the Security Council with alarming news, I badgered the interagency community. I called meetings of the Policy Coordinating Committee on Africa (PCC) and subjected the different agencies to all the alarming reports. This method persuaded the Bureau of Human Rights to join in support for a security operation, but IO, Defense, and the NSC remained unpersuaded.

During the first half of 1992, the budgetary crisis in the peacekeeping accounts and growing "conflict fatigue" effectively drove Somalia policy. Officially, Somalia remained a food problem, not a security problem. But no attempt was made to muzzle government employees like Andrew Natsios and myself from telling the truth about Somalia in public. We were joined by former ambassador to Somalia James Bishop, now deputy assistant secretary for human rights. As early as April 1992, Bishop was advocating military action in Somalia. Our public statements were designed to undermine official policy. The situation was clearly difficult for people in the other bureaus and agencies. They knew the facts as well as we and thus could neither contradict us nor shut us up.

Relentless badgering from Boutros-Ghali, the CNN effect, and a growing public outcry, including shrill congressional mail, persuaded our UN delegation to adopt a more flexible policy beginning in March 1992. Boutros-Ghali was authorized to send a special representative to Somalia, followed by 50 lightly armed Pakistani "cease-fire monitors."

As special representative he chose Mohammed Sahnoun, a highly regarded retired Algerian diplomat who had served as deputy secretary-general of the Organization of African Unity. Sahnoun negotiated a fragile cease-fire between the two principal warring factions, but he could not arrange for deployment of cease-fire monitors beyond the airport, where they were blocked by General Aideed's heavily armed militia. Sahnoun's presence demonstrated that a constructive role for a neutral outsider was possible, but this complex crisis required more than sending 50 military monitors. Unfortunately, Sahnoun and the Pakistanis could do little to alleviate starvation, given their narrow mandate.

Humanitarian outrage defeats bureaucratic resistance

By July 1992, the humanitarian crisis had become so dire that the political levels of the US government could no longer hide behind the stalemated bureaucracy. Shortly after the July Fourth holiday, I called yet another meeting of the African PCC to reassess positions. After listening to Andrew Natsios describe the latest horror stories, I began asking questions. I asked the Joint Chiefs of Staff representative if the military could begin planning for a possible airlift to deliver food to the more isolated towns in the interior. The response was, "We plan for operations like Desert Storm. We do not plan for humanitarian airlifts that can be done more cheaply through civilian charter." I asked the IO representative about the possibility of introducing a resolution in the Security Council authorizing "all necessary means" to break the blockade of food distribution by armed Somali factions. The response was, "We have already been burned by a similar resolution concerning Bosnia. Nobody in the Security Council would support such a resolution covering Somalia."[18]

Outside of the stalemated PCC process, things were happening. The "CNN effect" was escalating. Americans all over the United States were writing their representatives in Congress. Republican Senator Nancy Kassebaum, ranking minority member of the Africa Subcommittee, went to Somalia to see for herself. Upon her return, she and

Subcommittee Chair Paul Simon introduced a resolution calling for the use of armed security guards in Somalia to assure the delivery of food, mountains of which were sitting in the port. The resolution passed both houses of Congress unanimously.[19]

One regular attendee at PCC meetings was Walter Kansteiner, the young Republican director for African affairs on the National Security Council staff. He said little at meetings but reported back to his boss, National Security Advisor Brent Scowcroft. After the July meeting heard Andrew Natsios describe how food could not be moved even a mere two kilometers for delivery to starving Somalis because of armed thugs, we started to get positive signals from above. At a staff meeting in late July, Acting Secretary Eagleburger informed us that President Bush had instructed the State Department to be "forward-leaning" on Somalia.

That rather elliptical presidential directive broke the bureaucratic blockade. At the UN, we supported the secretary-general's proposal to supplement the 50 monitors with 500 armed food security guards. Public pledges were made for massive food deliveries. On 14 August 1992, without any interagency recommendation from the PCC, the White House made several announcements. The Defense Department would launch an emergency food airlift to Somalia. Ambassador Edward Perkins at the UN would begin consultations about "additional measures" to ensure the safe delivery of humanitarian relief. The United States would also be willing to provide military transport to Somalia for UN security forces, and Andrew Natsios was named the President's special representative for Somalia.[20]

Although the White House decision to become activist on Somalia was not based on formal recommendations advanced through the interagency process, we were struck that the president's directives covered the very subjects discussed at the PCC meeting ten days earlier. Thanks to Walt Kansteiner, the pointed questions I had asked agency representatives at that meeting had been answered by the president.

On 18 August, the US Central Command established a joint task force in Mombasa, Kenya, to operate the airlift, code named "Operation Provide Relief."[21] Thus began American leadership in Somalia. That the president acted shortly before the 1992 Republican presidential nominating convention, against a backdrop of increasing demands to do something, did not escape us. We did not question his motives. We welcomed wise decisions from our leaders any way we could get them.

The decision to intervene with force

Military food airlifts look good, show the flag in a dramatic way, and provide needed relief to people in the vicinity of airports. But a single Hercules C-130 sortie delivers only six tons of food. In Somalia, ten sorties a day from Mombasa barely dented the surface of the food problem. What the Somalis needed were a hundred ten-ton trucks per day from the overstuffed food warehouses in the port. While the airlift saved some lives, the armed thugs continued to block vital surface transportation.

Between the beginning of Operation Provide Relief in August and the US presidential election in November, the starvation problem in southern Somalia worsened. The 500 Pakistani security guards, part of the UN Operation in Somalia (UNOSOM), arrived only in September, delayed by the slow pace of negotiations with faction leader Aideed on their deployment. Even after their arrival, they were bottled up at the airport by the more heavily armed factions. A Security Council authorization on 28 August to increase the security force from 500 to 3500 could not be implemented.

In early November, an international consensus concluded that starvation in southern Somalia could be relieved only through armed intervention. Negotiating with the faction leaders, or "warlords," had proven useless. Even during his final months in office, after losing the election to Bill Clinton, President Bush maintained a lively interest in Somalia and requested an updated analysis with recommendations.

In the State Department, the Africa Bureau found willing allies in Under Secretary for International Security Affairs Frank Wisner and Assistant Secretary for Political-Military Affairs Robert Gallucci. Both had high-level contacts in the Pentagon and could tailor recommendations accordingly. In addition, Wisner had been the US ambassador in Egypt for five years and was on first-name terms with Boutros-Ghali.

Wisner began an immediate dialogue with Boutros-Ghali, who saw the Somalia crisis as a major challenge to the multilateral system. He also saw Somalia as an opportunity. A UN success in Somalia, he was sure, would solidly entrench the UN's international security function in world opinion. Unlike Bosnia, Cambodia, or Angola, Somalia had no ideological or political factors. It was purely humanitarian.

Boutros-Ghali proposed to Wisner that the UN peacekeeping mechanism mount a major armed intervention under Chapter VII of the UN Charter, with authorization to use force if necessary to assure food deliveries. US troops would not be part of the intervening contingent but would provide airlift and other logistical support. Boutros-Ghali had two reasons for excluding US troops. First, American political allergy to putting US military units in harm's way could cause the operation to be stillborn. Second, he saw the proposed Somalia intervention as an opportunity for enhanced UN leadership, which a US military presence on the ground would undoubtedly dilute.

Having gone through most of 1992 listening to JCS and DOD negativism about intervention in Somalia, the Africa Bureau considered Boutros-Ghali's proposal eminently reasonable. We therefore prepared the paperwork for the crucial 23 November meeting of the NSC Deputies Committee, highlighting his proposal as the lead option.

Admiral Jonathan Howe, deputy national security advisor, chaired the meeting. Under Secretary Frank Wisner represented the State Department, with me as his backup. The Defense Department sent Under Secretary Paul Wolfowitz, with Deputy Assistant Secretary for African Affairs James Woods as his backup. The Joint Chiefs of Staff sent Admiral David Jeremiah, the four-star deputy to Chairman Colin Powell.

The committee easily reached consensus on the need for a threat of force to turn the situation around in Somalia. After some discussion, it selected three options:

A. Expand the existing UNOSOM force to 3500 or more, provide heavier arms and equipment, and authorize lethal force as necessary.
B. Field a robust multinational force of 15 000 or more troops under UN command, with heavy arms and authority to use force. The United States would provide logistic support, as well as a rapid reaction force, with helicopter gunships on boats offshore to deal with emergencies.
C. Create a UN operation consisting mainly of American troops, with the United States in command, under a UN Chapter VII mandate.[22]

Howe called a follow-up meeting a few days later to see if the Deputies Committee could firmly recommend one option. When he was President Nixon's secretary of state, Henry Kissinger used to say that the bureaucracy always comes up with three options and that option B is always preferred. The Africa Bureau followed that formula, firmly believing that the middle option was best. We favored a robust operation without US forces on the ground. At this meeting three-star General Barry McCaffrey represented the JCS, replacing Admiral Jeremiah, who was unable to attend.

The general discussion revealed an overall preference for Option B. But McCaffrey made a totally unexpected statement. He said the UN would require at least six months of preparation before its intervention could begin. With Somalis dying of starvation at the rate of 5000 a week, a six-month delay was unconscionable. Only the US military had the capability to deploy the necessary forces in a matter of weeks. In what appeared to be something of an afterthought, McCaffrey said the JCS was not recommending Option C but merely making a statement of what was feasible and what was not.[23] After that bombshell, however, Option C had instantly become Bush's preferred choice.

Outside the White House Situation Room after the meeting, Frank Wisner and I looked at each other with a mixture of disbelief and euphoria. We speculated on why Chairman Colin Powell had authorized the JCS statement. Knowing him as I did from our two years together on the NSC staff during the Reagan administration, I concluded that he believed in the humanitarian objective of the proposed intervention and correctly expected the operation to be carried out with minimal casualties. I saw it as militarily a "piece of cake," provided sufficient force and muscle were applied. Some cynics thought perhaps the JCS were willing to go to Somalia "so they won't have to go to Bosnia."

The president accepted the JCS nonrecommendation, triggering a frenzy of meetings and activities about implementation. As the outgoing president, George Bush did not want to create a major burden for his successor Bill Clinton, although the president-elect endorsed the decision.[24] Accordingly, Bush called for the operation to be completed by 20 January 1993. He soon realized this deadline was unrealistic and modified his instructions to limit the operation to six months, with follow-on responsibility to be transferred to the UN.

Having devoted his annual speech to the UN General Assembly in October 1992 to the importance of multilateral peacekeeping and peacemaking,[25] Bush wanted the intervention in Somalia to bear a UN imprimatur, with an operation mandated by a UN Security Council Resolution. He ordered us to make every effort to persuade other governments to send troops to Somalia and to pledge their participation in the subsequent UN operation.

In meetings to plan the intervention, we always emphasized implementing the president's instruction to end the starvation and get out. There was little discussion of "nation-building" or reviving the various levels of government of a collapsed state. That would be part of the UN follow-on operation. On the other hand, the bureaucracy had no illusions. We knew that an international presence would be required for a lengthy period. We used terms like "limited trusteeship" to describe the patient, long-term effort needed to revive the Somali state.

During the many meetings of the Deputies Committee, I tried to inject two key points. One was the combative nature of the Somali nomadic tradition. I summed it up by saying, "We shouldn't forget that Somalis love to fight." Second, I insisted on the importance of coping with the totally intransigent Mohammed Farah Aideed. In Aideed's view, there was only one option. He had to be the head of state. He did not care how many Somalis would have to die to achieve that objective. I sincerely believed that if Aideed had not been on the scene, the Somalis might have reestablished a semblance of government with the help of Djibouti and other neighbors. At one deputies meeting, in response to my statements, Admiral Howe asked, "Do you mean that we will have to clean Aideed's clock?" I said yes. But the meeting quickly proceeded to other matters. Cleaning Aideed's clock was not part of our mandate.

Policy meetings included little discussion about cost and virtually none about a congressional strategy. At the Deputies Committee, a senior official of the Office of Management and Budget was usually present. After the president made his final decision to intervene in Somalia, a few minutes were devoted to cost. We knew that the US troop deployment would be between 28 000 and 32 000. Cost estimates of $500 million were bandied about. At one point, Admiral Howe turned to the OMB representative and asked how the operation would be financed. The response came: "We'll have to add it to the arrears." That was shorthand for unforeseen spending on special operations, requiring an eventual request to the Congress for supplemental funding.

The beginning of implementation

The first order of business after President Bush's decision was to negotiate the terms of reference for the operation with Boutros-Ghali. Secretary Eagleburger personally took on the task. After several meetings, they reached agreement on the following framework:

- The operation would be US-led under an enabling resolution of the Security Council pursuant to Chapter VII of the UN Charter. This phase of the operation was designated United Nations Interim Task Force (UNITAF).
- US forces would remain for a maximum of six months, during which time the UN would prepare to take over in Somalia with a regular peace enforcement operation called UNOSOM II.

- Every effort would be made to recruit other countries to contribute troops to join the Americans. Volunteer forces would be required for both the American phase of the operation and the UN phase to follow. The UN would recruit for both operations simultaneously.
- A special UN voluntary fund would be established to finance the participation of Third World contingents. This fund was the vehicle for bringing in Japanese and Saudi money.
- After the UN took over, most of the US forces would depart, but a 2500-man special US intervention force would remain on ships offshore ready to be helicoptered to hot spots for special rescue missions. Boutros-Ghali considered a US protective umbrella necessary to attract volunteer contingents for UNOSOM II.
- The sole US mission would be to break the hunger cycle. All necessary means were to be used to open distribution channels for the thousands of tons of food sitting in warehouses in Mogadishu harbor. The United States would not get involved in reconstituting the political system, disarmament, or encampment of militias. In short, its mandate was humanitarian and nothing more.

The ink was hardly dry on the Eagleburger–Boutros-Ghali agreement when a disagreement emerged over interpretation. Looking forward to May or June 1993, when UNOSOM II was scheduled to replace UNITAF, Boutros-Ghali understandably did not want his UN contingents facing the same heavily armed factions that his hapless Pakistanis faced in mid-1992. Consequently, he wanted the militias disarmed and expected the Americans to do that as part of their mission to open food distribution channels. Boutros-Ghali also knew that the ultimate objective was to reconstitute the Somali government, with all of its geographic components intact. He therefore wanted troops deployed throughout the country, not just in the southern famine zones.

Eagleburger quickly disabused Boutros-Ghali of these ideas. Certainly, force would be used if necessary to remove obstructions to food distribution, and UNITAF forces would defend themselves vigorously if threatened. But the mission would be peaceful if the Somalis cooperated. Eagleburger further asserted that the US troops' mission of ending starvation did not warrant their deployment outside the southern famine zones.

The Africa Bureau spent December 1992 coordinating a worldwide effort to attract volunteer contingents for UNITAF. It did not prove difficult. Eighteen countries, including Botswana and Nigeria in Africa, volunteered troops. I also undertook a special mission to countries in the Horn of Africa to ensure their cooperation for our use of their air and marine facilities. Here again, we found complete support in Djibouti, Eritrea, Ethiopia, and Kenya.

Under Secretary Frank Wisner supervised the diplomatic side of the operation, using the Africa Bureau as the main implementer and the Bureau of Political-Military Affairs (PM) as the main channel to the US military. Wisner persuaded retired US ambassador Robert Oakley to head up the civilian side of the US mission in Mogadishu. Oakley, who had served in Somalia as ambassador in the 1980s, had extensive experience in trouble spots. He asked his former deputy chief of mission in Mogadishu, John Hirsch, to give up his important assignment as consul general in Johannesburg to join him in Mogadishu as his number two. Hirsch did not have to be asked twice.

When the Bush administration left office at the end of January 1993, the Somalia operation was unfolding as planned. The main objective had been achieved. Within a matter of three to four weeks, the hunger cycle had been broken. Food and other commodities were moving normally to affected areas. Moreover, in March, Somali farmers in the southern twin rivers region took advantage of UNITAF's protection to harvest normal crops, thereby reducing the need for foreign food aid. Oakley carried out his mandate to the letter, making friends with all factions and encouraging reconciliation. His only concession to Boutros-Ghali was to ask the faction leaders to park their heavy weapons in secure areas under UNITAF supervision. But there was no attempt to disarm the militias.

Events after UNOSOM II replaced UNITAF in May–June 1993 have been analyzed at length by scholars and practitioners. Following the incident in October 1993 when sixteen American soldiers were ambushed and killed by General Aideed's faction, the entire Somalia intervention came to be described as a "disaster" for both the United States and the UN.

To those of us who had begun worrying about Somalia in late 1991, the results were far from disastrous. The saving of tens, possibly hundreds, of thousands of lives made the entire operation worthwhile, despite the enormous financial costs and the tragic loss of American lives in an unnecessary special operation. Even after the UN removed its last military contingents in 1994, the country did not revert to the widespread pillaging, raping, and killing that had ravaged the southern third of the country before the intervention. While Somalia remained without a central government as of late 1999, and conflict continued between factions in Mogadishu, the overall situation was significantly better than it had been toward the end of 1991.

Should we have treated Somalia as a special case?

Although it is inaccurate for journalists, scholars, and practitioners to categorize the Somalia intervention as a failure of conflict management, the US approach to conflict in Somalia in the Bush administration suggests some instructive lessons.

It has become almost a truism to say that early rather than late intervention in conflict is invariably less costly and more likely to succeed. This is especially true when early intervention prevents normal political conflict from degenerating into violence.

The most appropriate time for the United States to begin conflict management in Somalia would have been mid-1988. At that time, however, the leadership of the Bureau of African Affairs and the National Security Council Staff had thoughts only for the complex negotiations on Namibian independence. Despite the war then being waged by Siad Barre against the Somali people in northwestern Somalia, the problem was not considered particularly important to the United States. We continued to have access to the port and airfield at Berbera, and the Somali people were "naturally warlike," so why panic?

Between 1989 and 1991, we noted Somalia's internal wars and worried about them, but the Berbera strategic overhang made our approach much too timid. We offered to help the Somalis with negotiations, as we did with the other conflicts. When Siad Barre accepted but the Somali National Movement and other opposition groups refused, we backed off. Ethiopia and Angola, after all, were yielding better results. The pincer movement of General Schwarzkopf in Florida and the Italian government in Rome kept us diplomatically tied to support for Siad Barre, come what may, even though we had to hold our noses.

Alternative options in 1989–91 were to recruit other interested governments to exert pressure on the Somali opposition to negotiate, or to persuade the Italians and other friends of Siad Barre to ask him to step down to make way for a democratically elected regime. While it is far from certain that either of these approaches would have borne fruit, in retrospect they probably would have been better than our passive approach, which was the diplomatic equivalent of whistling past the graveyard.

Even if those hypothetical scenarios had not borne fruit, we might have ended with a more advantageous situation than what eventually ensued. It was rather naive of both ourselves and CENTCOM to believe that the facility at Berbera could remain available and usable as the internal situation in Somalia steadily deteriorated. On the contrary, our policy in 1989–91 guaranteed that we would both lose the use of the facility and eventually pay a much stiffer price in humanitarian costs than might otherwise have been the case. It was truly a "lose–lose" policy.

9
Superpower in Africa: Mediator or Meddler?

During the four years of the Bush presidency, US diplomatic interventions in seven civil wars engaged the Africa Bureau's full energies. If the administration had opted to do nothing about conflict in Africa, it would have incurred virtually no domestic political cost. Although its desire to cooperate with the Soviets compelled attention to Angola and Ethiopia, and pressure from the hunger lobby required us to deal with the Sudan, none of these cases obliged us to plunge so deeply into conflict resolution. Except for major investments in Angolan oil, the United States, after all, had few interests in these countries.

In the Bureau of African Affairs we decided to pursue conflict resolution without requesting policy approval from on high. Thus, some questions arise from our experiences:

- Was it worth the effort?
- Was the United States the right government to intervene?
- What does the experience demonstrate about the role of the US superpower as a third-party intervenor in Africa?
- Can a "bureaucratic handbook" for third-party conflict intervenors be written from our experience?

Intangible but real: the US moral influence

The United States has an image in Africa unmatched by any other country, notwithstanding the dominant French role in francophone countries.[1] As the sole remaining superpower, the United States exercises exceptional influence in Africa, particularly in conflict situations where frightened protagonists need psychological bolstering. In the seven internal conflicts I have described, one or both sides welcomed US involvement because of the perception that only the United States could provide the appropriate moral guarantees. Its capacity to project physical force, either by itself or through the United Nations, also exerted psychological pressure.[2]

Every case revealed the strength of US influence. In Angola in mid-1990, Portuguese mediation had made little headway until US intercession, with Soviet assistance, led to a quick breakthrough. When the United States began to mediate Ethiopia's Eritrean war in August 1990, the discussions promptly moved from procedural issues to substance. An unexpected consequence of this intervention was the collapse of the Ethiopian military, which anticipated an early end to the war once the Americans arrived. In Mozambique, the astute President Joaquim Chissano exploited the American presidency to convince his political allies that negotiations with RENAMO were the only viable option.

In actual negotiations, the influence of American experts was often crucial in breaking deadlocks and in injecting fresh ideas. This was especially true of the American military, who did such outstanding work in forging agreements in Angola, Mozambique, and Rwanda.

Even in cases like the Sudan where we were unable to move the parties toward negotiated settlements, some ideas introduced by the Bush administration Africa Bureau continued afterwards to animate ongoing discussions. In mid-1996 and again in 1999, for example, informal negotiations in the Sudan centered on US proposals advanced in 1990 for military disengagement in the south.

Perhaps the most felicitous result of our activism was the decision by the Organization of African Unity in 1993 to take responsibility for conflict prevention, management, and resolution in its own continent. Before that time, the OAU considered civil conflict untouchable because of the doctrine of noninterference in internal affairs, a doctrine rendered untenable by American leadership in the Namibia–Angola mediation.[3]

Conversely, US timidity and caution can have a negative impact, as in the case of Liberia, where our low profile probably contributed to the prolongation of that harsh civil war. While we were not responsible for the evil perpetrated by ethnic entrepreneurs and warlords in Liberia, one can argue that the war would have ended earlier if we had invoked the historical US–Liberia relationship to bring the parties to their senses.

Many Africans feel strongly, and quite correctly, that the United Nations must continue to be actively involved in conflict management in their continent. Africa has neither the resources nor the logistics to project military power when it is needed, although its ability to use diplomacy in conflict management has improved steadily since 1993.

Yet, US leadership in the UN Security Council remains crucial in determining how and when the international community will become engaged. The excruciatingly slow UN entry into the Rwanda genocide crisis during May–August 1994 was attributable mainly to US delaying tactics.

As these cases reveal, US efforts at conflict resolution in Africa during the Bush administration produced mixed results. How much of the success, and how much of the failure, can be attributed to US actions is difficult to assess. Some will argue that civil conflicts have their own life cycles and end, one way or another, upon reaching maturity. Acting as midwives at the moment peace seems ready to emerge may be the best third-party intervenors can do. As these cases demonstrate, nonetheless, US initiatives in Africa between 1989 and 1993 did make a difference.

Overall, our main contribution to African conflict resolution lay in encouraging disputants to think beyond questions of legitimacy, retribution, and power. This newly created ambience stimulated a trend toward democratization and good governance, which we preached as the main foundations of conflict prevention. Our efforts' most important impact was, perhaps, that by early 1993 the Africans themselves increasingly viewed conflict resolution and democratic political transition as high priorities.

Some lessons learned

Our involvement with African conflict during the Bush administration was not a one-term phenomenon. It had begun in the Reagan administration with negotiations leading to the independence of Namibia and continued into the first Clinton administration (1993–97), which made major efforts in Liberia, Burundi, and Sierra Leone. In addition, the Clinton administration has been the leader among donor governments in supporting the OAU conflict management mechanism established in 1993. The special US role in this area has, in effect, become bipartisan policy.

Though each conflict may have its own "personality" and require custom-tailored approaches, our experiences taught us some generally applicable premises.

1. Decision-making and willpower at the working level can make a difference

As assistant secretary, I was able to stretch the policy envelope to the maximum in addressing African conflict. In the Bush Africa Bureau, we pursued an activist approach, with considerable support from our embassies in Africa and extensive personal diplomacy on my part. We also worked to coopt other national security agencies. Had we chosen a passive policy, higher political levels probably would not even have noticed, much less criticized us. We did not justify our activist approach as "vital to US national security interests", but we did demonstrate that our methods were inexpensive and without negative side effects.

Our policy masters understood this approach, had confidence in our judgment, and let us do our thing. While the Bush–Baker team saw our approach as one of opportunity, another set of leaders might have rejected it as a "slippery slope" leading to expensive commitments. We were fortunate in our political leadership.

2. The network of US embassies in Africa and Europe is a vital element in an activist approach

Our efforts in Angola, Ethiopia, the Sudan, and Liberia benefited from information supplied, and actions taken, by US embassies in neighboring countries. Thanks to our embassy in Khartoum, for example, our knowledge of and relations with the Ethiopian and Eritrean insurgents greatly strengthened our contribution to peace in 1991. Diplomacy by our ambassadors in Gabon, Congo-Brazzaville, Zaire, and Cape Verde paved the way for Angolan negotiations in 1989. Information on the UNITA insurgents from our embassy in Kinshasa proved invaluable for the Angola peace process.

Extending the information network to embassies in western Europe, especially London, Paris, Brussels, Lisbon, Geneva, and the Vatican, also proved fruitful. London was a center for information on the Sudan, Somalia, and Ethiopia. Lisbon was a crossroads for Angolan politicking. The UN agencies and international private groups in Geneva provided valuable information and insights about African civil wars. Moreover, in the absence of sensitive US interests in these conflicts, there was no need to impose heavy secrecy on our activities.

3. Coopting the US national security community is essential

We used the national security coordinating system extensively to preempt opposition from other agencies and, more important, to solicit their advice and support. This approach was especially fruitful with respect to Defense, CIA, the NSC, USIA, and USAID. In Somalia, for example, between January and October 1992 we worked closely with AID's Office of Foreign Disaster Assistance to publicize starvation.

During implementation of the Angolan peace accords between June 1991 and September 1992, Defense, AID, and USIA contributed innovative and low-cost solutions to key problems.

4. Starting early is better than starting late

In Somalia we anticipated a severe crisis after the regime's destruction of rebellious Hargeysa in the northwest as early as 1988. But we were inhibited from getting tough with the regime by our requirement to maintain access to the naval and air facility at Berbera, a back door to the Persian Gulf. When we finally did intervene militarily in December 1992, the cost was steep, and we lost use of the facility anyway. Exerting "tough love" with friends at an early stage of conflict is the preferred way to prevent tragedy.

5. Talk to everybody

When the United States talks to insurgent groups, they gain instant legitimacy, a delicate move because we also need to maintain reasonable relations with the regime. Our posture in the seven conflicts was to talk to everyone and not worry about hurt sensibilities. In Mozambique we began a dialogue with RENAMO, snubbed by our predecessors, and thereby hastened the onset of negotiations. Two Sudanese regimes objected to our dialogue with the SPLA rebels in the south, but privately used our channel to send them messages. Our dialogue with the Ethiopian insurgents was crucial to our tactical analysis in the final days of the war.

6. Bring in the multilaterals early

If the United Nations is to implement an agreement, it should be in on the takeoff as well as the landing. We were wrong in the Angola negotiations to include UN peacekeeping and election monitoring as part of the implementation process without requesting UN experts to counsel the negotiators. They would have told the two Angolan parties to the agreement how inadequate and unworkable the arrangements would turn out to be. The same mistake was avoided in Mozambique through UN involvement in the negotiations.

7. Beware of signature obsession

Diplomatic mediators without a direct stake in the outcome are sometimes more interested in the signing of an agreement than in its substance, which can be inadequate and unworkable. The seriously flawed agreements in Angola and Rwanda demonstrated this truth. In Angola, the severe problem of sequencing should have been predictable. The Arusha agreement on Rwanda was a model on paper but had one problem: The real Rwandan power structure – the people with the guns in the army and the militias – were not part of the process. Mediators and observers should denounce such Potemkin agreements even if the protagonists are ready to sign. Frequently, such flawed agreements signal that the peace process is just another aspect of war for some protagonists, a resting and regrouping period between battles rather than a peaceful new beginning. Such was clearly the case in Angola, Ethiopia, Liberia and Rwanda.

Cross-border assistance to rebels

Internal rebellion cannot normally sustain itself without an external source of supply and safe havens for rest and medical treatment. Governments faced with the challenge of insurgency usually have easy access to weapons and logistics in international markets. As our case studies demonstrate, insurgents cannot function without the active collaboration of neighboring governments.

- The UNITA insurgents in Angola received assistance through South African–controlled Namibia and, from the United States, via neighboring Zaire.
- The RENAMO insurgents in Mozambique received arms from South Africa directly across the border or via neighboring Malawi.
- The Rwandan Patriotic Front (RPF) invaded Rwanda using bases and equipment in Uganda.
- The National Patriotic Front of Liberia (NPFL) insurgents received arms from Burkina Faso that transited cooperative Côte d'Ivoire.
- The Eritrean and Tigrean insurgents in Ethiopia received arms through supply corridors established in neighboring Sudan.
- The Sudanese Peoples Liberation Army (SPLA) received arms mainly from the Mengistu regime in neighboring Ethiopia but also from Uganda and Kenya.

As third-party intervenors, we observed this phenomenon with mixed feelings. Where we sympathized with the insurgents, as in the Sudan, Ethiopia, and Angola, we found it difficult to criticize the external suppliers, especially when we were among them. Where we found the insurgents repugnant, as in Mozambique and Liberia, it was easier for us to denounce the suppliers and try to embarrass them into stopping.

The Organization of African Unity, meanwhile, has never seriously discussed cross-border assistance to rebels, the ultimate interference in a neighbor's internal affairs. It remains a "dirty little secret," viewed as a given in civil wars.

We witnessed two types of insurgencies in Africa. In the first type, rebellions organized, equipped, and trained from the outside begin with an armed incursion from a neighboring country. The stated goal is invariably to topple a "repressive" regime and install a "democratic" replacement. The Liberian and Rwandan insurgents were quite vocal in making such claims.

In the second category insurgencies begin internally. Disgruntled, fed-up groups, whether armed by internal or external sources, unleash a cycle of guerrilla violence against established governing authorities. Angola, Mozambique, Sudan, Somalia, and Ethiopia fell into this category. Whatever their origins, however, insurgencies cannot sustain themselves without external aid.

In the case of Rwanda, I regret that we did not denounce the invasion from Uganda nor pressure the Ugandan government to force the RPF to withdraw. Had we done so, we could have pledged to inaugurate a diplomatic process to address the regional refugee problem. The RPF invaders were the children of Rwandan Tutsis who had been permanently expelled thirty years earlier. Nothing had been done throughout that period to help them gain the right of return. Nevertheless, when they entered northern Rwanda from Uganda they were not welcomed as liberators but were feared, even by the Tutsi minority. Morally justified as they were in their own minds, the RPF invaders thirty years later were essentially an alien body whose rejection by the majority Hutu population could only lead to tragedy. We should have tried to abort the invasion at an early stage and deal with the refugee problem through diplomacy.

The Liberian war was rooted in the corrupt and repressive Doe regime, only marginally legitimate after the rigged 1985 election. The NPFL invaders claimed the highest "patriotic" motives, but were unwilling to enter a democratic process until 1997, after war had destroyed the economy. We ignored assistance to the NPFL by Burkina Faso and Côte d'Ivoire during the first six months of the conflict for two reasons. First, the large Liberian exile community in the United States was anxious to see the Doe regime depart the scene, no matter what. Second, we knew little about NPFL leader Charles Taylor and were inclined to give him the benefit of the doubt. Although he was eventually elected president, having a reliable arms supply had encouraged him to delay the peace process until he could have his way. Had we been tougher with the suppliers, Taylor would have had to accept an earlier election.

When regimes in the first category were repressive dictatorships, as in Rwanda and Liberia, our inclination was to accept the invasions as a *fait accompli* and seek to correct the internal politics as part of the overall negotiations. The unhappy results in both cases indicate that this approach is too risky. Instead, we should adopt a policy that condemns such invasions instantaneously, insists that the invaders go back, and places maximum pressure on the OAU to characterize neighboring arms support as unacceptable. In addition, as part of a vigorous conflict prevention policy, the United States should focus appropriate intelligence assets on detecting preparations for such invasions. Hindsight reveals that RPF preparations in Uganda were hard to miss. And though less visible, preparations in the Liberian case could have been discovered if we had only looked.

In rebellions that begin from within, the insurgents sometimes have sympathetic tribal relatives living across the border who can be pressured for money, arms, and safe havens, as in Angola, Mozambique, and the Sudan. Neighboring governments often have to turn a blind eye to the cross-border activities of their own citizens or face political problems. Border controls are also difficult to enforce in very large countries.

Governments that feel threatened by hostile neighbors under insurgent attack may view assistance to rebels as an element of self-defense. Ugandan aid to southern Sudanese rebels, South African aid to Mozambican insurgents, and Ethiopian aid to Somali dissidents illustrate this phenomenon.

As a third-party intervenor, the US government must decide its policy toward assistance from neighbors to well-ensconced rebels on a case-by-case basis. At the very least, we should try to bring neighbors providing support to rebel groups into the peace process and exploit their leverage on the insurgents to the full. And we should not allow them to hide behind denials and obfuscation.

Enabling conflict prevention

American government efforts to engage in conflict prevention in Africa are conspicuous by their absence in this volume. The cases themselves deal with civil wars. To the extent that conflict prevention might have been possible in any of these, our record is one of lost opportunities.

In Liberia, for example, the 1985 rigged election generated the type of deep resentment that gave popular legitimacy to any attempt to overthrow the Doe regime. Charles Taylor's invasion and the subsequent humanitarian catastrophe were the inevitable fallout of that fraudulent election, which the US government viewed as "normal" in the West African context of the time.[4]

Somalia's terrible tragedy could have been foreseen and possibly prevented in 1990, when government forces destroyed the northwestern city of Hargeysa in an unsuccessful effort to stamp out rebellion. But our military interest in the Berbera naval and air facility inhibited our talking frankly to the Somali regime.

We might have been able to prevent the tragedy in Rwanda if we had focused our intelligence collection and analysis capability on the Rwandan Tutsi exile community in Uganda, especially those in command positions in the Ugandan army.

Our extensive conflict prevention efforts in Africa during the Bush administration, not described in this volume, demonstrated an implicit superpower role. In effect, the Africa Bureau's focus on conflict in those years created an environment conducive to conflict prevention that encouraged our embassies to do the same. Although we did not instruct our ambassadors to engage in conflict prevention activities, they knew from cables and weekly reports to the field that conflict resolution was a priority, and they acted accordingly.

Harmon Kirby, our ambassador in Togo, was one of several chiefs of mission whose work in conflict management was exemplary. In 1991, John Lewis, my country director for West Africa, expressed concern about Kirby's activities during Togo's difficult transition from military dictatorship to multiparty democracy, a transition marked by extreme political polarization and violence. In an effort to prevent the outbreak of civil war and to encourage a peaceful political transition, Kirby joined with his German and French colleagues to form an interventionist "troika." By unabashedly interfering in Togo's internal affairs, they managed to defuse tense situations and mediate between angry factions.

Lewis asked if we should not require Kirby to request instructions before engaging further in this activity. I told him a formal request for instructions would be a mistake. The AF Bureau would never be able to obtain clearance in the bureaucracy for a positive response, because Togo was not a country where US interests were at stake, and conflict prevention activities there could be seen by some as an open-ended US commitment. I therefore proposed that Lewis communicate informally with Kirby to tell him we were pleased with his activism and to encourage him to continue keeping us fully briefed on his activities.

Harmon Kirby's conflict resolution work was duplicated, in line with the AF Bureau's example, by a number of other US ambassadors. J. Daniel Phillips in Congo-Brazzaville played a key role in keeping that country's political transition on track amidst nonstop street demonstrations. Daniel Simpson in the Central African Republic singlehandedly prevented the military from sabotaging the multiparty election process. William Swing in South Africa was a human dynamo in informal shuttle diplomacy during the negotiations between the white minority government and the African National Congress. In Kenya, Smith Hempstone played a major role in efforts to persuade the government to accept multiparty politics. Overall, we were blessed with high-performing embassies, led by chiefs of mission who understood policy signals from Washington and had the courage to act.

The future of conflict management in Africa

By the time the Bush administration left office in early 1993, the Organization of African Unity had expressed the ambition to take the lead in conflict management. The doctrine of noninterference in internal affairs no longer provided a valid excuse to ignore violent conflict.

During the first Clinton administration, the OAU established a new entity called the Mechanism for Conflict Management, Resolution and Prevention. It provided a vehicle for intervention by the OAU secretary-general, with an emphasis on prevention based on the earliest possible warning. Since then, the secretary-general has been an active intervenor in a number of conflict situations, most notably in Rwanda, Burundi, Sierra Leone, and the Congo.

The first Clinton administration followed a constructive policy of helping the OAU conflict management mechanism build capacity. The Congress cooperated through the African Conflict Resolution Act of 1994, which authorized the expenditure of military assistance funds to support such capacity-building activities.

Outside the OAU, some interesting subregional conflict management initiatives have emerged, especially in the countries belonging to the Southern African Development Community (SADC). The SADC countries have pledged to support democracy and to act vigorously whenever democracy is threatened. This commitment was put to the test in Lesotho, São Tomé, and Mozambique, where the SADC governments demonstrated a willingness to project force to deter military coups.

In general, transition from single-party dictatorship to multiparty democracy in Africa will be slow and vulnerable to instability and violence, especially where economic transition is also in progress. Nonetheless, as democratization advances in Africa, outlets for nonviolent protest and criticism should increase, thereby diminishing incentives for violence. It is thus not surprising that the number of civil wars in Africa decreased between 1990 and 1999, notwithstanding the ongoing tragedies of Rwanda, Burundi, Somalia, the Sudan, Angola, and the Congo.

Conflict prevention clearly presents the major challenge to both the OAU and the international community in the early years of the twenty-first century and beyond. US policy is correct in assigning priority to developing African capacity to accept responsibility and assume leadership. At the same time, the influence of the sole remaining superpower remains significant in Africa. It is therefore difficult to imagine any actual or potential violent conflict in Africa to which the United States would not be able to make a useful diplomatic contribution at relatively low cost. The question, as always, will be one of political will.

Notes

[The official cables and memoranda cited in the notes that follow remain classified and unavailable to the public until released by the Department of State.]

Preface

1 The seven civil wars discussed in this volume were those in Angola, Ethiopia, Liberia, Mozambique, Rwanda, Somalia, and Sudan.
2 Herman J. Cohen, "Intervention in Somalia," in Allen E. Goodman, ed., *The Diplomatic Record* 1992–1993 (Boulder, Colo.: Westview, 1995); Cohen, "Political and Military Security," in John W. Harbeson and Donald Rothchild, eds, *Africa in World Politics* (Boulder, Colo.: Westview, 1995); Cohen, "African Capabilities for Managing Conflict," in David R. Smock and Chester A. Crocker, eds, *African Conflict Resolution: The U.S. Role in Peacemaking* (Washington, DC: United States Institute of Peace, 1995); Cohen, "Africa and the Superpower: An Agenda for Peace," in Gunnar M. Sorbo and Peter Vale, eds, *Out of Conflict: From War to Peace in Africa* (Uppsala, Sweden: Nordiska Afrikainstitutet, 1997).

1 Formulating a new US policy for Africa

1 Chester A. Crocker, *High Noon in Southern Africa: Making Peace in a Rough Neighborhood* (New York: W.W. Norton, 1992).
2 The multiagency and NGO effort to save lives in southern Sudan was coordinated by the United Nations under the name "Operation Lifeline Sudan," or OLS. The program was conceived by the late James Grant, an American who had been director-general of UNICEF since the Carter administration. Grant did more than anyone to keep OLS open and inspired us to engage in conflict resolution work.
3 The assistant secretary's freedom to convene PCC meetings in the Reagan and Bush administrations contrasted sharply with the situation in the first Clinton administration (1993–97), when the assistant secretary for Africa was required to seek permission from the National Security Council staff, with appropriate justification, before an interagency policy meeting could be organized. In my view, this restriction effectively inhibited creative initiatives in the administration's Africa policy, and placed control of day-to-day policy in the hands of an inexperienced and understaffed NSC directorate. Secretary of State Christopher should not have accepted this element of NSC control.
4 National Security Decision Directive 30 signed 15 January 1993. An unclassified version of the NSDD was issued by the State Department shortly thereafter. See *Dispatch: Fact Sheet – U.S. Policy for a New Era in Sub-Saharan Africa*, vol. 4, no. 3 (Washington, DC: US Department of State, 18 January 1993) p. 35.

2   Ethiopia

1   A small minority group in Ethiopia, the Jews were known as *Beta Esrael*, people of the House of Israel. They were also called *Oritawi*, adherents of the *Orit*, or Old Testament. "Falasha" is an Amharic word meaning "stranger." See *Selamta*, the quarterly magazine of Ethiopian Airlines, vol. 13, no. 1, January–March 1996, p. 18.

2   The organizations gave me a blank check when we first talked in May 1989, telling me, "If you want us to keep a low profile while you do your thing, just say so. On the other hand, if you want us to make a lot of noise, we can do that too."

3   We held the emperor in high esteem for his unstinting support in the Cold War, recognizing the importance of Ethiopia's having sent a battalion of troops to fight in South Korea during the 1950–53 conflict there. In addition, we harbored guilt feelings because the League of Nations had failed to act against Italy's military invasion of Ethiopia in 1937, despite Haile Selassie's personal and poignant appeal before the League's General Assembly in Geneva. Because of this strong friendship with the emperor, we tended to overlook the feudal system over which he presided, including tens of millions of landless peasants living in abject poverty under serflike conditions. This medieval socioeconomic system had made a violent revolution inevitable.

4   Henry Kissinger, "The Eternal Philosophical Problem of US-Soviet Relations," ch. 5, *White House Years* (Boston: Little, Brown, 1979) pp. 119–30, describes how the Brezhnev Doctrine led to major Soviet involvement in Ethiopia and Angola and thus made strategic dialogue between the superpowers difficult.

5   US Department of State, SECSTATE telegram 381414, 30 November 1989, to American Embassy Moscow. Following a meeting of Under Secretary of State for Political Affairs Robert Kimmitt and Soviet Ambassador Yuri Dubinin, Kimmitt was quoted as saying that Africa had proven the "best common ground for cooperation in regional conflicts" between the United States and the Soviet Union. Kimmitt made this statement even before anything really serious had taken place in either Ethiopia or Angola by way of peace efforts. His reference was to the quality of the dialogue between the two superpowers, which was particularly friendly on African issues.

6   First Annual Heads of State Conference, Cairo, Egypt, AGH/Res. 16(1) of 1964, Organization of African Unity, Addis Ababa.

7   American Embassy Khartoum, telegram 01459 of 8 February 1990. This is a memorandum of conversation between the deputy chief of mission and OLF Representative in Khartoum Dr Tadessa Ebba.

8   "Herman J. Cohen, Assistant Secretary of State for Africa, arrives in Addis Ababa for talks with the Ethiopian Government," *New York Times*, 5 August 1989, section I, p. 4.

9   Soviet Politburo member and former KGB head Victor Chebrikov visited Mengistu in January 1989. Chebrikov carried a letter from President Gorbachev urging a peaceful solution to the unwinnable Eritrean and Tigrean insurgencies and warning about the inevitable decline in Soviet military assistance.

10   "Small plane carrying Rep. Mickey Leland reported missing in Ethiopia enroute to refugee camp," *New York Times*, 8 August 1989, section I, p. 9.

11 "Ethiopian Government releases political prisoners," *New York Times*, 3 September 1989, section I, p. 16.

12 "Ethiopia's renewal of diplomatic relations with Israel," *New York Times*, 5 November 1989, section I, p. 4.

13 Hon. Toby Roth of Wisconsin, Extension of Remarks, *Congressional Record*, 11 October 1989, p. E 3368.

14 "Eritrean rebels begin long-expected offensive against Ethiopian Government," *New York Times*, 10 February 1990, section I, p. 8.

15 This reflected the growing importance of "democratization" in our overall policy toward Africa. The "liberalization of politics" was becoming a new conditionality for US development assistance.

16 Herman J. Cohen, Chairman, "Conclusions of PCC on Ethiopia, 14 August 1990," Memorandum to the Africa PCC dated 22 August 1990 (in Department of State archives).

17 "Text of Soviet Government Statement on Eritrea Fighting," Foreign Broadcast Information Service [FBIS], *Daily Report: Soviet Union*, 15 February 1990 (Moscow *Pravda* in Russan): "The Soviet Government calls insistently for the cessation of hostilities so as to create an opportunity to begin a search for mutually acceptable forms of national reconciliation at the negotiating table as quickly as possible."

18 *International Negotiation Network News*, volume I, no. 4, December 1989 (Conflict Resolution Program, Carter Center of Emory University, Atlanta, Georgia).

19 "About 15,000 Jews have descended on Addis Ababa," *New York Times*, 14 July 1990, section I, p. 3.

20 Memorandum from Herman J. Cohen to Under Secretary for Political Affairs Robert Kimmitt, "Ethiopian Peace Process: Meeting with Government and EPLF Officials," 5 October 1990, Department of State, Bureau of African Affairs (in Department of State archives).

21 The secretary was a bit out on a limb here because legislation required us to vote against World Bank and IMF loans to Ethiopia. However, when he offered to send appropriate signals to the World Bank, he did not promise we would vote in favor of loans to Ethiopia. We would merely refrain from actively discouraging such loans.

22 These details about the Ethiopian Jews during 1989–91 were taken from speech notes prepared by the Bureau of African Affairs for Deputy Assistant Secretary Irvin Hicks, who was active on the lecture circuit after May 1991. I found the notes in the State Department archives.

23 Gherman Ustinov, "Ethiopian Variant," *Izvestiya*, 29 March 1990.

24 US–Soviet Joint Statement on Ethiopia, Secretary of State cable 179226 of 4 June 1990. See also "President Bush and President Gorbachev issue joint statement on Ethiopia," *New York Times*, 4 June 1990, section A, p. 13.

25 The danger was not from EPLF antiaircraft fire, which they lacked, but from mortar rounds falling on Asmara airport, which was within EPLF capabilities.

26 Clifford Krauss, "US Aides Meeting Foes in Ethiopia," *New York Times*, 24 October 1990, section A, p. 9. This is a good background piece on the issue of US and Soviet involvement in the Eritrean peace process.

27 Herman J. Cohen, Assistant Secretary of State for Africa, "Ethiopia: Our Role in Talks," Memorandum to Under Secretary Robert Kimmitt of 5 October 1990, Executive Secretariat log no. 9022143.

28 Eritrean People's Liberation Front Political Bureau, Letter from Secretary General Isaias Afwerki to Assistant Secretary Herman J. Cohen, dated 7 October 1990 (in State Department archives).

29 Resolution 390 on Eritrea, adopted 2 December 1950, United Nations General Assembly, *Resolutions adopted by the General Assembly during the period 19 September to 15 December 1950*, Official Records, Fifth Session, Supplement no. 20 (A/1775).

30 "Eritrean legislative assembly votes for union with Ethiopia, ending federal status," *New York Times*, 16 November 1962, p. 3.

31 Heads of State conference, Cairo, Egypt, AGH/Res. 16(I) of 1964, Organization of African Unity, Addis Ababa.

32 US Department of State, SECSTATE telegram 032427, 31 January 1991, "Ethiopia: U.S. Strategy for GPDRE-EPLF Peace Talks." This roundup message to a number of interested American embassies, on the eve of a new round of peace talks scheduled for 18–19 February 1991 in London, provides a good overall review of the peace process to date.

33 Ibid.

34 "Ethiopia and the EPLF: On the Eve of Trilateral Talks," Memorandum from Department of State, Bureau of Intelligence and Research (INR) to Bureau of African Affairs, dated 15 February 1991 (in State Department archives).

35 *Proposal of the GPDRE on the Peaceful Resolution of the Problem in Eritrea*, Council of State, GPDRE, February 1991, Addis Ababa, Ethiopia.

36 "Ethiopian Government and Eritrean separatist guerrillas offer widely divergent peace proposals on second day," *New York Times*, 24 February 1991, section I, p. 11.

37 "Ethiopia: GPDRE/EPLF Washington Meeting, February 21–22," US Department of State, SECSTATE telegram 063520, 27 February 1991.

38 Department of State, Press Statement on the GPDRE/EPLF talks of 21–22 February 1991, Office of the Press Spokesman, Washington, DC, 22 February 1991.

39 Government of Ethiopia, *Resolution of the Third Emergency Session of the National Shengo of the Peoples Democratic Republic of Ethiopia*, Addis Ababa, 22 April 1991.

40 Department of Defense Appropriations for Fiscal Year 1991, section 8021. This was a classified amendment introduced by Senator Daniel Inouye (D) of Hawaii.

41 Soviet Foreign Ministry statement on Ethiopia (in English), TASS News Agency, Moscow, May 21, 1991, reported in FBIS, *Daily Report: Soviet Union*, London message LD2105201591 of 21 May 1991. The source for the information about the 21 May morning meeting was Kassa Kebede, who claimed he was present.

42 Statement by the Press Secretary, The White House, Office of the Press Secretary (Boston, Massachusetts), 24 May 1991.

43 Among many anecdotes concerning the Falasha airlift, one of the most remarkable was the story of the $35 million ransom. The airlift was delayed two hours while the GPDRE searched for the number of the Ethiopian government's account in the Federal Reserve Bank of New York. The Israelis deposited the money in this account, money that was all the Israelis' own. They did not call upon US money available in the Defense Department

appropriation. Months later, when Meles Zenawi was Ethiopia's provisional head of state, he told us they found the money still sitting in the Ethiopian government account. The efficient bureaucracy of the outgoing regime had made sure that the money remained under the control of the Ethiopian government and did not fall into "private" hands. Meles said that they returned the money to Israel because they did not want "blood money" in exchange for Ethiopian citizens. The Israelis confirmed the story and told us they would find a way to give an equivalent amount of money to Ethiopia in another form.

44 Before the conference ended, Tesfaye Dinka sent word that he would appreciate my support in his seeking political asylum in the United States. I had no hesitation in saying yes to this very civilized professional, who was doing his best for his country in trying circumstances.

45 Statement by Herman Cohen, Assistant Secretary of State for African Affairs, United States Information Service, American Embassy London, Press Release dated 28 May 1991.

46 Ibid.

47 Julian Ozanne and Michael Holman, "Ethiopian Peace Deal Threatened by Troops Dispute," *Financial Times* (London), 28 May 1991, p. 1.

48 James A. Baker III, *The Politics of Diplomacy* (New York: G. P. Putnam's Sons, 1995), pp. 478–86.

49 In August 1998, five years after Eritrea's independence, the two countries fell into a serious border dispute that led to major military clashes. The political rhetoric heard in Addis Ababa after the dispute erupted revealed the deep bitterness felt by the majority of Ethiopians over Eritrea's secession.

50 My Soviet counterpart Yuri Yukalev told me in April 1991 that Foreign Minister Shevardnadze considered it very important that the Soviets copreside with the United States over the London conference. They correctly anticipated that the international community would consider it a major event. Yukalev asked me to do everything possible to persuade the EPLF and the TPLF to accept the Soviets, to no avail. The Soviets sent a special delegation to London but never achieved any visibility. This was offset a few days later by the prominent Soviet role at the signing of the Angola peace agreements in Lisbon on 31 May 1991.

51 Hearings, 18 June 1991, House of Representatives, Committee on Foreign Affairs, Subcommittee on Africa.

3 Sudan

1 P. M. Holt and M. W. Daly, *The History of Sudan: From the Coming of Islam to the Present*, 3d ed. (Boulder, Colo.: Westview, 1979), provides a good overview of the Sudan's turbulent history. For an excellent summary of the Sudan problem after 1980, see World Vision, *Sudan: Cry the Divided Country*, Policy Papers, issue no. 1, Spring 1996.

2 US House of Representatives, *War and Famine in the Sudan*, Joint Hearings before the Subcommittee on Africa, Committee on Foreign Affairs, and the International Task Force, Select Committee on Hunger, 16 March 1990, serial no. 101–17 (Washington, DC: US Government Printing Office, 1991).

See also *Washington Post*, 3 January 1989, editorial, section A, p. 16, which accuses the Sudan government of using starvation as a weapon against the southern rebels.

3 "The Sudanese Army warns Sadiq to make peace or resign," *Washington Post*, 24 February 1989, section A, p. 14; and "Sadiq forms new government committed to making peace with the rebels," *Washington Post*, 24 March 1989, section A, p. 19.

4 "The Sudan Government signs a $250 million arms deal with Libya," *Washington Post*, 4 March 1989, section A, p. 18. Libyan interest in the Sudan intensified after 1979, when the Sudanese military government headed by General Nimeiry became the only Arab government to endorse the Camp David agreement between Egypt and Israel. Libyan leader Muammar Qaddafi thereafter did all he could to undermine the Nimeiry regime. As the result of a power-sharing agreement, Nimeiry and the southern political movements enjoyed peace until 1983 when Nimeiry moved toward political Islam. His infamous "September law" subjected all Sudanese to Sharia law (see note 5 below) and abolished the regional autonomy that had given the southerners limited self-rule in the three equatorial provinces. These moves reignited the civil war. Because of Nimeiry's endorsement of Camp David, Libya helped the southern insurgents, including an attempt to bomb Khartoum. Nimeiry was overthrown in 1985 and replaced by a democratically elected regime in 1986 under Sadiq el-Mahdi. When the new regime, which included the National Islamic Front in its coalition, turned cool toward Israel, Egypt, and Camp David, Libya switched sides and started helping Khartoum against the southern insurgents.

5 Sharia law is the main Islamic code covering family and criminal law. Applying Sharia law to all the populations of Sudan, including Christians and Animists in the South, was a primary issue in the civil war. This was especially true of the dreaded *Huddud*, which prescribed criminal penalties such as the amputation of limbs for theft.

6 *Washington Post*, 29 May 1989, section A, p. 17, describes how a fully loaded UN food train bound for the south remained in the north unable to travel for over a month.

7 For example, one project was the construction of a fifty-mile rural road. Obviously, we did not want to stop that one before the road was completed.

8 *Washington Post*, 1 July 1989, section A, pp. 1 and 2, reported the coup as marking the end of "one of Africa's few experiments in democracy." On the other hand, the editorial bid fond farewell to Sadiq by characterizing him as "exceptionally eloquent in discussing Sudan's problems, but stubbornly unwilling to take practical measures to solve them."

9 The regime's public posture was also pro-peace. For example, as the *Washington Post* of 2 July 1989 (p. A–31) reported, the "Sudanese army officers who overthrew the government of P.M. Sadiq announced their intention to honor foreign treaties and seek peace with the southern rebels."

10 Even the press had noticed our "wait and see" attitude. For example, the *Washington Post*, 9 July 1989, section A, p. 22, wrote: "The U.S. has assumed a quiet stance toward the new military regime that came to power in a coup led by 15 middle-ranking officers with close ties to Egypt."

11 In his conversations with the author and other US government officials, Ethiopian dictator Mengistu consistently described the problems of the Horn

of Africa as a war between the Arab/Muslim nations and the non-Arab/African Christian nations, such as Ethiopia. Just as the white *apartheid* leaders in South Africa used to talk about the "total onslaught of Communism," Mengistu talked about the "total onslaught of the Arabs." Hence, it was quite logical for him to assist the southern Sudanese rebels in retaliation for the passage of arms through Sudan to the northern Ethiopian rebels. The Sudanese held a mirror image view of the situation. Each was retaliating against the other.

12 US Department of State, telegram 26914, 26 January 1990.

13 *Al-Quwat Al-Musallaha* (the daily Armed Forces newspaper), Khartoum, 31 December 1989.

14 US Department of State, Washington, DC, telegram 44957, 10 February 1990.

15 Ibid.

16 Ibid.

17 United States Senate, correspondence from Wolf, Ackerman, and Humphrey to Dr. John Garang de Mabior, dated 13 February 1990, in the Sudan archives of the Bureau of African Affairs, US Department of State.

18 American Embassy Addis Ababa, telegram 1019, 1 March 1990, in the archives of the Bureau of African Affairs, US Department of State.

19 US House of Representatives, Committee on Foreign Affairs, Joint Hearing before the Subcommittee on Africa and the International Task Force of the Select Committee on Hunger, *War and Famine in the Sudan*, 15 March 1990 (Washington, DC: US Government Printing Office, serial no. 101–17).

20 Ibid.

21 "Media Reaction to US Assistant Secretary Cohen's Statement to Congress," American Embassy Khartoum, telegrams 3706 and 3708, 5 April 1990, in Bureau of African Affairs archives, US Department of State.

22 *New York Times*, 8 June 1990, Editorial, section A, p. 30. After denouncing the State Department for not criticizing the Sudanese government, the editorial praised our joint efforts with the Soviets to bring about a negotiated solution in Ethiopia.

23 American Embassy Khartoum, telegram 8564, 19 August 1990, in State Department archives.

24 *Sawt Al-Shab* (Sudanese weekly newspaper), 20 August 1990, quoted in Foreign Broadcast Information Service summary, 21 August 1990.

25 In the regime's view, excluding the southern provinces from the implementation of Sharia law and its Islamic punishments was a constructive gesture toward the Christian and Animist southerners. But John Garang and other southern leaders continued to point out that the proposal was unacceptable because Sharia law would still apply to the two-to-three million southerners living in the north.

26 United States Senate, Committee on Foreign Relations, *Emergency Situations in Sudan and Liberia*, Hearing before the Subcommittee on African Affairs, 27 November 1990, Senate Hearing 101–1163 (Washington, DC: US Government Printing Office, 1991).

27 Agence France Press dispatch, 19 January 1991, "Hundreds of Thousands March to Support Iraq," Foreign Broadcast Information Service report 231 of 19 January 1991, Washington, DC.

28   US Department of State, American Embassy Khartoum, telegram 719, 25 March 1991, "Sudan supports regional security arrangements, pledges cooperation and better relations with US."
29   Ibid.
30   Ibid.
31   *Washington Post*, 23 February 1991, section A, p. 6.
32   *Washington Post*, 16 March 1991, section A, p. 20.
33   Salim was well and favorably known to us through his long years as Tanzania's minister of foreign affairs. If any African could solve the Sudanese conundrum, he could. The fact that he was a non-Arabic-speaking African Muslim gave him good credentials with both sides in the Sudanese conflict.
34   That long-standing policy was clearly obsolete, because internal wars on the scale of Sudan's greatly harmed the other states in the subregion through refugee flows and arms proliferation.
35   US Department of State, telegram 116558, 11 April 1991, "Asst. Sec. Cohen Meeting with Sudan National Security Adviser Fatih Irwa."
36   Ibid.
37   US Department of State, American Embassy Khartoum, telegram 3418, 17 July 1991, "Khartoum Emb[assy]off[icer]s roughed up and threatened by security forces while at University of Khartoum."
38   US Department of State, telegram 238251, 20 July 1991, "A/S Cohen reviews the Horn, South Africa with Egyptian ambassador."
39   The most discussed policy difference between John Garang and Riak Machar concerned the future of the Sudan. Although he was beholden to the regime for arms, Riak preached a doctrine of southern secession and establishment of an independent state. Garang consistently spoke in favor of a new democratic Sudan that included the south. As the war continued into 1993, Garang's position moved toward supporting secession if a democratic Sudan clearly could not be achieved.
40   "U.S. officials fear that Sudan, backed by money and expertise from Iran, is emerging as a new Lebanon from which terrorist groups can launch operations and export Islamic revolution across Africa," *Washington Post*, 31 January 1991, section A, p. 13.
41   The two employees' "subversive activity" was maintaining radio contact with the American Embassy in Khartoum.
42   Committee on Foreign Affairs, House of Representatives, *Recent Developments in Sudan*, Hearing before the Subcommittee on Africa, 10 March 1993 (Washington, DC: US Government Printing Office, 1993).

4   Angola

1   Chester A. Crocker, *High Noon in Southern Africa: Making Peace in a Rough Neighborhood* (New York and London: W. W. Norton, 1992), pp. 293–99, describes in detail how the United States decided to arm the UNITA "freedom fighters" in Angola in keeping with the Reagan Doctrine of supporting anticommunist movements around the world against the Brezhnev Doctrine of support for Marxist regimes and movements.

2 The various agreements in the Crocker package are reproduced in Crocker, *High Noon in Southern Africa*, pp. 495–511.

3 "UNITA charges proposed peace settlement would permit thousands of Cubans to remain," *New York Times*, 30 November 1989, section I, p. 3; and "Treaty brokered by US makes no mention of 13-year civil war between Angola's Marxist government and UNITA guerrillas," *New York Times*, 14 December, 1989, section I, p. 1.

4 South Africa and Cuba were no longer allowed to assist their respective clients, UNITA and the Angolan government, but the United States and the Soviets were not bound by that agreement.

5 "President-Elect Bush makes first foreign policy commitment," *Washington Post*, 12 January 1990, section A, p. 1.

6 The conservative right was not happy with "constructive engagement" either, because the policy entailed having a civilized dialogue with Marxist Angola and Mozambique, as well as with South Africa. We just couldn't win.

7 Senate Foreign Relations Committee, Confirmation Hearings, 3 May 1989.

8 Despite our lack of real data, we suspected the South Africans had left UNITA a significant amount of both lethal and nonlethal supplies when they pulled out of Angola in August 1988. In addition, they continued to supply nonlethal material after their departure. US deliveries included Stinger antiaircraft missiles, antitank weapons such as the TOW, and, after land routes were cut off, fuel for UNITA's vehicles.

9 "National Reconciliation Efforts for Angola," Department of State, *Current Policy*, no. 1217, 27 September 1989.

10 Ibid.

11 Ibid.

12 Savimbi spoke to me from Jamba, in the far southeast corner of Angola, using the most sophisticated satellite telephone available.

13 *Current Policy*, no. 1217.

14 Afterwards, during discussions with francophone heads of state present in Gbadolite, I learned that in the French language versions of the discussions, the word *exil* was not uttered about Savimbi's future. They insisted that the French word they heard was *éloigner*, which means Savimbi would "step back" from active politics. That would have been perfectly consistent with Savimbi's own proposals of March 1989, when he said on Radio VORGAN that as a gesture to the MPLA, he would not participate in negotiations nor serve in an interim government. Unfortunately, the use of the word "exile" in public by too many heads of state made further discussions impossible.

15 "Angolan rebel leader Savimbi and Angolan President dos Santos sign cease-fire agreement that will end 14 years of civil war," *Washington Post*, 24 June 1989, Section A, p. 22; and "Analysis sees symbolic triumph for Angolan rebel leader Jonas Savimbi as African leaders show willingness to deal with him as equal to government," *New York Times*, 26 June 1989, section I, p. 3.

16 *Washington Post*, 1 July 1989, section A, p. 12.

17 "Angolan anticommunist leader Jonas Savimbi failed to appear at an African peace summit in Zaire September 18, 1989, causing some officials to doubt if a cease-fire in Angola's 14-year civil war can be revived," *Washington Post*, 19 September 1989, section A, p. 3.

18   "Lobby Gets Results for Savimbi," *Africa Report*, November 1989, is the most accurate description of how the pro-UNITA lobby managed to persuade the political levels of the need to insist on free and fair elections as a precondition for the cessation of US arms deliveries to UNITA. It was written from an anti-UNITA point of view.

19   "According to Congressional and Administration sources, Mobutu has unilaterally halted the secret shipment of US arms through his country to Savimbi," *Washington Post*, 4 October 1989, section A, p. 8.

20   Department of State, Bureau of Public Affairs, Office of Press Relations, "AF Press Guidance," 8 January 1990.

21   "Acceding to a request from President Bush, Angolan leader Jonas Savimbi said he will meet with Mobutu," *Washington Post*, 6 October 1989, section A, p. 34.

22   "A CIA cargo plane carrying military supplies to rebels in Angola has crashed there," *Washington Post*, 30 November 1989, section A, p. 1.

23   "US criticizes Soviet role in battling Angolan rebels," *Washington Times*, 19 January 1990, p. 2.

24   South African support for UNITA was the major subject of the Joint Commission meeting that took place in Capetown, South Africa, on 22 January 1990 at the height of FAPLA's offensive. While the signatories to the 1988 New York agreement all agreed that Cuban adherence to the troop withdrawal schedule was impeccable, the Angolans accused South Africa of violating the Geneva Protocol by continuing to supply UNITA by air. South Africa denied the charge, although their chief delegate, Foreign Ministry Secretary General Neil van Heerden, admitted that it was difficult to prevent "private" pilots from flying to Jamba from South Africa's many airstrips. US intelligence indicated that some flights were coming into Jamba from the south but was unable to identify the cargo. In any event, we felt that the number and size of the aircraft were too small to make much of a difference in the military balance.

25   "Dos Santos puts off trip to US under US pressure," *New York Times*, 24 January 1990, section A. p. 3.

26   *Swiss Press Review and News Report*, Swiss Eastern Institute (Jubilaumsstrasse 41, CH-3000 Berne 6, Switzerland), 16 April 1990, although written from a pro-UNITA perspective, has a good description of the dilemma faced by the MPLA regime from the UNITA sabotage activity.

27   *New York Times*, 10 February 1990, section I, p. 1 contains a full report of the Moscow ministerial meeting between Secretary Baker and Foreign Minister Shevardnadze.

28   *Africa Report*, November 1989.

29   "Angolans say US has rushed arms to rebels," *Washington Times*, 1 March 1990, p. A-7.

30   The Soviets had considered the Mavinga offensive the final opportunity for a military victory. Since the Angolans were not paying for the Soviet arms but merely signing promissory notes, the Soviets saw no economic reason for continuing their support.

31   James A. Baker III, *The Politics of Diplomacy* (New York: G. P. Putnam's Sons, 1995), pp. 224–28.

32   "Angolan peace talks to begin soon," *New York Times*, 8 April 1990, p. 3.

33 President Senghor talked to me about this when I was US ambassador to Senegal, 1977–80. As the father of "Negritude," Senghor saw the Angolan conflict as a struggle by the indigenous blacks, represented by UNITA, against the "mestizos and assimilados," represented by the MPLA.

34 The Joint Political Military Commission existed to supervise the implementation of the New York agreements of December 1988 for the withdrawal of South African and Cuban troops from Angola and the independence of Namibia.

35 "Cuba-US Bilaterals at Joint Commission Meeting 9/13/90," American Embassy Windhoek, telegram 1298, 14 September 1990.

36 Ruth Sinai, Associated Press, "Angola Dispute Lingering Vestige of the Cold War," Washington, 2 April 1990 (wire service copy), is an excellent summary of the war of the lobbyists.

37 *Background to the Fifth Round of Negotiations*, Free Angola Information Service, Washington, DC, 15 November 1990, a lobbyist bulletin on file with the Department of Justice. This particular issue gives a detailed account of the many charges and countercharges being tossed about by the different Angolan support groups in Washington in an effort to influence congressional action.

38 Baker, *Politics of Diplomacy*, pp. 599–600.

39 "Joint Statement on Angola," US Department of State, Office of the Assistant Secretary/Spokesman, 11 December 1990. The concept that the United States and the Soviet Union would pledge not to send arms to Angola and that the MPLA and UNITA would pledge not to receive any lethal materials became known as the "triple zero" option, which symbolized the end of the Cold War in Angola.

40 "Baker and Shevardnadze Hold Separate Meetings with Angolan leaders," *New York Times*, 13 December 1990, section A, p. 25.

41 The Soviets stop supplying the government, the United States stops supplying UNITA, and both parties agree to stop importing weapons from any source.

42 Actually, Lopo had a terrible earache, he told me, and was in a hurry to fly to Lisbon for treatment.

43 Text of the agreed Washington Concepts Paper:

(1) Upon entry into force of the cease-fire, all Angolan citizens will acquire the right to conduct and participate in free political activity, in accordance with the amended constitution and relevant laws to provide for multiparty democracy. Upon signing the cease-fire agreement, the parties will determine a date for free and fair elections.

(2) The Angolan Government will conduct discussions with all political forces in order to have their views on the proposed changes to the constitution. The Angolan Government will then work with all the parties to formulate the laws which will regulate the electoral process.

(3) The cease-fire agreement will obligate the parties to stop receiving lethal materials. The United States, Soviet Union and all other countries will support the implementation of the cease-fire, and will refrain from supplying lethal material to any Angolan party.

(4) The overall political control of the cease-fire process will be the responsibility of the Angolan parties working within the Joint Political

Military Commission (JPMC). The monitoring of the cease-fire will be the responsibility of the international monitoring group. The UN will be invited to provide monitors to assist the Angolan parties, at the request of the Angolan Government. The Governments which will provide the monitors will be selected by the Angolan parties, working within the JPMC.

(5) The process of creating the national army will begin with the implementation of the cease-fire and be completed by the time of the elections. The neutrality of the national army in the election process will be guaranteed by the Angolan parties working within the JPMC, with the assistance of the international monitoring group. The Angolan parties reserve until subsequent negotiations the discussion of what international assistance may be required to form the national army.

(6) Free and fair elections for a new government shall take place under the monitoring of international election observers, who will remain in Angola until they have certified that the election is free and fair, and the results have been officially proclaimed.

44 Department of State, telegram 423294, 15 December 1990, drafted by Richard Roth, deputy director for Southern African affairs, provides a summary of the discussions, the atmospherics, and the final outcome.

45 "Remarks by the Honorable James A. Baker III at the Angola Peace Accord Signing Ceremony 31 May 1991," US Department of State, Office of the Assistant Secretary/Spokesman, Washington, DC, press release, 31 May 1991.

46 Christine M. Knudsen and I. William Zartman, "The Large Small War in Angola," *Annals of the American Academy of Political and Social Science*, September 1995, pp. 135–38, analyzes the reasons for the failure of the Bicesse accords in October 1992 and addresses the flaws in the agreements.

47 "Rival Angolan groups bring their competition to the US," *New York Times*, 13 October 1991, section I, p. 6.

48 The White House, Office of the Press Secretary, press release, 16 September 1991.

49 "House votes to continue covert aid to rebels," *New York Times*, 12 June 1991, section A, p. 8. The vote appropriated funds for nonlethal equipment for UNITA.

50 "Most diplomats and political experts in Angola believe government has an edge," *New York Times*, 10 June 1991, section A, p. 6.

51 "Defectors accuse Savimbi of killing opponents," *New York Times*, 7 April 1992, section A, p. 17.

52 "Secretary of State Baker writes to US-backed guerilla leader Savimbi seeking explanation of killings and other human rights abuses," *New York Times*, 31 March 1992, section A, p. 5.

53 "Savimbi's response to Baker is that the deaths were part of a CIA plot to overthrow him," *New York Times*, 5 May 1992, section A, p. 7. Tito's alleged flirtation with the CIA and other foreign services to plot against Savimbi was considered the most plausible explanation for some time. Much later, it appeared more likely a question of Tito's having an affair with Savimbi's much younger wife.

54 Savimbi told travelers to Angola in 1995 that I had insisted on keeping the "Ninja" issue on the back burner in 1992, while he wanted to make it a

major *cause célèbre*. My personal recollection is that he was so sure he would win the election that he did not worry too much about the "Ninjas," which served as a convenient reason for complaining about the government.

55 Statement by the Deputy Press Secretary, The White House, Office of the Press Secretary, 30 July 1992.
56 "Angola's ruling party and former rebel movement agree to form coalition government," *New York Times*, 9 September 1992, section A, p. 9.
57 "Savimbi accuses the government of fraud, and hints at return to war if his party loses," *New York Times*, 4 October 1992, section I, p. 15.
58 State Department, Bureau of African Affairs, text contained in an unclassi-fied fax message from the American Embassy in Lisbon (Joseph Sala) to the Department of State (Richard Roth), dated 5 October 1992.
59 "Angola: Elections, UNITA," Statement by Richard Boucher/Deputy Spokes-man, Department of State, Office of the Assistant Secretary/Spokesman, 6 October 1992.
60 Department of State, Secretary of State, telegram 328040, to USLO Luanda, 7 October 1992.
61 "UNITA backs away from threat to go back to war provided UN investigates its complaints of cheating," *New York Times*, 8 October 1992, section A, p. 17.
62 "Anstee says no evidence of systemic or major fraud," *New York Times*, 18 October 1992, section I, p. 7.
63 "Angolan Elections," Statement by Richard Boucher, Spokesman, Department of State, 19 October 1992.
64 "Fierce Battle in Luanda," *New York Times*, 1 November 1992, section I, p. 12.
65 Memorandum of Conversation between Dr Jonas Savimbi and Assistant Secretary Cohen of 27 November 1992. In Department of State archives.
66 Resolution 811 of 12 March 1993, United Nations Security Council, New York.
67 "Angola-PC-7s Fly Ground-Attack in Civil War," in Daily Defense News Capsules via NewsNet, *Periscope*, Friday, 1 December 1995, describes how South African pilots flew Swiss-made trainer PC-7s fitted with 68-mm rock-ets against UNITA fighters with devastating impact.

5 Liberia

1 James Youboty, *Liberian Civil War: A Graphic Account* (Philadelphia: Parkside Impressions Enterprises, 1993), p. 37.
2 Reed Kramer, "Liberia: A Casualty of the Cold War's End?" in *CSIS Africa Notes*, no. 174 (July 1995), Center for Strategic and International Studies, Washington, D.C.
3 Youboty, *Liberian Civil War*, p. 48.
4 Kramer, "Liberia," p. 5.
5 Ibid., pp. 6–7. The emphasis on multiparty democracy, which was to gain strength in Africa starting in 1990, was virtually absent in Africa in 1985. Doe's action in declaring himself the winner of an election he probably lost was compatible with contemporary practice. All West African countries had either single-party elections or rigged multiparty elections. In short, in the 1980s, incumbent West African governments were turned out of office only through military coups. What happened in Liberia in 1985 was totally in context.

6   To describe that luncheon as "formal" was an understatement. Ladies wore their best Easter Sunday hats, and some men sported white tie and tails. Religion played a major role with invocation and benediction. It looked like an 1820 antebellum southern plantation festival.

7   State Department, telegram 156838, 18 May 1989, to the American Embassy Monrovia, "Gist of the 17 May 1989 PCC Meeting on Liberia."

8   The embassy's view was not shared by our colleagues at Defense, who predicted accurately that the insurgency would spread rapidly. They knew the abysmal state of training and morale in the Liberian Army.

9   In what was supposed to be a traditional tribal ritual, head of state Doe and his top lieutenants were reliably reported to have eaten Quinwonkpa's flesh after aborting the coup. Tom Woweiyu, a top Taylor lieutenant, told us the infiltrators' original plan was to stimulate a national anti-Doe uprising in Monrovia, followed by the entry of rebel forces into Nimba County. The infiltration part of the plan aborted.

10 In ethnic terms, it was logical for the Krahn leadership in the military to view the population of Nimba County as hostile. General Quinwonkpa, who attempted to overthrow the Doe regime in 1985, was an ethnic Gio from Nimba County.

11 American Embassy Monrovia, telegram 3054, 26 March 1990.

12 Youboty, *Liberian Civil War*, p. 44.

13 Ibid., p. 76.

14 Ibid., p. 97. Taylor was originally not charged with a crime in Massachusetts. He was incarcerated pending a judicial hearing on whether he should be extradited to Liberia. Since the Liberian government seemed incapable of delivering the evidence required for the court hearing, some observers think Taylor was probably "allowed" to escape after two years as a guest of Massachusetts.

15 American Embassy Abidjan, cable 10362, 12 May 1990, provides eyewitness accounts of cross-border rebel movements.

16 Youboty, *Liberian Civil War*, pp. 8–11, contains an interesting account by three captured NPFL rebels on how they were recruited in 1987 and sent for training to Libya via Côte d'Ivoire and Burkina Faso.

17 American Embassy Monrovia, telegram 4073, 21 April 1990.

18 *Financial Times* (London), 14 April 1990, p. 5.

19 Department of State, telegram 076292, to Embassy Abidjan, 9 March 1990.

20 As happened in Somalia a year later.

21 Department of State, Minutes of the Liberia PCC, 6 April 1990, in State Department archives.

22 Department of State, telegram 118182, 12 April 1990, to Monrovia contains the text of the department's statement suspending military assistance to Liberia because of "human rights violations by the Liberian Army."

23 American Embassy Monrovia, cable 3756, 13 April 1990.

24 Reuters news agency report, 7 May 1990, "Embattled Liberian Leader Meets Nigerian President."

25 State Department telegram 137386, 28 April 1990, to Lomé, and American Embassy Lomé, telegram 2383, 30 April 1990.

26 Department of State telegram 144199, 4 May 1990.

27 Department of State, telegram 149146, 9 May 1990.

28 American Embassy Abidjan, telegram 10369, 13 May 1990.

29 In their public rhetoric, the Americo-Liberian community in the United States bitterly criticized the US government throughout the Liberian crisis. They attributed Liberia's tragedy solely to the refusal of the United States to get rid of Doe in 1985 in the aftermath of the rigged election. Instead of forgetting about the past and looking to formulate constructive solutions to Liberia's problems, they filled their testimony at congressional hearings and other public discussions with venom toward the US government. Instead of ignoring their criticism, as I should have, I began to respond that Doe would never have come to power if the Americo-Liberian rulers of Liberia had not inflicted a form of "apartheid" on the majority "tribal people" who produced Doe. The record of the House Africa Subcommittee hearing on Liberia of 16 July 1991 provides just one example of these totally unproductive exchanges. Dr Sawyer was an exception to this general pattern.

30 Department of State, Memorandum from Herman J. Cohen to Under Secretary Robert Kimmitt, 24 May 1990, in State Department archives. We persuaded South Korea to stop selling arms to Doe, but the Israelis were unwilling to make such a commitment. Our dialogue with Côte d'Ivoire was particularly unproductive. Abidjan denied complicity in the arms flow to the NPFL but acknowledged maintaining communications with the NPFL for "humanitarian purposes." Technically, Côte d'Ivoire told the truth about arms, as it was not supplying arms to the NPFL but allowing free and unrestricted passage of arms between Burkina Faso and Taylor.

31 Memorandum from Acting Assistant Secretary of State for Africa Jeffrey Davidow to Under Secretary Robert Kimmitt, 4 June 1990, in State Department archives.

32 Kramer, "Liberia," p. 1, contains a quote from a 1993 interview with Bush's national security advisor, Brent Scowcroft: "It was difficult to see how we could intervene without taking over and pacifying Liberia with a more-or-less permanent involvement of US forces. Our attention was dedicated toward other areas most involved in ending the cold war. You can only concentrate on so many things at once." Haiti in the 1930s appeared to be the paradigm feared at the NSC level. If Scowcroft and Gates had only asked for some advice, they would have understood how misguided this view was.

33 Speaking notes for Assistant Secretary Herman Cohen in preparation for the Africa PCC meeting, 12 June 1990, in State Department archives.

34 Senate Foreign Relations Committee, Subcommittee on Africa, *Hearings on Sudan and Liberia*, 27 November 1990, Statement by Assistant Secretary Herman J. Cohen.

35 Youboty, *Liberian Civil War*, pp. 196–97.

36 In subsequent years, Taylor claimed I had promised to "get Doe out of office" provided the NPFL refrained from capturing Monrovia. When I suggested to Taylor that he leave open an escape route for the AFL, I said Doe would probably leave, once he saw his troops melting away to exile in Sierra Leone. I never promised to make Doe leave in return for a Taylor promise that the NPFL would not invade Monrovia. Taylor never made such a promise. During most of July, as the city slowly starved, I kept hoping the NPFL would take over Monrovia and get it over with. But Taylor's troops had no experience with frontal assaults, and Prince Johnson's INPFL forces

were harassing them. They failed to capture Monrovia because they lacked the capability.

37 "L'initiative de paix de la CEDEAO au Liberia: Une Chronologie," *Bulletin de l'Ouest Africain*, no. 3 (June 1995), pp. 6–7, published by the Secretariat of the Economic Community of West African States in Lagos, Nigeria.

38 Department of State, Memorandum from James K. Bishop to Assistant Secretary Cohen, "Briefing for PCC Meeting, July 12, 1990," in State Department archives.

39 Kramer, "Liberia," p. 8. For a detailed firsthand account of these events, see also Dennis Jett, "Evacuation during Civil War, Liberia 1990," in Joseph G. Sullivan, ed., *Embassies under Siege* (Washington and London: Brassey's, 1995), pp. 132–47.

40 "L'initiative de paix de la CEDEAO au Liberia," pp. 6–11.

41 We had found $3 million in available Economic Support Funds (ESF) that could be transferred to peacekeeping accounts for further transfer to ECOWAS, a multilateral organization. Since ECOWAS had never before received US funding of this type for military purposes, it had to be certified by a Presidential Determination (PD) of eligibility.

42 The entire gruesome operation was captured on videotape, some of it aired by the British Broadcasting Corporation.

43 Memorandum from Ambassador Donald Petterson to Assistant Secretary Cohen, 4 September 1990. (Petterson had succeeded Ambassador Bishop as director of the Liberia working group.)

44 Kramer, "Liberia," p. 8.

45 Memorandum from Herman J. Cohen to Under Secretary Robert Kimmit, 8 November 1990, "Liberia – PCC Recommendations."

46 This was the clearest signal yet that Côte d'Ivoire would do everything possible to prevent interference in Taylor's quest for power. The exercise also demonstrated that the permanent members of the Security Council have less power than most observers believe. They can use their veto power to block Council initiatives, but they cannot make things happen unless they obtain nine votes in favor. Thus the three African members and the nonaligned in general have a blocking majority of their own.

47 Youboty, *Liberian Civil War*, p. 549.

48 State Department telegram 328047, 3 October 1991, to Monrovia contains a relatively optimistic analysis of the situation after Yamoussoukro III by Alan McKee, director of West African affairs.

49 Most foreign heads of state or government invited to visit Washington make "official visits" or "official working visits." These usually involve a one-hour business meeting in the White House Cabinet Room followed by a one-hour luncheon in the White House dining room. A "state visit," in contrast, involves considerable pomp and more time together for the two heads of state, with a glamorous "state dinner" as the main social event.

50 Robinson was a Republican political appointee. Unlike other such appointees I had known, he was very knowledgable about Africa. As president of the African Development Foundation during the Reagan administration, he had extensive experience in Liberia and thus knew all the politicians quite well.

51 Section 552 of the Foreign Assistance Act (FAA) gives the President authority to transfer ESF funds to peacekeeping operations and to draw up to $25 million annually in stocks and services from any agency for peacekeeping purposes.

52 State Department, telegram 328047, 3 October 1991.

53 Department of State, Memorandum from Alan McKee to Assistant Secretary Cohen, 22 January 1992, "Liberia Policy Review."

54 Department of State, telegram 362553, 5 November 1992, to US embassies in West Africa.

55 "Liberians Free 71 Foreigners; US Offers Aid," *International Herald Tribune*, 22 April 1996, p. 2, from Associated Press and Reuters.

56 See note 32.

57 In late 1990 and early 1991, President Houphouet-Boigny of Côte d'Ivoire also proved important to us as an influence on Jonas Savimbi, president of the UNITA movement in Angola.

6 Rwanda

1 Gérard Prunier, *The Rwanda Crisis: History of a Genocide, 1959–1994* (London: Hurst, 1995). This is probably the best compilation of research on the origins and events surrounding the 1994 Rwandan genocide.

2 In 1972, human rights was not as big an issue in US foreign policy as it later became. As director of the office that dealt with Burundi at the time, I found it difficult to arouse interest in what was happening there. The media were indifferent, and the US Congress hardly noticed. The selective genocide against educated Burundi Hutu ended only when Tanzanian President Julius Nyerere closed the railway from Burundi to Dar Es Salaam, cutting external communications.

3 During one of my many meetings with South African Foreign Minister Roelof "Pik" Botha in 1991, I raised the subject of South African arms shipments to Rwanda, noting that Rwanda had a heavy debt load and did not need added debt for arms purchases. Botha replied: "Don't worry about debt. The Rwandans pay cash."

4 Prunier, *The Rwanda Crisis*, p. 91. According to Prunier, the regime knew in advance of the impending invasion from Uganda but took no preventive measures because it wanted an excuse to increase internal political and ethnic repression against pro-democracy forces.

5 France's assistance to the regime was openly acknowledged as covered by its military cooperation agreement, but Uganda's involvement was clandestine. The Ugandan government continued to deny any role on the RPF side in the conflict. To the Ugandans, the moral justification for the RPF invasion was the Rwandan government's refusal to allow refugees to return to their homeland, in violation of international conventions. More important, Ugandan President Yoweri Museveni owed a debt of gratitude to the Tutsi officers and men who played an important role in his own victorious guerrilla war against the corrupt and repressive Obote regime from 1981 to 1986. Museveni also needed to find a solution to the problem caused by the unpopularity of the Rwandan refugees in Uganda. Helping them return to Rwanda thus served an internal Ugandan political objective as well.

6   Prunier, *The Rwanda Crisis*, p. 105. Fashoda is the location in central Sudan where French military explorers advancing eastward from Sahelian West Africa were turned back by British forces, advancing southward from Khartoum, during the scramble to divide up Africa in the late 1800s. The French apparently saw the RPF invasion as, in effect, an anglophone effort to destabilize francophone Africa and expand the Anglo-American sphere of influence at France's expense.

7   I would have gone way out on a limb here, as no bureaucratic groundwork for such a threat had been established in Washington. Uganda's economic growth was one of the few relative success stories in Africa, and we were thus not about to undermine these good results by cutting Uganda's foreign assistance.

8   See, for example, Howard Adelman and Astri Suhrke, *The International Response to Conflict and Genocide: Lessons from the Rwanda Experience, Study 2, Early Warning and Conflict Management* (Copenhagen: Joint Evaluation of Emergency Assistance to Africa, March 1996), p. 6.

9   Ibid., p. 9.

10 Ibid., pp. 6–7, concisely describes France's "dual policy" of providing continued military support to the regime and encouraging negotiations.

11 Astri Suhrke, "UN Peacekeeping in Rwanda," in Gunnar M. Sorbo and Peter Vale, eds, *Out of Conflict: From War to Peace in Africa* (Uppsala: Nordiska Afrikainstitutet, 1997), pp. 97–113, provides an excellent description of how the Arusha accords moved the country inexorably toward genocide.

7   Mozambique

1   In such situations, the National Security Council staff often finds itself caught in the middle. In my case, as a State Department officer on loan to the NSC, I had to tread carefully not to demonstrate visible bias toward my home agency.

2   In 1983, a US embassy officer in Mozambique had been expelled from the country by the FRELIMO government, which caught him in the alleged act of spying on the Cuban embassy. Although a minor event in the history of such operations, it sent a signal that the regime was on the "other side" in the ideological battles of the Cold War. That "Marxist" image was still quite strong in 1987–88.

3   Cameron Hume, *Ending Mozambique's War: The Role of Mediation and Good Offices* (Washington, DC: United States Institute of Peace Press, 1994), p. 8. Hume provides a good description of FRELIMO's self-inflicted problems derived from attempts to impose book-learned scientific socialism on an extremely underdeveloped Third World society.

4   The "total onslaught" theory began to unravel with the December 1988 New York agreements and the resulting departure of Cuban troops from Angola. When US–Soviet relations warmed up under President Bush and the Berlin Wall was dismantled, the theory collapsed completely. That *apartheid* itself began to unravel in 1990, at about the same time as Soviet communism, was thus not entirely coincidental.

5 Hume, *Ending Mozambique's War*, p. 21, quotes Assistant Secretary of State Chester A. Crocker telling the Senate Foreign Relations Committee on 24 June 1987 that RENAMO "lacks a political identity where it really counts, in Mozambique itself."

6 The briefing occurred on 3 March 1987. Reagan had been keeping a low profile since November 1986, when the Iran-Contra scandal began to involve the presidency. Reagan's activites were reopened to normal press coverage in March 1987, with the RENAMO briefing one of the first to be announced. This led to a spate of articles on the bureaucratic battles over Mozambique. See, for example, the *New York Times*, 16 March 1997, section I, p. 9, headed, "State Department has succeeded in ending efforts of conservatives and others to undercut policy of seeking better relations with Mozambique."

7 RENAMO's popular base was eventually substantiated by the free and fair UN-sponsored election of 1994 in which RENAMO captured 35 per cent of the vote.

8 For the first six years of Reagan's presidency, a series of CIA officers had served as senior director for African affairs on the NSC staff. When I took the position in January 1987, I was the first non-CIA person to handle Africa for the president and the national security advisor. In December 1986, in the aftermath of the Iran–Contra affair, Frank Carlucci was appointed the new national security advisor and General Colin Powell the new deputy. To demonstrate that a real change was taking place, Carlucci and Powell fired virtually all of the NSC staff, including the unimplicated CIA officer in charge of Africa, who was simply caught up in the wholesale purge.

9 Getting such an invitation is not a simple process. Within the State Department, the competition for official visits among the various geographic bureaus can be fierce, with Africa often losing out to higher priority countries. The competition is repeated in the NSC when the lists of recommended visits comes over from State.

10 Chissano was favorably impressed and actually flattered by Crocker's briefing in advance of his meeting with Reagan. Nine years later, when I met with Chissano in Maputo in May 1996, he was nostalgic about the 1987 visit, rehearsing in detail what he had considered a conspiracy between US bureaucrats and himself to overcome resistance from his own colleagues.

11 Hume, *Ending Mozambique's War*, p. 21.

12 Ibid., ch. 2, provides a concise play-by-play account of the steps leading from the 1989 prenegotiations to the July 1990 beginning of actual negotiations.

13 Sant'Egidio's involvement, though a surprise, was really quite logical. The order had programs in Mozambique and knew the terrain well. Its contacts covered both government and RENAMO. The involvement of President Moi and Bethuel Kiplagat on the side of RENAMO remains somewhat murky. To the best of my knowledge, contacts were made through Protestant church connections. Moi is close to his Protestant denomination, and Kiplagat had always been closely associated with the All Africa Council of Churches. RENAMO chief Afonso Dhlakama may have developed confidence in Moi and Kiplagat via his connections with American evangelicals.

In any event, the Kenyan government was the only African entity willing to help RENAMO with travel, passports, lodging, and the like.

14 During our first discussion about my becoming assistant secretary, Baker asked me, "How are your relations with Senator Helms?" I replied that as NSC director for Africa during 1987–89, I had gotten along relatively well with Helms. I had made a point of keeping him and his staffers briefed on African issues of interest to them, especially Angola. Baker then said that he had consulted Helms before offering me the job, and Helms had replied, "Cohen is OK, even though he is a Foreign Service officer."

15 Senate Foreign Relations Committee, Subcommittee on Africa: Hearings, 3 May 1989 (not printed but transcript carried by USIA African Wireless File as AEF 303 of 3 May 1989). See also State Department Press Guidance of 4 May 1989.

16 Hume, *Ending Mozambique's War*, p. 31. Also, "President Bush calls for negotiations to end Mozambique's 10-year civil war; issues plea after White House meeting with Chissano," *New York Times*, 14 March 1990, Section A, p. 15.

17 Looking over the heads of the FRELIMO hard-liners, Chissano also knew that Mozambicans were thoroughly fed up with the war and increasingly disenchanted with FRELIMO because of its failure to end the conflict. The timing was thus right for a persuasive pitch by Bush.

18 Hume, *Ending Mozambique's War*. This excellent book provides a complete description and analysis of the twenty-seven months of negotiations.

19 Hume, *Ending Mozambique's War*, pp. 100–1.

20 We also developed a good working relationship with Mugabe on the Persian Gulf War. In January 1991, just as the United States was beginning to use force against Iraq under a UN mandate, Zimbabwe started a two-year stint on the UN Security Council. I was sent to urge Mugabe to continue the strong support of the previous African group on the Security Council. I expected him to demonstrate his strong "nonaligned" credentials and berate the United States for playing bully again. But Mugabe surprised me, saying Zimbabwe would support the Chapter VII action against Iraq without reservations, because "we don't want big countries like Iraq gobbling up small countries like Kuwait."

21 "De Klerk visits Mozambique; claims SAG has cut off aid to RENAMO," *New York Times*, 17 December 1989, Section I, p. 24.

22 *New York Times*, 5 October 1992, Section A, p. 10.

8 Somalia

1 Terrence Lyons and Ahmed I. Samatar, *Somalia: State Collapse, Multilateral Intervention, and Strategies for Political Reconstruction* (Washington, DC: Brookings Institution, 1995), p. 14, notes: "By 1969, it had become increasingly clear that Somali parliamentary democracy had become a travesty, an elaborate, rarefied game with little relevance to the daily challenges facing the population."

2 Lyons and Samatar, *Somalia*, p. 14: "The military leaders, led by General Siad Barre and organized as the Supreme Revolutionary Council (SRC), at first received a tumultuous welcome."

3 Siad Barre consistently took this line with visiting Americans, both military representatives from CENTCOM and diplomats traveling from Washington. When I visited Mogadishu in 1983 to inaugurate a program of military intelligence exchanges, I gave Siad an intelligence briefing that emphasized the absence of any evidence of Ethiopia's planning to attack Somalia. He was not persuaded. Two Ethiopian provincial governors who were Somali ethnics had informed him, he said, that an invasion would take place within a few months. Siad continued to predict an Ethiopian invasion right to the end of his regime, in a desperate effort to obtain lethal equipment.

4 Lyons and Samantar, *Somalia*, pp. 15–18.

5 Guerrilla tactics in the city of Hargeysa illustrated the intense hatred of the Siad Barre regime. Central government civil servants were dragged out of their homes and murdered. Wives of SNM guerrilla fighters followed behind to finish off any wounded central government employee who might still be alive.

6 See Chapter 5 on Liberia.

7 Lyons and Samantar *Somalia*, pp. 28–29.

8 For a detailed account of this dramatic evacuation, see James K. Bishop, "Escape from Mogadishu, 1991," in Joseph G. Sullivan, ed., *Embassies under Siege* (Washington and London: Brassey's, 1995), pp. 148–62.

9 Lyons and Samantar, *Somalia*, p. 28.

10 See Chapter 2 on Ethiopia.

11 Lyons and Samantar, *Somalia*, pp. 18–19, state: "Somali opposition movements lacked the institutional bases and political vision to cooperate once Siad Barre had been overthrown."

12 Lyons and Samantar, *Somalia*, p. 29, observe: "Many Somalis regarded the Djibouti talks as an Italian attempt to move its new allies in the Manifesto Group, including Ali Mahdi, into the positions recently vacated by their old ally, Siad Barre."

13 The Security Council in late 1988 approved the Namibian peacekeeping operation implementing Resolution 435. As senior director for Africa on the NSC staff at the time, I was informed that the United States would have to come up with an additional $25 million during FY1988 to cover our share of the operation's cost. With the support of National Security Advisor Colin Powell, this was done by a presidential stroke of the pen, transferring the required amount from the Defense Department budget to the State Department's UN Peacekeeping account, with absolutely no opposition or fuss.

14 In January 1991, every foreign embassy in Mogadishu except Egypt's evacuated its personnel and closed its doors.

15 Herman J. Cohen, "Intervention in Somalia," in Allan E. Goodman, ed., *The Diplomatic Record 1992–1993* (Boulder, Colo.: Westview, 1995), p. 54.

16 For example, House of Representatives, Select Committee on Hunger, Hearings, 30 January 1992 (Washington, DC: US Government Printing Office).

17 For example, United States Senate, Committee on Foreign Relations, Hearings, 19 March 1992, *The Horn of Africa: Changing Realities and U.S. Response* (Washington, DC: US Government Printing Office, 1992). This was but one of several 1992 hearings before committees in both houses.

18 I found the technique of asking pointed questions from the chair in PCC meetings fairly effective in focusing the debate and calling the attention of otherwise passive agencies to the dilemma.

19   Cohen, "Intervention in Somalia," pp. 53–54, 59.
20   Ibid., pp. 60–61.
21   The Kenyan government agreed quickly and without any quibbling to our request to use Mombasa. This illustrates the dilemma we faced in our bilateral relations with Kenya. President Moi's resistance to democratization, accompanied by human rights abuses, caused us to take the lead in cutting Kenya's economic assistance in 1992. On the other hand, Kenya never failed to grant us access to military facilities when we needed them.
22   Cohen, "Intervention in Somalia," pp. 63–65.
23   I was present at the meeting as Under Secretary Wisner's backup. This represents my personal recollection.
24   President-elect Bill Clinton, written statement, *Reuter Transcript Report,* 3 December 1992.
25   Thomas L. Friedman, "Bush Address to the UN Urges More Vigor in Keeping the Peace," *New York Times,* 22 September 1992, p. A-1.

9   Superpower in Africa

1   It would be unfair to describe the special influence of the United States in African conflict management without mentioning the special role of France in Africa's French-speaking countries. It is no coincidence that this volume does not include among its seven case studies any former French colonies in Africa, although it does analyze the situation in the former Belgian colony of Rwanda, where French influence was strong prior to the civil war in that country. In its former colonies, France remains the dominant external influence in matters involving conflict management. But unlike the United States, which tends to act as a neutral third-party intervenor, France tends to intervene as the "big brother" settling a family dispute, using its extensive military presence, economic and military assistance, and attendant leverage to promote stability in most of its former colonies. Whether France has helped promote conflict management and resolution, however, is not as clear. For the best overview of the French role in Africa, see Francis Terry McNamara, *France in Black Africa* (Washington, DC: National Defense University Press, 1989).
2   US or UN force projection in Africa began to fade as a psychological element in Africa after the 1993 disaster in Somalia. Since then, the United States has resisted efforts to expand military peacekeeping operations in Africa.
3   David R. Smock and Chester A. Crocker, eds, *African Conflict Resolution: The U.S. Role in Peacemaking* (Washington, DC: United States Institute of Peace Press, 1995), provides a good survey of Africa's efforts to take responsibility for its own conflict management.
4   In the 1980s, all elections in West Africa were more or less rigged, so why should our good friend Liberia have been any different? The Doe regime, after all, could not have been more helpful to the United States in every aspect of our foreign relations, including US use of Liberia's airport for military transit to all parts of Africa.

Index*

---

*This index was prepared by Susan Fels.